LexisNexis
Questions and Answers

Corporations Law

5th edition

LexisNexis
Questions and Answers

Corporations Law
5th edition

Anil Hargovan

BA LLB (Natal), LLM (Monash),
Associate Professor, School of Management and
Governance
University of New South Wales, Sydney

LexisNexis
Australia
2022

LexisNexis

AUSTRALIA	LexisNexis
	475–495 Victoria Avenue, Chatswood NSW 2067
	On the internet at: www.lexisnexis.com.au
ARGENTINA	LexisNexis Argentina, BUENOS AIRES
AUSTRIA	LexisNexis Verlag ARD Orac GmbH & Co KG, VIENNA
BRAZIL	LexisNexis Latin America, SAO PAULO
CANADA	LexisNexis Canada, Markham, ONTARIO
CHILE	LexisNexis Chile, SANTIAGO
CHINA	LexisNexis China, BEIJING, SHANGHAI
CZECH REPUBLIC	Nakladatelství Orac sro, PRAGUE
FRANCE	LexisNexis SA, PARIS
GERMANY	LexisNexis Germany, FRANKFURT
HONG KONG	LexisNexis Hong Kong, HONG KONG
HUNGARY	HVG-Orac, BUDAPEST
INDIA	LexisNexis, NEW DELHI
ITALY	Dott A Giuffrè Editore SpA, MILAN
JAPAN	LexisNexis Japan KK, TOKYO
KOREA	LexisNexis, SEOUL
MALAYSIA	LexisNexis Malaysia Sdn Bhd, PETALING JAYA, SELANGOR
NEW ZEALAND	LexisNexis, WELLINGTON
POLAND	Wydawnictwo Prawnicze LexisNexis, WARSAW
SINGAPORE	LexisNexis, SINGAPORE
SOUTH AFRICA	LexisNexis Butterworths, DURBAN
SWITZERLAND	Staempfli Verlag AG, BERNE
TAIWAN	LexisNexis, TAIWAN
UNITED KINGDOM	LexisNexis UK, LONDON, EDINBURGH
USA	LexisNexis Group, New York, NEW YORK
	LexisNexis, Miamisburg, OHIO

A catalogue record for this book is available from the National Library of Australia

ISBN:	9780409349474 (pbk).
	9780409349481 (ebk).

Inquiries should be addressed to the publishers.

Typeset in Sabon and Optima.

Printed in Australia.

Visit LexisNexis at www.lexisnexis.com.au.

Contents

Contents

Preface

The fourth edition of this book was published in 2013. Much has changed in corporate law since that time, with both temporary law reform in 2020 (arising from the impact of the Coronavirus pandemic on the economy) and permanent law reform. On 1 January 2021, a number of changes to Australia's insolvency framework came into effect, pursuant to the Corporations Amendment (Corporate Insolvency Reforms) Act 2020 (Cth). The reforms, which represent the most significant changes to insolvency laws in 30 years, replace the former 'one size fits all' insolvency approach under the Corporations Act 2001 and introduced a new debt restructuring procedure in Pt 5.3B of the Corporations Act for eligible small businesses that are financially distressed. Key features of this law reform are discussed further in Chapter 10.

At the time of writing, the federal government announced potential reform which, if enacted, will impact upon the operation of schemes of arrangements — the current law on schemes is discussed in Chapter 10. Similarly, in August 2021, the government also announced a review by an independent panel of experts on the operation of the safe harbour provision under insolvent trading law — this topic is discussed in Chapters 6 and 10. Further developments may arise in these areas of law.

Other significant statutory reform includes changes made to the regulatory regime on corporate fundraising by the introduction of a new Pt 6D.3A of the Corporations Act which deals with crowd-sourced fundraising. The impact of this reform, with reference to the legal definition of a proprietary company, is discussed in relevant parts of this book. Another important reform relates to the stiffer civil and criminal penalties introduced for breaches of the Corporations Act by the Treasury Laws Amendment (Strengthening Corporate and Financial Sector Penalties) Act 2019 (Cth). For example, the penalty for a contravention of s 184 (directors' and officers' duties) has increased from a maximum of five years to 15 years' imprisonment. Other reforms, falling outside the scope of this book, include targeting 'phoenix' transactions (the Treasury Laws Amendment (Combating Illegal Phoenixing) Act 2020 (Cth)), amendments made to online meetings, electronic notices, electronic executions and continuous disclosure reforms. The latter reforms arise from the Treasury Laws Amendment (2021 Measures No 1) Act 2021 (Cth), in effect from 14 August 2021.

Case law developments in corporations law continue at a rapid pace. Each chapter has been reviewed and updated to include important recent decisions. There has been a steady stream of corporate insolvency cases and cases concerning directors' duties. One significant area of development has been the clarification of the meaning of company officer, with a recent High Court decision in *ASIC v King* included in Chapter 6. Other significant recent High Court decisions deal with the law on procedural irregularities (*Weinstock v Beck* included in Chapter 5), the law on financial assistance (*Connective Services Pty Ltd v Slea Pty Ltd* included in Chapter 7) and deeds of company arrangement in voluntary administration (*Mighty River International Ltd v Hughes* included in Chapter 10). Several other Appellate level decisions have been included dealing with the division of corporate power between the board and members (*Australasian Centre for Corporate Responsibility v Commonwealth Bank of Australia* in Chapter 5), directors' power to issue shares (*Mualim v Dzelme* in Chapter 6), the meaning of informed consent arising from a breach of fiduciary duties (*Coope v LCM Litigation Fund Pty Ltd; Mualim v Dzelme* in Chapter 6) and with the meaning of insolvency (*Quin v Vlahos* in Chapter 6).

The Australian Securities and Investments Commission (ASIC) has had several significant enforcement victories in the *Storm Financial* case (*ASIC v Cassimatis* included in Chapter 6), *AWB Ltd* case (*ASIC v Flugge* included in Chapter 6), *Vocation Ltd* case (*ASIC v Vocation Ltd* included in Chapter 6) and in the *Sino-Australia* case (*ASIC v Sino Australia Oil and Gas Ltd (in liq)* included in Chapters 6 and 9). There are many other case examples in Chapter 6 illustrating ASIC's success with its stepping-stone approach to enforcement of directors' duties.

It pays to repeat the warning that was given in previous editions: the suggested answers in this book are not perfect, 'model' answers. There are no doubt issues and arguments that have not been covered. Good answers do not simply raise every possible issue, but rather focus on the most important issues in that particular situation. This will be a reflection of the specific facts involved, the client being advised and the content and emphasis of the individual subject. Students who seek to blindly reproduce these answers in real exam questions are unlikely to score high marks as every exam question has its own points of significance and the answer must be tailored to suit the specific facts and the contours of the subject involved. An experienced marker will pick a pre-prepared answer easily and the marks will be lowered as a result.

I want to thank the authors of the earlier editions — Robyn Donnelly who wrote the first and second editions of this text and Jason Harris who wrote the third and fourth editions. I also want to thank the editorial team at LexisNexis, particularly Annabel Adair and Jocelyn Holmes whose eye for detail and efficiency kept the update on track. I also owe gratitude to all of my past and present students at UNSW whose engagement inspire my teaching and help to make company law an exciting course to deliver. Lastly, I thank Kalyani, Satyen and Rahul for their love and support during the time spent working on this edition.

Anil Hargovan

School of Management and Governance,
University of New South Wales, Sydney

August 2021

Table of Cases

References are to paragraphs

Table of Cases

Table of Statutes

References are to paragraphs

Table of Statutes

Table of Statutes

Chapter 1
Answering Law Questions

Introduction

1-1 This chapter is different from the rest of the book because it contains neither questions nor suggested answers. The purpose of this chapter is to encourage students to consider how they approach answering questions on corporate law, *because the style and structure of written communication is as important as the underlying message that is being communicated*. A clearly written and well-argued answer is much more persuasive than a poorly written paper that argues the same points. Merely covering the 'right' cases or statutory provisions is not sufficient to produce a well-argued paper.

By the time most business and law students study corporate law they are in their second or third year of university. As relatively senior students the key focus of assessment tasks is no longer the accuracy of your legal approach — this is taken for granted. You should be able to examine a question and identify what the issue is, what legal rules apply to that issue and attempt to apply those principles to the facts of the question.

Planning your answer in advance, even in exams, is a useful way to promote clear and persuasive writing. This chapter will discuss a number of issues regarding what you can do to better prepare for exams and assignments and hopefully improve the impact of your writing. It is also important to note that the matters discussed are of general advice only and each course/lecturer/faculty is likely to have different writing requirements and assessment expectations. Check with your faculty's guide to writing before proceeding.

Different types of questions

1-2 It is important to identify the type of question that you are being asked and to adopt planning and writing strategies suitable for that type of question. It is also important to consider what types of information are usually sought in different types of questions.

Law subjects generally use three main types of questions for assessment tasks, and each of these will be discussed below.

Problem

1-3 Problem-based questions typically involve consideration of a specific fact scenario that requires an assessment of the legal rights and liabilities of the parties involved in the problem scenario. Problem questions may require consideration of several legal issues or may focus on one or two major issues, depending on the scope of the question.

Where there are multiple issues it is important to identify which issue is the most important and then to prioritise the remaining issues to ensure that you do not run out of time (in an exam) or space (in an assignment question).

For example, consider the following question:

> Manda is the managing director of Go East Pty Ltd, a fashion boutique, and holds 30% of the shares. The other shareholder (with 70% of the shares) in Go East Pty Ltd is Jane (who is not a director) and her husband Lee, who is a non-executive director (although in Manda's experience all of Lee's decisions as a director are discussed with Jane). Manda, Jane and Lee have been friends for a long time and have until recently been very happy with the running of the company. However, recently Manda has become concerned that Jane and Lee are misappropriating money from the company. Manda becomes alarmed when creditors start complaining that their bills are unpaid despite the fact that Manda has sent company cheques to cover all unpaid amounts. Soon after a board meeting when Manda asks Lee questions about his unusually large spending on the company's credit card, Jane informs Manda that she is calling a shareholders' meeting next Friday to remove Manda from the board of directors and to appoint herself as a director under the company's constitution.
>
> Manda seeks your advice as to her rights and potential liabilities.

This apparently simple question involves numerous corporate law issues including:

- insolvent trading (because the company seems unable to pay its debts as and when they become due and payable);
- breach of directors' duties (because Lee may have acted for an improper purpose or under a conflict of interest);
- whether Jane's and Lee's conduct was oppressive on Manda;
- whether Jane is a shadow director (because Lee acts in accordance with her wishes); and
- whether Jane's proposed shareholders' meeting is properly called (because of the inadequate notice).

Even in a three-hour exam most students would struggle for time to fully discuss each of these issues. More importantly, trying to cover each of these issues is likely to result in a superficial answer for each of them which will result in a basic or poor mark overall.

It is important to determine which of the above possible issues is the most important. This will usually be determined by reference to the conduct of the course (for example, was insolvent trading emphasised or only mentioned in passing? How much attention was given to the duty to act for a proper purpose compared with the conduct of shareholders' meetings?). Once the priorities have been determined, students should then proceed to discuss the issues in order of priority as emphasised in the course.

It is important to ensure that each issue is at least 75% dealt with before moving on to the next issue. Students rarely obtain high marks for briefly discussing several issues without going into detail on any particular issue. However, it is also important that students recognise that it is generally easier to obtain the first 75% of the marks than to obtain the remaining 25% (it is much easier to obtain a pass or credit than to obtain a high distinction). Thus, it is often better to write your exam answers so that they are 75% complete (with space remaining in the examination booklet) and then to move on to the next question. Once each question is answered to 75% you can then finish off the remaining 25% of each question. This will ensure that if you run out of time you have maximised your marks.

However, much will also depend upon the wording of the question, the marks available (for example, a 20-mark question will require a detailed discussion whereas a 5-mark question may only require the identification of issues) and what other questions are required (most exams will not involve multiple large questions on the same issue).

Solving problem questions

1-4   The key to an effective answer to a legal problem question is the application of relevant legal rules to the given factual scenario. A logical and persuasive application of law should provide a conclusion that is supported by the balance of legal authority. One method of achieving this outcome is to use the MIRAT method. There are various other similar methods such as IRAC (issue, rule, application, conclusion). The most important message of these methods is to focus on how the law may apply in the particular fact scenario posed by the question.

The MIRAT method is outlined below:

- **M** — identify what the material facts are, although *don't formally list these facts in your answer* as that would be repeating the question. It is sufficient to mentally identify what facts may give rise to a legal issue (for example, facts involving discrimination against a shareholder might suggest that the question concerns Corporations Act 2001 (Cth) s 232 oppression).
- **I** — identify the relevant legal issue(s). This may take the form of a question such as: 'Is the issue here whether the directors have breached their statutory duties owed to the company?'. This can be one of the first sentences in your answer.
- **R** — identify the legal rules that are relevant to the legal issue(s) raised by the question. This will typically involve consideration of

both statute and general law and should generate a list of matters that must be satisfied in order to establish the application or contravention of a particular rule. A short statement of the main principle should be sufficient. Depending on the course requirements, *it is usually not necessary to summarise the rules in any detail* (particularly in open book exams). Ensure that you do not simply copy the content of the statute. Nor will copying material from the text produce a high mark. Remember, the marker has a copy of the textbook too! It is therefore important to show what you know in your own words to demonstrate your understanding.

• A — apply the legal rules to the facts in the problem. *This is always the most important part of the answer and will determine the bulk of the marks.* This involves working through the elements of liability or 'test' identified in the rules section above. The application of the rules to the problem facts should seek to explain why a particular element of liability is proven by a particular fact or range of facts. It is also important to use cases that interpret or explain the rules that you are applying. While citing cases as supporting particular rules is useful, cases should also be used to compare and contrast the fact situation in the question (for example, 'Unlike in the *Adler* case, the facts in this question demonstrate that the directors did appropriately balance the potential risks involved because they sought an independent valuation of the assets that were being purchased with the corporation's funds').

• T — tentative conclusion, which should be the answer to the question posed in the issue section above.

Most course co-ordinators will encourage the use of headings in assessment tasks but it is important to verify style and formatting requirements with your individual course authority.

Essay

1-5 The ability to write persuasively on a specific topic is an important communication skill that will prove invaluable in your business or legal career.

Essay questions involve providing a commentary on a particular theme or question. It is common to use essay questions for assessing how well students understand particular issues (such as lifting the corporate veil or problems arising in corporate governance) or how well students understand the interaction of multiple concepts (such as 'Discuss the relevance of the traditional shareholder wealth maximisation norm with the modern trend towards corporate social responsibility').

When answering an essay question, it is important that students take the time (usually 5–10 minutes) to plan their answer so as to prevent a 'stream of consciousness' response. Answers to essay questions that are unplanned usually miss key points and will often be repetitive. The plan to answering an essay question will typically involve an introduction, body and conclusion.

The introduction should be limited to no more than two or three paragraphs as its purpose is to set up the framework of the question (not to restate the question) by stating why the issue/question is important/topical/problematic, and briefly to summarise how the paper will answer the question.

The body of the essay should proceed from some form of definition or identification of the key issues involved in the question (for example, the body of an essay concerning increasing corporate governance standards may begin with a definition of corporate governance) and then proceed to work through the elements of the issue (such as for/against arguments or advantages/disadvantages of a particular view). It is important in the body of an essay to engage with the weaknesses in the argument presented. Students can assume that the marker will be aware of the range of issues involved in the question so students should not think that refraining from mentioning points that seem to go against their view will make their argument stronger. A rough rule of thumb is to argue 75% of the body for a particular view and then spend 25% of the body acknowledging and seeking to overcome disadvantages/negative points in the argument. Remember, in law there is often no one 'right' answer!

The conclusion for an essay should tie all of the arguments/points together by seeking to make a defining statement that answers the question/problem posed. As a general guide, the arguments presented in the body of the essay should make the conclusion obvious. If the reader is still unsure of the conclusion by the end of the essay then the student has failed to provide a persuasive argument in the body of the essay. Should you find that you have competing answers in your conclusion (which is not unusual in a law answer), then state which answer you prefer and explain the reason why.

Of course, each course is different and students should consult their course co-ordinator as to their style and formatting preferences.

Short answer

1-6 Short answer questions will usually require between half to one-and-a-half pages depending upon the topic and student writing style. The key to answering short answer questions is to get to the point! Identify what the question is concerned with, define the key concepts and answer the question, preferably with reference to the relevant statutory provision and/or cases that discuss the concept. Short answer questions are typically narrow in scope so there is no need to give a lengthy introduction to the topic.

Short answer questions can take the form of straightforward explanations of particular principles or concepts (for example, 'How is good faith established in applications to bring a statutory derivative action?'), or may require some critical analysis (for example, 'Compare the court's approach to veil piercing in the UK with that taken in Australian cases').

Research and preparation

1-7 Preparation, particularly by undertaking effective research and working through practice questions, is the key to success in legal assignments and exams. The level of preparation required is determined by the type of assessment task you are undertaking.

Success in exams will involve preparation through end of semester (or term) revisions and completion of the weekly reading and tutorial/ seminar questions. Students are advised to attempt practice questions under conditions similar to those that will be used in their exams (that is, open or closed book and limited time). It is one thing to gain a general understanding of the material by passive learning through listening to lectures or to tutorial answers being explained by the lecturer. It is quite a different thing to attempt to apply that knowledge to a random problem or essay question in a limited timeframe.

It is typical for students to not know the precise topics covered in exams, aside from a general understanding that particular weeks (for example, weeks 2–10) could be included in the exam questions. In this situation, it is important for you to cover each topic in your exam preparation. Being selective about what topics will be examined, especially based on what was covered in exams in previous semesters, is a dangerous game that can lead to failure if the lecturer changes the focus (as they often do). Allocate your preparation time according to the level of detail given to each topic. Ideally, you should aim to spend at least a week preparing for a final exam, and this is based on the assumption that you have completed all of the work during semester (or term).

The key to preparation prior to an exam is not merely to go over the material covered in the course but to also identify your strengths and weaknesses. This is best done by attempting practice questions under exam conditions. Forcing yourself to give a clear and well-argued answer in 30–50 minutes (the typical time allocated for each final exam question) is very challenging and will typically reveal areas where you feel more or less confident. After identifying your weaknesses, undertake further revision of those topics by going over the readings again. It is also a good idea to seek out alternative textbooks, and legal reference materials (such as legal encyclopaedias like *Halsbury's Laws of Australia*), to further improve your understanding of the topic. After doing this, retake the same problem question under exam conditions to see if you feel more comfortable with the material.

Essays and assignments require a different type of preparation because students usually have several weeks to answer the question. This means the lecturer will often require research outside of the prescribed textbooks. There are several books that can help with conducting legal research, particularly electronic legal research. Check your law library catalogue or ask your law librarian for assistance.

Referencing

1-8 Referencing in exams is usually very basic because of time constraints. The answer guides produced in this book usually give the full case name and citation, but full citations are typically not required in exams. It is normally enough for students to identify the main case name (for example, *Salomon's* case), although it may also be useful to put the year of the decision to make sure that you are referring to the correct case. Abbreviations of the statutory provisions, such as CA for Corporations Act 2001 (Cth), are also usually acceptable. However, check with your course authority about referencing expectations.

Lastly, it is also useful to make your case and statutory references stand out from the text, so use underlining or highlighting to make the references bolder. This will make it easier for the marker to identify whether you have correctly understood the legal issues raised by the question.

Tips for success

Time/space management

1-9 In an exam you only have limited time so allocate your time between each question and leave yourself a 5–10-minute buffer for each question so that you can go back at the end of the exam and improve your answer where possible. Stick to your time allocations! Missing out on questions because you mismanaged your time is the easiest way to lose valuable marks.

In an assignment you will typically have a limited word allocation, so similarly allocate the bulk of your space to what you think is the most important issue raised by the question.

Planning for a clearly written and argued paper

1-10 Always take a few moments at the start of an exam to plan your answer. Identify what the main strands of your argument will be and then consider what is the best order in which to discuss those points. Consider using headings to guide your discussion and your reader. Headings have an added bonus of constraining repetition as you can deal with a point under the relevant heading and then move on to the next point without repeating yourself.

Are there points/issues that overlap with other points/issues? If so, consider discussing them together either at the start or at the end.

Don't try to do too much (quality over quantity)

1-11 It is usually preferable to address a limited number of issues in depth than to try and cover every issue but only in a superficial manner. Be guided by what issues were emphasised in your particular course, as these issues are more likely to be emphasised in an exam question.

Chapter 2

Registration and its Effects

Key Issues

2-1 Most corporations are now formed by the administrative act of registration by the Australian Securities and Investments Commission (ASIC) under s 119 of the Corporations Act.

Once a company is formed it becomes a separate legal person with attributes which closely, although not perfectly, resemble a natural person with full legal capacity: s 124.

The consequences of the company being a separate legal entity are that the company's property is separate from that of the people who register it and any other persons who become members from time to time. This is commonly referred to as the 'corporate veil' because the members are separated from the company itself. The limited liability of members is a related concept to the corporate veil. Members have limited liability if they purchase shares in a company that is limited by share capital and they have fully paid for their shares: s 516. Members who hold partly paid shares are liable to contribute an amount up to the full price of the shares. It is in this sense that the members enjoy limited liability; namely, they only stand to lose the amount of capital they have contributed or agreed to contribute under their shareholding (or guarantee, for a company limited by guarantee).

The separate legal entity principle was famously confirmed in the leading decision in *Salomon v A Salomon & Co Ltd* [1897] AC 22 which was applied in *Macaura v Northern Assurance Co Ltd* [1925] AC 619; and *Lee v Lee's Air Farming Ltd* [1961] AC 12. These decisions have been applied in Australia on numerous occasions, including by the High Court of Australia in *Industrial Equity Ltd v Blackburn* (1977) 137 CLR 567 in its legal treatment of companies within the same corporate group. More recently, the New South Wales Court of Appeal referred to *Salomon's* case as a 'fundamental tenet of company law': *Alexandria Landfill Pty Ltd v Transport for NSW* [2020] NSWCA 165 at [361].

The recent passage from the Supreme Court in the UK in *Sevilleja v Marex Financial Ltd (Rev 1)* [2020] UKSC 31 at [122] reinforces some very basic and longstanding points as a consequence of *Salomon's* case:

A company is a legal person distinct from its shareholders, which has its own assets which are distinct from theirs. A share in a company is an item of property owned by the shareholder, which is distinct from the assets owned by the company.

The separate legal entity principle in *Salomon's* case has been castigated as 'one of the greatest instruments of fraud ever invented' but it survives as a necessity of modern economic life: *Gilbert v Molineux* [2021] QCAT 176 at [16].

There are limited instances at common law and under statute which allow the courts to look beyond the separation between the company and its members and directors. This is commonly called lifting or piercing the corporate veil. This is usually done to shift legal responsibility from one legal entity (for example, a company) to another (for example, a parent company, major shareholder or director of the company). You should be familiar with *Gilford Motor Co Ltd v Horne* [1933] Ch 935; *Jones v Lipman* [1962] 1 WLR 832; *Re FG (Films) Ltd* [1953] 1 WLR 483; *Smith Stone & Knight Ltd v Birmingham Corp* [1939] 4 All ER 116. For a useful discussion of the main cases, see the decision in *Briggs v James Hardie & Co Pty Ltd* (1989) 16 NSWLR 549 (particularly Rogers AJA) and more recently by the New South Wales Court of Appeal in *Burrows v Macpherson & Kelley Lawyers (Sydney) Pty Ltd* [2021] NSWCA 148 which also affirmed that 'it is well settled that mere control is not sufficient to disregard corporate identity' (Lemming JA at [124]). You should also be familiar with the statutory veil piercing under the Corporations Act — in particular, s 588G, which imposes personal liability on directors for insolvent trading.

Apart from limited liability there are some other attributes of a company which are advantages for the conduct of business enterprises; namely, it can sue and be sued in its own name; it can acquire, hold and dispose of property; and it has perpetual succession. Furthermore, as a vehicle for investment it has the benefit of a formalised and controlled system of internal management, responsibility and accountability to protect the investors' interests and, in the case of public companies, the transferability of shares enables investors to change their investment choices to avoid risk.

The Corporations Act permits different classes of companies which are differentiated according to their *liability* (for example, limited by shares, limited by guarantee, etc) and their *ownership* (for example, proprietary, public, foreign, etc).

The essential difference between non crowd-sourced funded *proprietary* companies and *public* companies is that proprietary companies are prohibited from soliciting funds, either debt or equity finance, from the public via a disclosure document, and there may be restrictions on the disposal of shares by shareholders in such companies: s 113. Public companies may solicit funds from the public and they will often list their company on the Australian Securities Exchange (ASX) to facilitate this process. Shares in public companies are usually freely transferable and the transfer is further facilitated by listing on the ASX.

In order to acquire a corporate structure a person can either purchase an existing company by acquiring all of the shares in such a company, or incorporate a new company. It is now possible to incorporate either a proprietary company or a public company with only one member: s 114. However, in the case of a public company, it is still necessary to have at least three directors, two of whom must ordinarily reside in Australia: s 201A.

Until 1 July 1998, incorporating a new company involved the preparation of two documents forming the company's constitution. These were the memorandum and the articles of association.

Since 1 July 1998, companies can be incorporated merely by the lodgment of an application for registration. The application for registration now requires, among other things, the inclusion of all of the information that would have been contained in a company's memorandum: s 117. These matters include the type of company, the members, directors and secretary. The rules for the internal administration of the company would formerly be contained in the articles of association. An optional model set of articles was provided in a schedule by the former Corporations Law. This too was repealed but substituted by a series of default internal management rules called 'replaceable rules'. The rules are specific sections of the Act which may be replaced by a specific provision in the company's written constitution (if one is adopted by the company) and a complete list of them can be found in s 141. A breach of a replaceable rule is not itself a breach of the Corporations Act: s 135(3).

A new company need not have a constitution (unless it is a mining company or a publicly listed company). If it does not, then its internal administration will be governed by the replaceable rules or, if it is a single member company, those rules set out in ss 198E, 201F and 202C. Alternatively, it may choose to have a constitution which is in substitution of all or some of the replaceable rules: ss 134–136. Some of the key replaceable rules are mandatory for public companies and cannot be removed by a constitution: s 135(1)(b)(iv).

The content of and the law surrounding the company's constitution will be examined in **Chapter 5**.

Before attempting the questions below, check that you are familiar with the following issues or terms:

✓ What is meant by the concept of 'a separate legal person'?

✓ What is meant by the 'capacity of a natural person'?

✓ What is meant by 'corporate veil'?

✓ What is the purpose of limited liability?

✓ In what circumstances will the corporate veil be lifted?

✓ What is the role of ASIC in incorporation?

✓ What is the difference between a proprietary company and a public company?

Question 1

> Mei has a successful computer retail business in Sydney. Her customer base is broadening because she manages the business well and her customers like the quality of service and expertise provided by Mei. Her income is rising, as is her income tax, but she wants to expand the business. One of her loyal customers tells her that she could incorporate as a sole trader.
>
> Mei comes to you for advice. She wants to know if this is true and, if so, what it would mean if she did incorporate, and what the costs and benefits are of doing so.
>
> **Time allowed: 30 minutes**

Answer Plan

This is an essay-style question, but it may be answered partly in a standard essay style and partly with numbered or bulleted paragraphs in an effort to list the pros and cons of incorporation. You would be expected not only to list the characteristics of incorporation but also to explain them in a fashion that could be understood by someone like Mei, a business person.

You should explain the following:

- A proprietary company may be formed with only one member who may also be the company's sole director (unless it is a crowd-sourced funded company, in which case, two directors will be required: s 113). Public companies may now also be incorporated with only one member, but they still require three directors: s 201A.
- Incorporating means the creation of a separate legal entity through registration with ASIC. Once registered, the company may undertake

most of the activities that a natural person may do, including owning assets and operating a business.

- There is a procedure involved in incorporating: the preparation of an application for registration and possibly a constitution is necessary, and fees will be payable to ASIC.
- Mei's business would need to be transferred either by sale or lease to the new registered company and thereafter the new company would beneficially own the business. Mei would no longer 'own' the business, although she would be entitled to the price of the business from the company as part of the sale to the company.
- The new company would have similar capacity to a natural person and, depending on the type of company formed, particular powers to borrow money and limited liability. Each of the attributes of the company ought to be enumerated and explained.
- Despite the benefit of limited liability, there are circumstances in which liability may be imposed upon Mei directly as a result of the common law and the Corporations Act.
- The affairs of the corporation are controlled by the Corporations Act which is administered by ASIC.

Answer

Single person companies

2-2   Mei has sought advice concerning the capacity to incorporate a company with only one member. Up until the amendments brought about by the First Corporate Law Simplification Act 1995 (Cth), it was not possible for sole traders to incorporate. It was always necessary for there to be more than one person to form a company. In the case of a proprietary company, it was necessary to have at least two members and two directors. In the case of a public company, it was necessary to have at least five members and three directors. Due to significant law reform in 1995, in respect of all companies it is now permissible to have only one member: s 114. The number of directors required is set out in s 201A. In respect of a proprietary company, there need only be one director (unless it is a crowd-sourced funded company); in respect of a public company, there still needs to be three directors. If a proprietary company has just one officeholder, they do not need to follow replaceable rules or have a constitution.

Accordingly, if Mei wishes to form a corporation as a sole trader, it is more appropriate to advise her to form a proprietary company. To incorporate a public company, she would need to find and remunerate two other directors, and she may find that the financial reporting requirements for public companies are too onerous and costly to warrant the benefit of public company status. As the business develops, she can always consider changing the status of the company to a public company under Pt 2B.7.

Under s 112, a proprietary company may only be one limited by shares or an unlimited company with share capital. It is unlikely that Mei would be interested in the latter form given the risk it would pose to her personal assets and that it would negate the purpose of limited liability.

If Mei chooses to incorporate, then the act of doing so would mean that a separate legal entity would be created: *Salomon v Salomon & Co Ltd* [1897] AC 22. As confirmed in that case, it makes no difference that Mei is the dominant (or in this case, the only) shareholder; the company would be separate from her and would have its own legal rights and obligations as though it was a company formed by others.

If the purpose of incorporating was to run the computer retail business, then Mei would need to transfer the business to the company. This could be done by a contract of sale of the business from Mei to the new company. It is possible to transfer a lesser interest in the business to the company, such as a lease, and, apart from the difference in legal title, the company would have the beneficial rights to the business and its income subject to lease payment obligations to Mei. Such a leasehold interest, being a type of property, would be the property of the company. Mei would be left with the freehold title, if any, and an agreement to receive lease payments. Under an arrangement where the business is sold to the company, the company would receive the full legal title to the business in return for either the payment of money (which the company probably would not have) or the promise of money (a loan to the company) or perhaps by the issue of shares to Mei up to the value of the business.

In *Salomon's* case, the sale price of the business to Salomon and Co was a combination of loan by Salomon to the company that was secured against the assets of the business and the issue of fully paid shares in the company. In this way, Mr Salomon became a secured creditor of the company, despite his status as founder, director and major shareholder of the company.

The process of registration

2-3 Mei will need to either register a new company or purchase a shelf company that is already registered but has never traded. A pre-registered shelf company can be purchased from any one of a number of businesses that are involved in helping start up companies (known as 'promoters', discussed in **Chapter 3**). After purchasing the shares in a shelf company, Mei could then pass a resolution making herself the sole director and must notify ASIC of all changes to the company's details (such as change of name and address) within the strict timeframes set out in the Corporations Act.

Mei could alternatively register a new company online by herself (via the Australian government's Business Registration Service (BRS)) or with the aid of a private service provider (PSP). A PSP may be her accountant, solicitor or another business who provides online services with ASIC and charges a fee for their services above what ASIC would charge.

The checklist for registering a company involves considering the type of company (limited or unlimited liability) with the former being appropriate for Mei for asset protection; choosing the company's name (or for it to be known by its Australian Company Number (ACN)); the capital structure; Mei's name as sole member and details relating to the company's registered office and principal place of business. Mei may wish to reserve a business name prior to applying for registration so as to ensure that her preferred name is available. Mei's business name will also need to be registered under the national Business Names Register which is operated by ASIC.

Apart from the preparation of registration and perhaps constituent documents, there is also the need to prepare documents to transfer the business to the company. There is a fee payable to ASIC for the registration of the company in addition to any fees payable to register transfers of land or lease documents and, inevitably, there will be stamp duty payable on the transfer documents.

Mei as sole director and sole shareholder, of course, is not required to have a constitution: s 134. She need only prepare and lodge the online application at BRS for registration. If she does this and her company is a single member/single director company, then her company's 'constitution' is governed not by the new replaceable rules, but by special rules set out in ss 198E, 201F and 202C. Mei is free, however, to have a constitution so long as it does not override the terms of these sections. The special rules contained in these sections are facilitative, however, and it would be unlikely that Mei would wish to override them.

Once the transfer is complete, then the business would belong to the company (let's call it Techno Pty Ltd).

Once Techno Pty Ltd comes into existence then Mei needs to be aware that the business is now the property of the company and it is no longer her property: *Macaura v Northern Assurance Co Ltd* [1925] AC 619. Mei's only proprietary interest is as a shareholder of Techno Pty Ltd. Shares are personal property: s 1070A. The company would pay tax as a taxpayer at the current company rate and Mei would only pay income tax on her earnings as an employee/director of the company (see *Lee v Lee's Air Farming Ltd* [1961] AC 12) or on any dividends received from her shares.

The company would have all of the powers of a natural person to enter contracts and perform civil acts: s 124. Generally, the company would also have perpetual succession, which means that if Mei dies then the company still exists — there would just be a need to appoint a new director: s 201F. Companies come into existence on the day specified in their certificate of registration (ss 118 and 119) and they continue to exist until such time as they are deregistered by ASIC. It matters not that within their 'life span' members die or are replaced. Just as any natural person is capable of suing or being sued, so can a company, and it also has the power to acquire, hold or dispose of property in the same way that natural adult persons can do: s 124.

Limited liability

2-4 Any debts that are incurred by Techo Pty Ltd in conducting the business would be the debts of the company and not of Mei herself. In this sense, Mei's liability is limited in that she can only be required to pay any uncalled capital in relation to her shares: s 516. If her shares are fully paid, a likely position if they are issued to pay the purchase price of the business, then she is not liable to pay anything more to the company in the event that there are debts owed by the company in a winding up. During the company's life, creditors of the company cannot sue members or directors for debts owed by the company because of the separation or corporate veil between the company and its members. This separation between the company and its members completes the concept of the separate legal entity doctrine (as illustrated in *Salomon's* case).

There are some instances where the corporate veil will be lifted or pierced and liability for the company's debts will be imposed upon directors. Sometimes the courts will look beyond the corporate veil to make directors liable, but the circumstances are limited; for example, this may occur where the company is formed to evade an existing obligation: *Gilford Motor Co Ltd v Horne* [1933] Ch 935; *Jones v Lipman* [1962] 1 WLR 832. The Corporations Act also provides instances where the corporate veil will be breached to expose directors to personal liability. The relevant provisions for Mei would be under ss 588G–588U, which make directors personally liable for debts incurred by the company when it is, or is likely to become, insolvent.

Of course, creditors of Techno Pty Ltd may not always be willing to deal only with the company. Because of limited liability, creditors, particularly those who will potentially be large creditors such as banks under loan arrangements, will require some additional security for the credit made available to the company. In many cases they will require that a director of a company will either provide a security for the company's debt or a personal guarantee in relation to the company's debts. Thus, if the company defaults, then the creditor will not need to argue that the court must breach the corporate veil, but it will simply pursue the director under any guarantee, or recover against the secured asset.

Regulatory framework

2-5 Finally, the affairs of Techno Pty Ltd would be subject not only to the laws which would have governed Mei personally in the running of her business, but additionally they would be governed by the Corporations Act. This could involve possible investigation or control by ASIC, certainly the obligation to keep financial records, and sometimes to lodge financial reports: Ch 2M. If Techno Pty Ltd complies with the Corporations Act, its contact with ASIC will be minimal — such as the requirement to lodge an annual return. In this sense, Mei, in order to ensure compliance, will need to be aware, from time to time, of the compliance requirements of the Corporations Act or, at least, to engage a professional who will advise her on these matters.

Examiner's Comments

2-6 Given that this is a straightforward essay question without any problem to solve, it is in some ways difficult to identify areas where elaboration will be warranted. Incorporating a new company and the consequences which flow from this generally are all interesting matters to develop, so long as you don't go beyond the original purview of the question; namely, advising Mei in the context of what she needs. However, there are three areas in particular which are useful additions to an answer such as this, particularly if a wider approach is taken to the 'costs and benefits' of incorporation.

A discussion of the competing theories about the nature of the corporate personality

2-7 English and Australian courts are committed to the theory that a corporation is a separate legal entity. Its concomitant benefit is that of limited liability and there are a number of economic arguments that support the principle of limited liability as producing not only specific but general benefit to society; namely, that limited liability encourages business activity by eliminating certain business risk.

The separate entity theory has a number of shortcomings. The consequences of the theory can be that unscrupulous individuals may hide behind the corporate veil and reap the benefits of their position within the company while avoiding responsibilities to third parties under the principle of limited liability. This potential for abuse has led to the courts adopting certain stances in relation to the lifting of the corporate veil. In Australia we have seen substantial legislative inroads to the separate entity theory. In particular, as a response to some major corporate collapses in Australia, there has been an additional Part added to the Corporations Act to protect employee entitlements: Pt 5.8A. These provisions go some way to protecting the position of employees as creditors of companies as they do not have the same means available to them as are available to other creditors. Trade creditors may limit their exposure to companies by having credit limits and payment terms, while other creditors are in a position to take security to protect their position. Employees, while they had priority of repayment in a winding up under s 556, often found that there were insufficient funds to pay their salaries, wages or other entitlements when a company was wound up in insolvency.

Particular problem for single member companies

2-8 Nowhere is the problem of the separate entity theory more acute than for the single member company. The controller of the company must make decisions as a director which are for the benefit of the company as a whole. They must treat the property of the company separately from their own and they must record their decisions in relation to the company's affairs, when in reality they probably feel as though they are making decisions in relation to their own property.

The reform which permitted the incorporation of single member companies was largely to remedy the kinds of situations which arise where a sole trader convinces another, usually his or her partner, solicitor or accountant, to be a member of a company simply to make up the required number of incorporators. These additional members thought of themselves as purely nominal members and they took no active part in the management of the company. They would also overlook, however, the fact that under the law they owed duties and responsibilities which could not be excused by arguing that they were only nominal or 'sleeping' directors — as illustrated in the result in *Statewide Tobacco Services Ltd v Morley* (1990) 2 ACSR 405. Cases such as *AWA Ltd v Daniels t/as Deloitte, Haskins & Sells* (1992) 7 ACSR 759 reasserted the liability of officers and directors of companies, and s 180(1) of the Corporations Act is now clear in its application to all such persons.

While the single member company resolves the position of the 'sleeping' director it probably pushes the separate entity theory to its limit. The issue of sleeping directors is discussed further in **Chapter 6**.

Internal administration for single member companies

2-9 The provisions of ss 198E, 201F and 202C go some way to remove the unreality of standard rules for administration. These sections provide rules that overcome the need for plurality for certain corporate functions and the division of powers and enabling the single member/director to conduct the affairs of the company more easily. The question that arises for all new companies, no matter what their status, is whether they should have a constitution. This issue is dealt with more fully in **Chapter 5**.

 Keep in Mind

- Do not fall into the trap of saying that Mei incorporates herself. Mei does not turn into a corporation; rather, Mei remains a person and the corporation is a new and separate entity.
- A company, even a 'one-person company', is a distinct entity from its owner: *Salomon v A Salomon & Co Ltd* [1897] AC 22.
- The circumstance that a company may ultimately be owned or controlled by one person will not affect its status as a legal entity that is distinct from its members or controllers. This basic legal principle has been reinforced on numerous occasions by the High Court

of Australia: *Hamilton v Whitehead* [1988] HCA 65; (1988) 166 CLR 121; *Andar Transport Pty Ltd v Brambles Ltd* [2004] HCA 28; (2004) 217 CLR 424.

- As a consequence of *Salomon's* case, '[t]he company is liable for its contracts and torts; the shareholder has no such liability': *Prudential Assurance Co Ltd v Newman Industries Ltd (No 2)* [1982] Ch 204 at 224.

- The company owns its assets and the shareholders have no legal or equitable interest in and are not part owners of those assets: *Macaura v Northern Assurance Co Ltd* [1925] AC 619.

- Do not overlook the need to actually transfer the business in some way to the new company, otherwise Mei will still be operating the business herself and be liable for taxation for the income from the business.

Question 2

> The separate legal entity theory for corporations involves the notion of a corporate veil.
>
> Is the protection provided by the corporate veil justifiable?
>
> **Time allowed: 40 minutes**

Answer Plan

There is no problem analysis required for this question. What is required is an exposition of your understanding of the effect of the legal principle that a corporation is separate from its members. You should:

- explain the attributes of a corporation;
- explain what is meant by the corporate veil;
- identify the problems for third parties which arise from the existence of the corporate veil;
- identify circumstances where the corporate veil will be ignored or lifted either at common law or under statute.

Answer

2-10   At common law, a company is considered to be a separate legal entity from its members. Incorporation is now an administrative procedure and once a company is registered and a certificate of incorporation is issued then a company comes into existence: s 119. That company has all of the significant attributes accorded to companies under the common law; namely, it:

- is capable of performing all the functions of a body corporate;
- is capable of suing and being sued;
- has perpetual succession; and
- has power to acquire, hold and dispose of property.

That a company is a separate legal entity was clearly established in *Salomon v Salomon & Co Ltd* [1897] AC 22. The separate legal entity theory means that the company is a separate and distinct legal person from its members or those who formed it. It necessarily flows from this that the company's property (of which it has the power to acquire, hold and dispose) is also distinct from the property of its members. If it is accepted that it is a separate legal entity and its property is distinct from the property of its members, then it also follows that the property of the members of a company cannot be used to pay the company's debts. In other words, the members have no liability for the company's debts; their liability is only to pay the amount that they promise to pay when they subscribe for shares or under a guarantee: ss 516 and 517. This is what is meant by limited liability.

In order to maintain the distinction between the property of members and the property of the corporation, a fictional barrier is set up between the company and its members, including the directors, to ensure that members' property is not used to satisfy corporate debts; this fictional barrier is called the 'corporate veil'. Practically, it means that if a company has insufficient funds or assets to satisfy its debts then the members cannot be forced to pay them even when the members have in fact acted on behalf of the company in incurring the debts: s 516. The effect of the corporate veil is squarely represented by the statement of Lord Sumner in *Gas Lighting Improvement Co Ltd v IRC* [1923] AC 723 at 740:

> Between the investor, who participates as a shareholder, and the undertaking carried on, the law interposes another person, real though artificial, the company itself, and the business carried on is the business of the company, and the capital employed is its capital and not in either case the business or capital of the shareholders. Assuming, of course, that the company is duly formed and is not a sham, the idea that it is mere machinery for effecting the purposes of the shareholders is a layman's fallacy. It is a figure of speech, which cannot alter the legal aspects of the facts.

While the reality of the matter is that the corporate form is indeed the 'mere machinery for effecting the purposes of the shareholders', especially in the case of small companies or quasi-partnership companies, the legal form persists in the fiction of a separate personality.

There are competing theories about corporations, in particular the economic view or the enterprise theory wherein the company is viewed as a group of investors with a common view to making a profit using the most efficient means possible. Courts in England (*Prest v Petrodel Resources Ltd* [2013] UKSC 34) and Australia (*Andar Transport Pty Ltd v Brambles* (2004) 217 CLR 424) are, however, through the doctrine of precedent, committed to the separate legal entity theory.

The corporate veil represents a major problem for unsecured creditors of companies. Neither the common law nor the Corporations Act requires that companies must have a minimum capital before they are permitted to incorporate. In Australia, this meant that there was a proliferation of '$2 companies', being companies with an issued capital of only two shares of $1 each (or one $2 share). Unless the company acquired valuable assets then unsecured creditors were faced with the possibility that, if a company did not pay, there was only $2 in the company coffers to satisfy the debt, even though the company's directors had requested the credit. Unsecured creditors had no control over how a company dealt with its assets, even though the company's activities (at the behest of its directors) were conducted in such a way as to prejudice the amount of funds available to satisfy unsecured creditors.

The problem for creditors was not seen as a major problem by the courts or by the legislature as it was thought that creditors were in the best position to determine the likelihood of a company being able to repay the debt. Thus, if the company is under-capitalised, the creditor will often require a personal guarantee or some other security for the repayment of the debt before credit is extended. This is not always the case and will depend on the relative bargaining positions of the creditor and the company. The problem for creditors is also compounded by the modern tendency for business to be conducted by complex corporate structures involving groups of related corporations, holding companies and subsidiaries. Creditors may find it difficult to really determine, particularly in small or frequent transactions, which corporate entity he or she is dealing with and thus the creditor may assess the creditworthiness of one member of the group as being good, whereas he or she is in fact dealing with a separate legal entity within that group who is in a very poor financial position: *Qintex Australia Finance Ltd v Schroders Australia Ltd* (1990) 3 ACSR 267.

Further, not all persons who are potentially owed money by a corporation are persons who can assess the creditworthiness of the corporation. Persons who are injured by the corporation and have a legal claim against it or employees are not in a position to determine whether or not the corporation can pay.

Courts in England have, on rare occasions, found justification to shift the focus away from the separate legal status of the company based on a range of statutory and common law principles. These precedents provide no coherent method for categorising when the corporate veil may be lifted and represent at best an ad hoc application of legal rules to meet the requirements of particular fact situations: see the discussion by Rogers AJA in *Briggs v James Hardie & Co Pty Ltd* (1989) 16 NSWLR 549; more recently in the UK in *Prest v Petrodel Resources Ltd* [2013] UKSC 34. However, they do suggest that the legal principle of the corporate veil has some degree of flexibility.

For example, it can be argued that the company is a mere agent of another and this may allow for the principal to either obtain a benefit offered to the agent or to accept responsibility for the conduct of the agent: *Smith Stone & Knight Ltd v Birmingham Corp* [1939] 4 All ER 116; *Re FG (Films) Ltd* [1953] 1 WLR 482. Agency can of course be proved by an express agreement between two companies (similarly, two companies may be found to be working in partnership with one another). Cases such as *Smith, Stone & Knight* represent examples of an implied agency relationship. The evidence to establish an implied agency has to be more than just a relationship of control between the two companies. As Rogers AJA noted in *Briggs v James Hardie & Co Pty Ltd* (1989) 16 NSWLR 549, control is an ordinary incident of the relationship between parent and subsidiary companies. If one company (the parent or principal) uses another company (the agent) to carry out its activities and the agent company is clearly working for the benefit of the principal (perhaps as evidenced by the fact that it has beneficial right to the profits generated by the business activities as demonstrated by its lack of capital, assets, employees or means to carry on the activities in its own right), then it is possible that a court will look through the corporate fiction and identify those activities as being the activities of the principal: *Re FG (Films) Ltd* [1953] 1 WLR 483.

The English authorities have been closely examined in Australia and while recognising that there is a tension between economic realities and strict legal doctrine, the courts have been very conservative in their approach to lifting the corporate veil: *Pioneer Concrete Services Ltd v Yelnah Pty Ltd* (1986) 5 NSWLR 254; *Qintex Australia Finance Ltd v Shroders Australia Ltd* (1990) 3 ACSR 267. Both of these cases have defended the corporate veil in situations where there is a corporate group in which a parent or holding company controls the affairs of a subsidiary. However, in *Spraeg v Paeson Pty Ltd* (1990) 94 ALR 679, the Federal Court saw fit to lift the corporate veil in circumstances where the degree of control over the associated company was so great as to justify imposing orders on the parent company for breaches of the former Trade Practices Act 1974 (Cth) (now Competition and Consumer Act 2010 (Cth)).

Another example of a situation where the court may lift the corporate veil is when the corporation is clearly formed to evade an existing legal duty: *Gilford Motor Co Ltd v Horne* [1933] Ch 935; *Jones v Lipman* [1962] 1 WLR 832. The legal duty must be an existing one, and not some perceived future liability. Accordingly, it is permissible to form a company to undertake a business venture which has possible financial risks and it is the intention of the incorporators to avoid those financial risks by using the corporate form with limited liability: *Adams v Cape Industries plc* [1990] Ch 433.

The judicial uncertainty at common law for the grounds of veil lifting can be contrasted with the position taken by the Australian parliament which provides for a number of specific statutory grounds for lifting the corporate veil.

The most important ones are as follows:

• Sections 588G–588U: Liability for a company's debts is imposed upon directors who trade or permit a company to trade when it is insolvent.

- Sections 588V–588X: Liability for the debts of a subsidiary company is imposed upon the holding company when the subsidiary company engages in insolvent trading.
- Section 197: Directors of trustee companies may be held personally liable if they have not obtained indemnities from the beneficiaries of the trust fund.
- Chapter 2M Div 6: Holding or controlling companies must present consolidated accounts to reflect the financial position of the group as a whole and to reveal any contingent liabilities between members of the group under guarantees or other cross-securities.

The statutory provisions go some way to protecting the position of creditors and potential investors, but they do not fully protect others such as employees or potential claimants in tort. However, when companies are being wound up, the claims of employees are preferential debts and are paid ahead of other creditors: s 556. Part 5.8A of the Corporations Act now lifts the corporate veil and provides access to any person who enters transactions which defeat or compromise the recovery of an employee's entitlements to salary, wages, superannuation or other award or injury compensation.

Other legislation, such as workers' compensation and third party or public liability insurance, can give some protection to claimants in most cases. However, there is still no general access under the Corporations Act to the controllers of companies who make decisions which result in either civil or criminal wrongdoing to others. Similarly, a wrong committed by a subsidiary company will go uncompensated if the subsidiary company has insufficient assets, notwithstanding that its holding company is wealthy.

In summary, the corporate veil is an important foundation concept that underpins the operation of modern company law but it is not inviolable. The law contains numerous statutory and common law examples where the principles may be avoided or disregarded for a limited purpose. The justification of the principle is not undermined by specific examples of unfairness to third parties as other areas of law provide some measure of protection.

Examiner's Comments

2-11 This question, like Question 1, is of a general essay type. Possible areas upon which a student may elaborate would be to provide more examples of situations in which the corporate veil can be used and abused. Recent events in Australia concerning the restructuring of the James Hardie group of companies would provide a good example where assets were moved between companies with the effect that companies bearing liability for disease caused by asbestos were left with insufficient assets as the asset holding companies were moved offshore.

It may be useful to refer to *Donnelly v Edelsten* (1992) 109 ALR 651, where the court refused to lift the corporate veil in circumstances where the company was incorporated to avoid possible future liabilities. Given that the corporate structure is essentially a creature of business designed to spread and limit risk, it was legitimate to use such a structure to limit the risk of a business enterprise which may possibly carry the risk of financial loss in the future. These are the risks that a sole trader would not wish to bear and which a corporate structure can sometimes alleviate, unfortunately for creditors of companies. The distinction to be drawn between the *Donnelly v Edelsten* case and cases such as *Gilford Motor Co Ltd v Horne* is that the *Edelsten* case is about avoiding possible (maybe even probable) future obligations, while the *Gilford Motor Co Ltd* case was about evading existing obligations.

The lament in these cases is that creditors suffer as a result of the interpolation of the corporate veil between them and the decision-makers on questions of raising credit. Consequently, it may be useful to elaborate on the various other devices designed for the protection of creditors. You would have already touched on this by setting out the various statutory means of lifting the corporate veil, such as in s 588G.

Creditors are also given ultimate protection by virtue of their position ahead of members in priority of payment in a winding up and, of course, creditors are in a position to assess the ability of the company to repay and to require security if necessary. This protection can be illusory if the company has a large debt situation and the creditors are unsecured.

Potential judgment creditors may protect their position by asking the court to grant a Mareva injunction to prevent a company from dissipating its assets to avoid the payment of a judgment debt.

Finally, it would be useful to include some discussion of the theory of the corporate veil. Economic theories tend to support the corporate veil and the related principle of limited liability by arguing that such a system encourages diverse investment and entrepreneurial risk-taking. A system of unlimited liability would lead investors to be wary of making investments in new businesses as it would increase their exposure to personal liability. It would also increase monitoring costs as investors closely monitor companies in which they invest to manage risk of personal liability. Other theories (for example, communitarian perspectives) argue that the corporate veil is a device to shift liability onto those that can least afford it such as tort victims. However, the role of other laws (such as tort laws and accident compensation laws) can also assist these parties.

🔔 Keep in Mind

- '"Piercing the corporate veil" is an expression rather indiscriminately used to describe a number of different things.' So commenced Lord Sumption's analysis of the expression in *Prest v Petrodel*

Resources Ltd [2013] UKSC 34, indicating the difficulty in finding a common objective for veil piercing at common law.

- Do not fall into the trap of asserting that the courts will lift the corporate veil where it can be shown that a company has been set up to limit liability.
- Do not assume that the court will lift the corporate veil simply because a company has insufficient assets to pay its liabilities.
- Do not assume that shifting liability or benefits between separate legal entities necessarily involves ignoring the corporate veil.

Question 3

Short answer questions:

(a) What are the basic differences between proprietary and public companies?

(b) What is the difference between a company limited by shares and a company limited by guarantee?

Time allowed: 10 minutes for each question

Answer Plan

Short answer questions are designed to elicit a concise and accurate description of terms or phrases commonly used in the discipline. These questions are concerned with classification and structure of corporate forms, and students should point out not only the meaning of the terms used according to common law but they should also refer to relevant parts of the Corporations Act.

Answer (a)

Purpose

2-12 Proprietary companies were designed to meet the needs of smaller businesses, which wanted the benefit of limited liability from incorporation. Non crowd-sourced funded proprietary companies are restricted to a maximum of 50 members not including employee members: s 113(1). Proprietary companies can operate their business in a similar way that public companies can, including appointing a board of directors, conducting regular members' meetings and issuing shares to raise money.

Funding

2-13 Proprietary companies may not solicit funds from the public generally, unless they are crowd-sourced funded. The general restriction is contained in s 113(3), which prohibits a proprietary company from engaging in any conduct requiring disclosure under Ch 6D. The disclosure provisions contained in Ch 6D are the requirements for the lodgment of a disclosure document or prospectus, this being the means by which funds are solicited from the public generally. It is also possible as a result of the replaceable rule in s 254D that existing shareholders of proprietary companies will have pre-emption rights on new share issues by their companies. The constitution of proprietary companies may contain restrictions on who can purchase shares in the company and how these may be purchased.

Share transfer restrictions

2-14 Proprietary companies may place restrictions upon the transfer of their shares, whereas public companies can have no such restrictions. Indeed, directors of proprietary companies can have a discretion to refuse to register a transfer of shares: s 1072G.

Plurality of members

2-15 Proprietary companies may now be incorporated with only one member (s 114) and need only have one director (except if crowd-sourced funded, in which case a minimum of two directors are required): s 201A. Public companies may now also be incorporated with only one member (s 114) but still need to have three directors, two of whom must ordinarily reside in Australia: s 201A. Public companies are required to hold an annual general meeting under s 250N, although proprietary companies may also choose to conduct regular members' meetings.

Disclosure

2-16 Proprietary companies generally have less stringent requirements for the disclosure of their affairs, and the disclosure level depends on whether they are small proprietary companies or large proprietary companies: ss 45A(2) and 292(2). Public companies, conversely, have more extensive disclosure requirements to ASIC and their members: see Ch 2N. Public companies may list on a securities exchange, and if they do then a further disclosure regime may apply under the Corporations Act (s 674) and also under the Listing Rules of the relevant exchange.

 # Examiner's Comments

2-17 There are some further practical differences between proprietary and public companies. The proprietary company must use the word 'proprietary' or 'Pty' in its name: s 148. Directors of a proprietary company tend to have a different security of tenure as directors than those in public companies. A director of a public company may be removed before the end of his or her term by an ordinary resolution of members notwithstanding anything in the constitution: s 203D. Removal of a director of a public company by the other directors is expressly prohibited by s 203E. Section 203B is a replaceable rule for proprietary companies to permit the removal of a director by members. However, there is no equivalent provision to s 203E preventing removal by other directors. There appears to be no restriction to having a rule for removal of a director by other directors in the constitution of a proprietary company.

Directors of public companies have different requirements about disclosure and voting on matters where there is a conflict of interest: ss 191, 194 and 195.

Further, public companies are regulated by Ch 2E of the Corporations Act, which purports to prevent the giving of financial benefits to related parties, whereas proprietary companies (except if crowd-sourced funded) are not so regulated.

Buy-backs and takeover rules differ also as between proprietary and public companies.

The accounting and reporting requirements for proprietary companies, while being substantially less than those for public companies, are subject to whether the company is classed as a small proprietary or a large proprietary company. While keeping in mind that this is a short answer question, it is worth noting the different reporting requirements for proprietary companies. These are set out in s 292.

Answer (b)

2-18 A company limited by shares and a company limited by guarantee have several important differences, each of which comes from a fundamentally different capital structure. A company limited by shares has equity capital that is divided into one or more shares that are issued to members in order to raise money for the company. Shares are the personal property of each member (s 1070A) and may be traded, mortgaged or held on trust. Share capital may also be divided into different classes, each with different rights which will attract different prices according to the desired financial and risk exposure of each investor. Companies with share capital therefore have a flexible way of raising new equity capital.

Companies limited by guarantee must be a public company (s 112); however, they do not have the same flexible range of fundraising options as companies limited by shares. The capital structure of a company limited by guarantee is not divided into tradable shares but rather is based on promises given by members to contribute to the company's liabilities upon a winding up (that is, a guarantee): s 517. The guarantee given by each member is limited to a particular amount (usually a small amount such as $10). A company limited by guarantee therefore cannot raise money by issuing more equity capital. It is for this reason that companies limited by guarantee are usually run for charitable and other not-for-profit purposes.

Examiner's Comments

2-19 This answer could discuss the differences in reporting obligations between the two types of companies. While companies limited by guarantee are public companies which usually have greater disclosure obligations, companies limited by guarantee may be either large or small companies limited by guarantee. Small companies limited by guarantee are defined in s 45B and are generally not obliged to prepare financial and directors' reports unless directed to do so by the members or by ASIC: s 292(3).

The regulation of corporate names is another variation between the two forms of companies that could be discussed. While proprietary companies must have 'Pty Ltd' after their name on all public documents (s 148), companies limited by guarantee may be exempted by ASIC from having Ltd after their name in certain circumstances: s 150.

 # Keep in Mind

- Do not simply refer to sections of the Corporations Act or copy out the text of the legislation without more. Answers in this form do not demonstrate any understanding of the differences.

 # Question 4

> There are a number of different types of companies referred to in the Corporations Act.
>
> What are the basic differences and can a company convert to a different status at any time?
>
> **Time allowed: 35 minutes**

Answer Plan

First, I would explain that companies can be classified according to their public or private status and then they may be classified according to the liability of their members. This can be done either diagrammatically or by listing.

It would then be necessary to explain briefly each type of classification by describing each of the following:

- proprietary company;
- public company;
- company limited by shares;
- company limited by guarantee;
- unlimited company; and
- no liability company.

The most common change of status is from private to public, so it would be logical to discuss these processes next by examining the legislative provision permitting such change and then outlining the procedures for the company to effect the change.

 # Answer

2-20 Companies that are incorporated under the Corporations Act are classified into types according to different qualities. The most common classification is between public and proprietary companies. Section 9 of the Corporations Act defines a public company as being a company other than a proprietary company, meaning that a company must be either public or proprietary; there is nothing in between.

Historically, the distinction between proprietary companies and public companies was size. The proprietary company, originating from the English 'private' company, was a corporate form for small, often family, businesses and it was less heavily regulated than the public company. The public company, on the other hand, was the corporate form used for enterprises with conceivably large numbers of members or investors. Because they would be likely to solicit funds from the investing public they are more heavily regulated in terms of their disclosure and fundraising activities.

Proprietary companies are required to use the word 'Proprietary' or 'Pty' in their name to indicate that they are subject to less disclosure and also to disclose their true nature to potential creditors: ss 148 and 149. Notwithstanding this 'small private' and 'large public' distinction, a proprietary company can be a very large enterprise with assets that exceed many public companies. They are by far the most popular business structure and they outnumber public companies by approximately 50 to 1. Of course, both public and proprietary companies must have the word 'Limited' or 'Ltd' in their name, again as a reminder to creditors that liability is limited: ss 148 and 149.

The main differences between proprietary and public companies are contained in s 113. There is an upper limit to the number of shareholders in that a proprietary company cannot have more than 50 non-employee shareholders (unless if crowd-sourced funded), and it can only be a company with share capital, but it can be either limited or unlimited in the liability of its shareholders: s 112. It cannot solicit funds from the public (s 113(3)) but it can offer shares to existing shareholders or employees: s 113(3)(a). Except for crowd-sourced funded proprietary companies, if a proprietary company exceeds its limit of 50 members or purports to be other than a company with share capital or if it solicits funds from the company, then apart from any contravention of the Corporations Act the company may be forced to convert to a public company: s 165.

Commonly, proprietary companies have a restriction on the transfer of shares in their constitution. Restrictions on share transfers are not a prerequisite for proprietary status, but they are still common because this reflects their basic use as a corporate form for small businesses which originated from sole traders, families or partnerships. There is a minimum size for all companies of one member: s 114. That member may be another corporation such as exists in a holding company and subsidiary company structure. Public companies will still need to have three directors, and directors have to be natural persons: s 201A.

Public company status requires a greater degree of disclosure in reports to members and ASIC. Because of the variability in the size of the enterprise of companies regardless of their status, proprietary companies have been divided into a further sub-category of small proprietary and large proprietary companies. This sub-categorisation entails different levels of disclosure and reporting dependent on the size of the enterprise.

The other major form of categorisation under the Corporations Act is by way of the liability of members.

Company limited by shares

2-21 Section 9 defines a company limited by shares as a company where the liability of the members is limited to the amount unpaid on any shares held by them. Thus, the company must state a share capital in its application for registration and how many shares there are: s 117(2). The value of each share, being the total share capital divided by the number of shares, was formerly called the 'nominal' or 'par' value. Par value has now been abolished and the original subscribers simply state how much they will pay for each share of their shares. A company limited by shares is the pinnacle form of the limited liability principle. Creditors of a company limited by shares do not have access to the personal property of the members because of the corporate veil. Members are only liable to lose the amount of their shares in a winding up or they may be required to pay the debts of the company only up to the amount, if any, unpaid on their shares: s 516. This type of company is the most common form for business enterprises and it must use the word 'Limited' or 'Ltd' in its name to indicate to potential creditors that it is a limited liability company: s 148. It is the most useful form for a profit-making venture because the subscription for shares provides the working capital for the venture.

Company limited by guarantee

2-22 Section 9 of the Corporations Act defines a company limited by guarantee as one where the liability of the members is limited in the memorandum to the amounts that the members agree to contribute to the company if and when it is wound up. Thus, this company does not have a share capital and does not have start-up funds in the form of subscriptions for shares. This type of company is not very useful for a trading venture and is often more suitable for a club or association which will gain funds from other sources. It is also a common form for insurance companies where funds will be acquired from insurance premiums.

In this type of company, the members' liability is still limited as it is in the company with a share capital, but the liability will only arise when the company is being wound up and then the liquidator will call upon the member to pay up to the amount promised or guaranteed under the memorandum. A company limited by guarantee can only be a public company: s 112. A company limited by guarantee may be classified as a small company limited by guarantee (s 45B) which means that the company is not generally obliged to produce annual financial reports and directors' reports (s 292(3)).

Unlimited company

2-23   Section 9 defines an unlimited company as one which has no limit on the liability of its members. While the company is a separate legal entity and has all of the benefits associated with separate personality, creditors will have access to the personal property of members in a winding up if the company has insufficient funds to meet its debts. This is not a popular form of corporation. It may or may not have a share capital; if it does, then it is not subject to restrictions on the return of capital to its members as other limited liability companies are. (The doctrine of maintenance of capital prevents a company from returning capital to members as it defeats the claims of creditors in a winding up. This is examined in **Chapter 9**.) This form of company is used for investment holdings such as mutual funds. Thus, a mutual fund which holds investments can distribute the income to members without breaching any rules about returning capital to members.

This form of company is also useful for certain professional organisations that want the flexibility of a separate legal personality, but the rules of their professions prevent them from limiting their liability. Accountants and lawyers come within this category.

No liability company

2-24   Because of the speculative nature of mining exploration, investors in these companies would evade calls to make further payments on the unpaid portion of their shares to minimise their losses if they thought that the venture was not successful. In order to normalise this phenomenon, previous legislation accepted that this would occur and provided that, in the event that calls on shares were unpaid, the shareholder would forfeit those shares. Section 9 of the Corporations Act therefore defines a no liability company as one where the company does not have a right to enforce calls on the unpaid capital contributions of shareholders. Section 254M(2) further provides that shareholders are not liable to pay and that if they choose not to pay then the shares will be forfeited: s 254Q.

Only companies whose sole purpose is mining or mining exploration can be no liability companies: s 112(2). Restrictions on the activities of no liability companies are further set out in s 112 and the note to that section. These companies must have the words 'No Liability' or 'NL' in their name (s 148(4)) as a warning to potential investors and creditors.

There are special rules about the payment of dividends and surpluses on a winding up. No liability companies must be public companies: s 112.

Changing a company's status

2-25 Changing the status of a company is governed by Pt 2B.7 of the Corporations Act. Essentially, the company must pass a special resolution and then comply with ss 163 and 164. In short, the requirements merely ensure that the company, in wishing to change, actually fits the description of the type of company that it wishes to become. Existing companies that have a constitution may need to fulfil additional requirements under their constitutions.

The Corporations Act permits only certain changes of status: s 162. In allowing a change of status ASIC is concerned that there is no material prejudice to creditors or to existing shareholders. Changes of status and the necessary change of name are notified in the ASIC database and the *Gazette*. They are also subject to appeal.

Examiner's Comments

2-26 Probably the best area to expand on in this answer is to give some reasons why a company might wish to change its status. Conversion from proprietary company to public company may be forced upon the company because of an increase in non-employee shareholders, or because of a desire to be able to solicit funds more broadly. A public company may wish to convert to proprietary status if it finds the cost of compliance with the higher disclosure requirements is too high. Provided it can comply with the other prerequisites for a proprietary company status, a change of status may deliver cost cuts. There may be legislation, such as tax legislation, that benefits certain types of companies that would justify a change of status.

There are other categories of classification within the Corporations Act which are not concerned with the public status or liability of the company, but which will greatly affect the company's activities. The classification is according to ownership or purpose. Under ownership classifications, companies are classified as holding or subsidiary companies and various degrees in between. There are also categories of related entities or entities controlled by other entities. The purpose of these classifications is essentially to ensure a more rigorous system of financial reporting. Companies with interests and potential or contingent liabilities through corporate relationships now are required to declare these relationships so that potential investors or creditors have a better view of the company's financial position when it is part of a corporate group. These accounting and audit requirements represent a statutory inroad into the corporate veil in that there is now a degree of transparency which reveals the controlling forces of companies which are part of a group: Ch 2M Div 6.

The purpose of a company can affect the way in which it is treated under the Corporations Act. Just as mining companies or companies with charitable objects can have special status or licence, companies formed to manage trusts or investment companies are subject to special restrictions imposed either by state laws or by Ch 5C of the Corporations Act.

 Keep in Mind

- Apart from the special conditions in s 112 for proprietary companies and the provisions relating to no liability companies, the Corporations Act does not require that certain types of companies have any particular status. The definitions of each type of company in s 9 all refer to the fact that the key to the status of the company is in the application for registration. Thus, the Corporations Act does not dictate choice of company status, save for the restrictions just mentioned.
- The other common error is to assume that all public companies are also listed companies. Many public companies are listed, but there is no requirement for listing. Listing on the ASX is an additional step for a public company, which expects that it will frequently use its ability to solicit funds from the public. Listing simply provides a mechanism and public place to offer and trade securities (shares or debentures) in the company. In order to be listed, the company must comply with the ASX Listing Rules and formally apply to the ASX to be listed.

 Question 5

Buster Crabbe is a scallop fisherman in the coastal waters of southern New South Wales. The stocks of scallops in these waters are limited and subject to protective legislation to ensure regeneration. Hence, the Scallop Fishing and Marketing Act provides for a quota system. Under the quota system, a person must apply for a quota which will permit him or her to catch 50 tonnes of scallops in a calendar year. Further, the Scallop Marketing Authority will purchase any scallops up to the quota limit for each person.

The Act also provides for a number of offences. It provides that it is an offence to sell scallops caught in New South Wales coastal waters to any person other than the Scallop Marketing Authority and it further provides that it is an offence to catch more than the quota limit. Each offence carries a fine of up to $100,000.

Buster has the physical capacity to catch more than 50 tonnes of scallops in a year and wishes to make more money from his business. His daughter tells him that by incorporating a company he could double his catch.

Is she correct? Advise with reference to company law.

Time allowed: 30 minutes

Answer Plan

This is a simple application of the separate legal entity principle.

The company as a separate legal entity

- Companies are separate legal entities from the members and directors and managers.
- The importance of the legal principles in *Salomon's* case.
- Companies have all of the powers of a natural person.
- Buster Pty Ltd is not the same as Buster Crabbe and would thus be entitled to apply for its own quota under the Act.

Corporate veil piercing

- Consider whether there may be grounds to look beyond the corporate veil.

Answer

The company as a separate legal entity

2-27 This question is a simple demonstration of the basic concept that a company is a separate entity from its incorporators or members. This has a number of consequences in this situation.

Crabbe is able to incorporate a proprietary company with only one member (s 114) and only one director (s 201A). The proprietary company type would be most suitable for Crabbe as it has the least administrative and maintenance requirements under the Corporations Act.

Once incorporated, the new company has the capacity and power of an individual (s 124) and can apply for its own fishing quota in addition to any quota held by Crabbe. The word 'person' in legislation will include humans and corporations unless it is expressed not to apply to corporations or it cannot apply because of the nature of a corporation: Acts Interpretation Act 1901 (Cth) s 22; Interpretation Act 1987 (NSW) s 21.

The property of the company (the quota) is separate to the property of its members (*Salomon v Salomon & Co Ltd* [1897] AC 22; *Macaura v Northern Assurance Co Ltd* [1925] AC 619), and the new company can even employ Crabbe to perform the fishing for it: *Lee v Lee's Air Farming Ltd* [1961] AC 621.

Once registered, the company is a real entity and a corporate veil exists which shields the member(s) from liability to outsiders. The company is not a sham merely because it seeks to take advantage of this: *Sharrment Pty Ltd v Official Trustee* (1988) 18 FCR 449; *Peate v FCT* (1964) 111 CLR 443; *Salomon v Salomon & Co* (above). Its certificate of registration is conclusive evidence that all the procedures required for legal formation have been complied with: s 1274(7A).

Lifting the corporate veil

2-28 Crabbe needs to be made aware of the possibility, despite the doctrine of separate legal personality, that there are circumstances where the court may lift the corporate veil. The relevant fishing authority or his competitors may well initiate proceedings or agitate for proceedings to be brought against him wherein this issue will be debated.

There are two possible arguments that could be developed to warrant a lifting of the corporate veil. One argument is that Crabbe has used a corporate form to avoid the effect of a law and thereby negate the policy behind the law. This policy is aimed, arguably, at protecting fishing resources in the long term. A similar method of reasoning can be discerned in *Daimler Co v Continental Tyre and Rubber Co (Great Britain) Ltd* [1916] 2 AC 307. In this case, the court lifted the veil on a company incorporated in Great Britain during the Great War to see that the controllers were citizens of a country with whom Great Britain was at war. Trading with persons from a country against whom war had been declared was prohibited under the Trading with the Enemy Act 1914 (UK).

Some statutes will expressly prohibit 'double dipping' of this nature; however, our question is about some hypothetical legislation, so we don't know if this prohibition exists.

The other possible argument is that the company is acting as an agent for Crabbe. This argument is similar to the reasoning in *Smith Stone & Knight Ltd v Birmingham Corp* [1939] 4 All ER 116. For this argument to succeed it would be necessary to point to facts which clearly establish that the corporation is merely acting as the agent either under an express agreement or an implied agreement. In *Smith, Stone & Knight Ltd v Birmingham Corp* (above), the plaintiff successfully argued that its subsidiary was incapable of carrying on the business which was threatened by actions of the local council and that the plaintiff, as parent company, was in fact carrying on the business.

Similarly, in *Re FG (Films) Ltd* [1953] 1 WLR 483, a subsidiary of an American company was held to be acting as an agent of its parent company in the production of a film seeking registration under the Cinematographic Films Act 1938–1948 (UK). The finding was based upon the facts that the subsidiary did not have the necessary capital, cash flow or employees to have produced the film. In *Spraeg v Paeson*

Pty Ltd (1990) 94 ALR 679, the court held that the corporate veil would be lifted from a subsidiary to reveal that it was the parent company that was carrying out the transaction for the purposes of imposing sanctions under the former Trade Practices Act 1974 (Cth).

Of course, this conclusion is contrary to the basic principle in *Salomon's* case (above). Given the reluctance of courts in Australia to depart from *Salomon's* case, the argument may well flounder: see *Pioneer Concrete Services Ltd v Yelnah Pty Ltd* (1986) 5 NSWLR 254.

The distinguishing point between Crabbe's situation and these cases is that Crabbe and Buster Pty Ltd are not parent and subsidiary companies. Certainly, a parent company will be classified as a controller of its subsidiary depending on the percentage of shares held. In the case of a single member company, there is no issue about who controls the affairs of the company. The risk of the argument succeeding would clearly be higher if Buster Pty Ltd had no assets with which to conduct its fishing and no formal arrangement with Crabbe as an employee or subcontractor to do the fishing for it.

If Buster Pty Ltd is under-resourced to carry out its quota, then the court may well entertain the argument that Buster Pty Ltd is an agent for Crabbe himself. However, the stronger argument is perhaps based upon the first point — that the law, or its policy, will require that the veil be lifted as activities such as this thwart the clear policy of fishing management.

Examiner's Comments

2-29 This is an excellent example of how the ease of incorporation can be misused to thwart legitimate regulation. It would demonstrate a clear understanding of the limits of the separate entity doctrine to discuss the effect of these excesses upon policy in Australia and the United States.

Another area to discuss is whether using a corporate vehicle to avoid the effects of legislation is the same as evading an existing legal obligation as maintained in *Gilford Motor Co Ltd v Horne* [1933] Ch 935 and *Jones v Lipman* [1962] 1 WLR 832. Whether a statute that imposes a penalty for certain activities creates a corresponding legal duty in an individual to refrain from those activities is an interesting jurisprudential argument.

Keep in Mind

- Do not fall into the trap of saying that because the legislation refers to 'persons' and this covers corporations (see Acts Interpretation Act (Cth)), Crabbe could still only have one quota. Crabbe, by forming a corporation, is not 'incorporating himself'; he is actually creating another, albeit artificial, legal being.
- In relation to lifting the corporate veil, avoid arguing that the company is a sham. To say that it is a sham is to argue that the company is not

a real company at all, but some disguise or pretence of a company. The company is real because of the process of registration and the evidentiary effect of the certificate of incorporation. Lifting the corporate veil is a process whereby the court examines the activities which are said to be the activities of the company to see if they really are activities of that company or whether they are more correctly the activities of the director or member of the company.

- Another common error is simply to argue that, if the corporation exceeds the quota, then the corporation will be liable for the fine and not Crabbe himself. This is a short-sighted argument, because if the corporation continually exceeds its quota there is bound to be some other part of the legislation which enables the relevant authority to refuse quotas. Further, if the corporation is fined and is unable to pay the fine, then it is likely that it will be wound up in insolvency.

Chapter 3

Promoters and Starting a Company

⊙ Key Issues

3-1   In the previous chapter we discussed the separate legal existence of a registered company. However, in order for the company to be registered, there are various steps that must be taken such as completing the application for registration, finding and appointing the directors and officers and doing all things necessary to bring the company to life. This is the role of the promoter. The definition of a promoter in relation to a corporation is a little vague. Generally, a promoter is the person involved in starting or registering a new company. Promoters are specifically dealt with under Ch 6D in relation to the preparation of disclosure documents and prospectuses. These requirements are dealt with in **Chapter 9** of this book. This chapter deals with the role of promoters in forming a company and the activities in which they engage prior to incorporation on behalf of the company.

The term 'promoter' includes a range of persons who may undertake all or some of the activities involved in forming a company such as registration of the company, preparation of constituent documents, obtaining directors and shareholders, raising capital and negotiating preliminary agreements. The meaning of the term is to be found in common law as there is no definition of promoter in the Corporations Act, although the term is used in the Act. For a review of the leading authorities on promoters and their fiduciary duties, see *Meriton Apartments Pty Ltd v The Owners Strata Plan No 72381* [2015] NSWSC 202.

Because companies are formed not only to start a new enterprise but also to take over existing enterprises, there is much scope for persons involved in the start up or acquisition of a business to abuse their position and make personal gains. The facts of *Salomon v Salomon & Co Ltd* [1897] AC 22 reveal a very common example of the activity of a promoter. Salomon sold his existing enterprise to a newly formed company in circumstances where possibly Salomon knew facts about the business which, if revealed to the company as a separate legal entity, may have militated against the company purchasing the business. In Salomon's situation the new company was comprised of other members (albeit, members of his family); however, with the ability to incorporate a single member company, the position of a promoter becomes indistinct from the company and challenges the doctrine of separate legal personality. While there is virtually no situation where the new single member company will assert its rights against the promoter (its only member), issues may arise if the company issues shares to new members or is sold to new members.

Persons who have not had an active role in forming the company but who allow others to do the promotion and who also profit from the venture have been held to be promoters: *Tracy v Mandalay Pty Ltd* (1953) 88 CLR 215.

The special position of a promoter in relation to the newly formed company attracts the classification of a fiduciary relationship. Thus, a promoter owes duties of good faith, honesty and candour to the company. The promoter must declare any conflicting interests to the company promoted and cannot make any secret profits: *Erlanger v New Sombrero Phosphate Co* (1878) 3 App Cas 1218; *Gluckstein v Barnes* [1900] AC 240.

A promoter who breaches any duty to the company by failing to make disclosure will be liable, and the company may seek a variety of remedies such as rescission of any contracts and recovery of any profits from the promoter, damages for deceit or an order that a constructive trust exists in respect of any property acquired by the promoter in breach of his or her duty.

Promoters may also have a separate liability to investors in a company under the provisions of Ch 6D.

In addition, as recognition of the position of promoters who take up shares in new mining companies without paying cash, the provisions of s 254B(3) rank these shares as repayable after the return of capital to cash contributories. Section 254B(4) also ranks promoters' shares with later priority to other shares.

Given that it is the promoter who is generally involved in setting up the corporation and starting up or acquiring the business of the corporation, it is common for promoters to enter into contracts in advance of the corporation coming into existence. Simple matters such as ordering stationery or acquiring premises for the business of the corporation are often activities that are carried out prior to incorporation. The contract may even be to acquire the business that will ultimately be conducted by the corporation. These contracts are called 'pre-registration contracts' and at common law they posed problems of enforceability against the newly formed corporation and the promoters because an agent could not be said to bind a non-existent principal: *Kelner v Baxter* (1866) LR 2 CP 174; *Black v Smallwood* (1966) 117 CLR 52.

Part 2B.3 of the Corporations Act is a statutory code that purports to overcome the common law difficulties encountered in the majority of earlier cases. It governs liability in respect of these contracts to the exclusion of the common law. Thus, where a person enters into a contract on behalf, or for the benefit, of a company before it is registered, then in certain defined circumstances the company will be bound by that contract when it is registered. For detailed analysis of s 131, see *DGF Property Holdings Pty Ltd v Di Federico (No 3)* [2020] NSWSC 510.

In order for a company to be bound by a pre-registration contract it must be registered (or a substitute company must be registered) and it must ratify the contract. In simple terms, 'ratify' means to agree after the event. There is a time limit for ratification. The parties to the contract (the third party and the promoter) will either agree to a time limit for ratification in the contract or the time limit will be a 'reasonable time'. For analysis on the ratification requirement, see *DGF Property Holdings Pty Ltd v Di Federico (No 3)* (above); *DGF Property Holdings Pty Ltd v Di Federico (No 4)* [2021] NSWSC 157. For an example of where incorporation and ratification of a pre-registration contract did not incur within a 'reasonable time', see *L-TAG Technologies Co Ltd v SA Cement Supply Pty Ltd* [2014] SADC 120.

The code in Pt 2B.3 sets up a system of primary and secondary liability. Thus, if the pre-registration contract is made and the company (or a company which is reasonably identifiable with it) comes into existence and ratifies the contract, then the contract is primarily enforceable against the newly formed company: s 131(1). If the company is not ultimately incorporated, or if it does not ratify the contract, then the person who executed the contract will bear primary liability for the contract: s 131(2). Recognising that companies may unreasonably refuse to ratify, or that promoters may enter into contracts that are unreasonable or extremely difficult for the newly formed company to comply with, the court may order that either the company or the person who signed the contract should pay or contribute to payment of any obligations under the contract: s 131(3). There is also provision for the release of a promoter from any liability under the contract: s 132.

Before attempting the questions below, check that you are familiar with the following issues or terms:

✓ What kinds of persons will be classified as promoters?

✓ What duties are imposed on promoters and to whom are they owed?

✓ What sanctions or remedies are available for a breach of a promoter's duty?

✓ What is a pre-registration contract?

✓ Who is liable under such a contract?

Question 6

Mary purchased shares in a newly formed company set up by Alf and Syd, on the basis of extravagant promises made by them about the potential profitability of the company. About 12 months later, the company is not doing well and the value of Mary's shares is falling dramatically. She discovers that the company's business was actually sold to the company on registration by Alf and Syd and was only worth half of what the company paid for it.

What legal action, if any, can Mary take over this?

Time allowed: 25 minutes

Answer Plan

This question is concerned with the duties and obligations of company promoters and the potential liability that may flow from statements made to induce persons to purchase shares.

Are Alf and Syd promoters?

- Role of promoters.
- Definition of promoters.

Duties of company promoters

- If Alf and Syd are promoters, what duties do they owe to the company and to its shareholders (if any)?
- Have any of their duties been breached?

Remedies for breach of duty

- What remedies are available for such a breach?

Answer

3-2 This question concerns the role and potential liability of company promoters. The question does not provide details concerning the nature of the company that Mary has purchased shares in so it can be assumed that it is a public company.

Are Alf and Syd promoters?

3-3 The term 'promoter' is not defined in the Corporations Act; however, the term has been extensively discussed at common law. The classification of promoters of companies covers a wide range of persons involved in the incorporation of and initial dealing with new companies. The classic statement of the meaning of the term is that of Cockburn J in *Twycross v Grant* (1877) 2 CPD 469 at 541:

A promoter, I apprehend, is one who undertakes to form a company with reference to a given project and to set it going, and who takes the necessary steps to accomplish that purpose.

Quite clearly, Alf and Syd would fall within this definition as they were the persons responsible for forming the company. Forming a company would involve performing the administrative procedures necessary for registration of a company.

Duties of company promoters

3-4   Given that, as promoters, Alf and Syd are in a position where they may make personal profit or gain from a newly formed company (they propose to sell their business to it), the law imposes fiduciary duties upon them to act in good faith and to avoid conflicts of interest. Good faith implies a high degree of honesty and candour such that if the promoter does have a conflict of interest, then that conflict must be fully disclosed to the company whether there is in reality a profit to be made or not: *Erlanger v New Sombrero Phosphate Co* (1878) 3 App Cas 1218; *Gluckstein v Barnes* [1900] AC 240.

The duties owed by the promoters are owed to the new company (*Erlanger's* case) which is, of course, a new and separate legal entity. Mary is not the new company, but a shareholder, and so the disclosure must be made to the company. *Erlanger's* case sets out the procedure to be followed by promoters in making disclosure. Appropriate disclosure can be made by full disclosure to the board of the new company. However, frequently it emerges that the promoters are also directors of the new company. In such a case, disclosure must be to a board of directors that is independent of the promoters. If the board of the new company is comprised only of Alf and Syd, or if they are the majority on the board, then clearly there is no independent board.

In *Salomon v Salomon & Co Ltd* [1897] AC 22, Salomon, as a promoter, was in a similar position vis-à-vis the board of Salomon and Co Ltd, as the board was made up of his wife and children who were obliged under the articles to vote as he directed. In that case, the purchase price of the business was held to be fair, but the court also said that the requirement to disclose would be satisfied where there was no independent board, if there was disclosure to all members of the company and unanimous assent to the transaction.

Thus, in the absence of the independent board, Alf and Syd should have disclosed their interest to Mary and the other shareholders of the company and obtained their consent before the sale of the business to the company.

In this case, therefore, the promoters have breached their duty to the company by not making full disclosure to the new company. Ironically, because the duty is owed to the company then a breach of the duty may only be pursued by the company, even though in practical terms the disclosure need only have been made to Mary as the only other member of the company. The disclosure that had to be made to Mary is *not* a personal right or duty owed to her and, strictly, it does not give her any personal right to sue if it is not made.

If the right belongs to the company, Mary's option is to embark upon a derivative action under Pt 2F.1A. (Derivative actions and other member remedies are specifically dealt with in **Chapter 8** of this book.)

Remedies for breach of duty

3-5 If either Mary can, or the company decides to, bring action against Alf and Syd for the breach of their duty as promoters, then a possible remedy for the breach would be rescission of the contract for the sale of the business and restitution of the parties to their pre-contract positions.

Rescission as a remedy will not be available:

- if it is not possible to restore the parties to their pre-contract position (which may be likely given that the company has operated for some time already on the basis that the contract would not be compromised);
- if third parties have innocently acquired rights to the property;
- if rescission is not done promptly after the failure to disclose is discovered; or
- if the company does something which ratifies or affirms the contract after the facts are disclosed.

If rescission is available, then the promoters have to return any moneys received from the sale and, of course, the company must hand back the business to the promoters: *Erlanger's* case.

Mary or the company (depending on who initiates the proceedings) would need to act promptly in order to secure rescission as a remedy. If she or the company can prove fraud on the part of the promoters, then damages are also available: *Re Leeds and Hanley Theatres of Varieties Ltd* [1902] 2 Ch 809.

If rescission is not available because restoration of the parties to their original position is not possible (which is probable given the facts and the likelihood of dealings with third parties), then equitable damages against the promoters may be the next most suitable remedy. Equitable damages would be measured in part by any profit made by the promoters.

Whoever brings the action needs to be careful that the contract is not affirmed in any way; if it is, then any profit made by the promoters would not be recoverable as this would conflict with the position taken by the company. An affirmation of the contract is an agreement to it on the now disclosed terms; you cannot agree to the profit in one breath and expect it to be repaid in the next — this is called 'approbating' and 'reprobating': *Tracy v Mandalay Pty Ltd* (1953) 88 CLR 215.

Mary needs to act quickly to bring a derivative action or to convince the board of the new company (assuming it has more than Alf and Syd as members) to sue for a breach of duty and to seek either restitution or equitable damages to recover profits made by Alf and Syd on the sale of the business.

It may also be possible for Mary to commence proceedings against Syd and Alf if it can be proved that they made misleading statements in the company's prospectus. Section 728(2) of the Corporations Act provides that a person making a forward-looking statement in a disclosure document must have reasonable grounds for making the statement, otherwise it will be deemed to be misleading. Given the extravagant nature of the profit statements, it may be found that there were no reasonable grounds for making these claims that induced Mary to buy shares in the new company. Furthermore, s 711 requires a prospectus to set out the interests held by promoters in the property of the company. If Syd and Alf failed to disclose their profit gained by selling their property to the newly formed company, this may constitute a breach of s 711 which would be a material omission under s 728(1)(b), possibly allowing Mary to sue Syd and Alf under s 729 for compensation. As Syd and Alf would have known about the property's true value, it is unlikely they would have a defence under s 731(2).

Examiner's Comments

3-6 This problem gives rise to issues involving directors' duties to the company. Alf and Syd may be directors at the time that the contract to buy the business is executed unless it was a pre-registration contract. If they were directors, then they are subject to the fiduciary and statutory duties that attach to that position. In particular, the purchase of the business from themselves would constitute a conflict of interest with a need to disclose appropriately to the company.

As a member of the company, Mary also has access to a range of personal remedies which are discussed in **Chapter 8**.

Keep in Mind

- Do not equate the company's interests with those of Mary. While they have something in common, the duty of the promoter is owed only to the company. Mary is a mere shareholder. While you may not yet have studied members' remedies, it would flow from the basic principle that the company is a new person with its own rights and obligations, including the right to sue, and that the company would be the appropriate person to sue for any breach of a duty owed to it.
- Do not assume that because Mary is doing badly in the deal she can sue on her own behalf. The promoters owe her no duty personally. Perhaps Mary should have been more wary before she handed over her money to the promoters.

Question 7

Rogers Traders Pty Ltd had an authorised capital of $250,000 divided into $1 shares. Mr and Mrs Rogers were shareholders and directors. They each owned 500 shares. The remaining shares were not issued. The paid-up capital is $4.

Mr Rogers contracted on behalf of the company to buy a block of harbourside land and build luxury apartments on it. He intended to incorporate a new company called Luxor Ltd. Rogers Traders would then sell the land to Luxor at a profit. Luxor would develop the land with funds obtained from members of the public who would buy apartments off the plan.

Rogers Traders was unable to pay for the land so Rogers convinced Smith and Jones to buy shares in Rogers Traders on the promise that they would then own the land through their shareholding and reap the profit from the sale to Luxor.

Luxor was incorporated, but instead of selling the land to Luxor at a profit (and to avoid capital gains tax) Rogers sold the package of the land, development plans and consent to Luxor. Under the terms of the sale, the land was sold at cost and the development plan and consent became available to Luxor when it purchased the shares in Rogers Traders owned by Smith and Jones at a profit. Thus, Luxor purchased shares in Rogers for an amount that was equal to the profit that was originally envisaged by Rogers on the sale of land to Luxor.

Luxor raised equity capital to build the apartments and ultimately new directors were appointed to Luxor's board.

Can the board of Luxor do anything about recovering this profit?

Time allowed: 30 minutes

 # Answer Plan

The problem posed relates to the circumstances both before and shortly after the new company's formation. The new company now has different controllers and it wants to look to earlier participants in its formation and start-up period for compensation.

Are they promoters?

- Are any of these parties promoters: Mr and Mrs Rogers, Smith and Jones?

Have they breached their duties as promoters?

- Have they breached their duty to the new company, even though their original plan to make the profit was not carried out?

What remedies may be available?

- What is the appropriate remedy given that the land acquired was acquired at the appropriate value?

Answer

3-7 The question is concerned with the legal rights of the new Luxor board of directors, particularly if they may have any cause of action against the former controllers of the company, which raises issues of promoters' duties.

Are they promoters?

3-8 Luxor is in the position of having acquired land from Rogers Traders at a price involving no profit to Rogers Traders, and it has also acquired shares in Rogers Traders at an overvalue from two shareholders (Smith and Jones). These two transactions in themselves would not give rise to any cause of action. The sale of the land is unremarkable in itself and the sale of the shares, while overpriced, could possibly be categorised as a bad bargain. What makes the transactions possibly subject to challenge is the identity of the other parties to them. Mr Rogers is clearly a controller of Rogers Traders and he is also a promoter of Luxor: *Twycross v Grant* (1877) 2 CPD 469. As a promoter, Mr Rogers owes fiduciary duties of disclosure to Luxor.

Smith and Jones are not directly involved in the process of setting up or incorporating Luxor. It has been held, however, that persons who are not necessarily involved in setting up the new company but who are aware, and supportive, of the plan may well be classified as promoters: *Tracy v Mandalay Pty Ltd* (1953) 88 CLR 215.

The facts of *Tracy v Mandalay* (above) bear some resemblance to the current problem. The new company, Mandalay, bought land at cost and shares at overvalue from another company in a device which was a substitute for a plan to sell land to Mandalay at a profit. The shareholders entered into the arrangement with a view to first making a profit on the sale of the land to Mandalay and second with a view to profiting from the sale of their shares. The shareholders did not actively participate in the setting up of Mandalay, but they were aware of the design at all times. The shareholders in that case were in the same position as Smith and Jones in the current problem. The High Court in *Tracy v Mandalay* (1953) 88 CLR 215 at 242 (referring also to *Emma Silver Mining Co v Lewis & Sons* (1879) 4 CPD 396 at 407) said:

> In the first place, the defendants left Park [the promoter] to get up the company upon the understanding that they as well as he were to profit by the operation; they were behind him; they were in the position of undisclosed joint adventurers; and in respect of their interest his obligations and theirs are in our opinion indistinguishable. The defendants in fact were, partly by

assisting Park and partly by leaving him to do the best he could for them as well as himself, in the position of promoters of the company.

Mr Rogers, as a shareholder in Rogers Trading, stood to make a profit from the purchase and sale of the land and therefore had an interest in the deal and any substitute deal which would deliver a profit. As such he had a conflict of interest in respect of his position as promoter of Luxor and he should have disclosed that interest to an independent board of Luxor. The practicality of doing this in circumstances where there is no independent board can be overcome by disclosure either to all the members of the company or to the ultimate shareholders. New or prospective shareholders can be informed either through a statement of disclosure in the articles or in a prospectus issued to potential investors if it is a public company: *Lagunas Nitrate Co v Lagunas Syndicate* [1899] 2 Ch 392.

Smith and Jones would also be categorised as promoters under the extended definition of promoters in *Tracy v Mandalay* (above). They, too, have the same duty of disclosure to the new company as is imposed on Mr Rogers.

Potential remedies

3-9 Luxor would be able to sue Rogers, Smith and Jones for the breach of their duties as promoters. Generally, the making of a secret profit from direct dealings with the new company would permit the new company to seek rescission of the contracts. Such a remedy would not be appropriate in Luxor's case since it has already taken steps to develop the site and raise money through the subscription of shares. Indeed, it may well be said that it has lost its right to rescind because of delay or because third parties have acquired interests in the property. In *Tracy v Mandalay* (above), rescission was not available to the new company, but the promoters were liable to repay the secret profit made on the deal in equitable damages. Accordingly, Rogers, Smith and Jones would probably find that they would also have to repay any profit made on the deal.

 # Examiner's Comments

3-10 This question further highlights the problem of disclosure to a company which probably, at the relevant time, did not have an independent board. The question does not reveal who the directors of Luxor are, but even if they were Mr and Mrs Rogers originally, in this kind of deal it would be envisaged that Luxor would pass into the ownership and control of other persons. Otherwise, Rogers would never get the money for the land. Disclosure to the ultimate shareholders in a prospectus therefore would be the only practical means of disclosure. It would be useful to point out that using new corporations to distance oneself from bad bargains is a real problem for corporate regulators.

Disclosure in a prospectus of this kind of deal would discourage investors and thus there is a strong motive for promoters not to disclose but to take the risk of new controllers perhaps deciding to take legal proceedings. The availability of criminal proceedings under s 728(3) in relation to a prospectus is crucial as a deterrent to this kind of activity.

Keep in Mind

- Do not overlook the position of Smith and Jones because they are only shareholders. While they don't fit the traditional idea of a promoter, they will fall into the class of persons considered as promoters because of their knowledge of and acquiescence to the scheme.

Question 8

> Bernard is an accountant skilled in preparing budgets and cash flow statements for new businesses. He is hired by four former university friends to prepare budgets and cash flows for a new company that is to be set up. Bernard goes to the printer and orders stationery for the new company and signs on behalf of the as-yet-to-be incorporated company. Bernard does the work and is paid. The new company, Mates Pty Ltd, is formed, but it does not pay for the stationery which Bernard ordered.
>
> Who is liable to pay the stationery account?
>
> **Time allowed: 15 minutes**

Answer Plan

This is a simple application of the statutory code contained in Pt 2B.3.

You need to identify the key facts that attract this statutory code:

- Is it a company that is not yet registered?
- Is it a contract entered on behalf, or for the benefit, of this as-yet unregistered company?
- Does the company become registered?
- Does the company ratify the contract?
- If the company neither becomes registered nor ratifies, is there any means of claiming liability from the company?

Answer

3-11 Part 2B.3 of the Corporations Act is designed to provide an exclusive set of rules to determine liability under pre-registration contracts. A pre-registration contract is one that is made on behalf, or for the benefit, of a company before it is registered: s 131(1). The contract between Bernard and the printer is a pre-registration contract. It may be argued that Bernard was not able to sign a contract *on behalf of* the as-yet unregistered company, although making it clear that he was acting for someone else (that is, the company that was being set up) assists Bernard in bringing his situation within the scope of s 131: *BJ McAdam Pty Ltd v Jax Tyres Pty Ltd (No 3)* [2012] FCA 1438. Similarly, he may not have had authority to sign a contract on behalf of the promoters (the four university friends). However, the contract is apparently for the benefit of the proposed company. This and the fact that the company is yet to be incorporated are the key attributes that bring this situation within the scope of the section.

In order for the company to be bound by the contract it must be ultimately registered and it must ratify the contract: s 131(1). From the facts it appears that the company was formed and registered. It is called Mates Pty Ltd.

There is no stated fact that the company has or has not ratified the contract. If it did ratify the contract, it would be primarily bound and the failure to pay under the contract is a breach of contract between Mates Pty Ltd and the printer. The company could be sued for the breach. If it is not ratified then Bernard, being the 'person' who entered the contract, is liable to pay damages: s 131(2). The damages are simply measured by the amount that the company would have to pay had it been liable under the contract.

This seems unduly harsh on Bernard. However, Bernard can gain some comfort from s 131(3). Subsection (3) is designed to ameliorate the effect of s 131(2) which makes the 'person' who entered the contract liable rather than the company. If the company is registered but refuses to ratify the contract, thus making the 'person' (Bernard) primarily liable to pay the amount under the contract, then the court may make a range of orders to shift the liability of the contract to the company. This subsection states:

> ... the court may do anything that it considers appropriate in the circumstances, including ordering the company to do 1 or more of the following:
>
> (a) pay all or part of the damages that the person is liable to pay
> (b) transfer property that the company received because of the contract to a party to the contract
> (c) pay an amount to a party to the contract.

If the stationery was specially printed for that company, it would be unlikely that a court would order that the goods be returned to the printer as they would have little value to anyone but the company. A contract such as this is likely to be for a small amount; accordingly, it is unlikely that the company would be unable to pay.

The most likely outcome would be an order that the company pay the amount due under the contract.

Examiner's Comments

3-12 It would be useful to explore the other option under s 131; that is, what would occur if the company ratified but did not pay. Simply, there would be a breach of the contract as stated in the answer. Section 131(4), however, contemplates such a position and dictates that the 'person' (Bernard) may be ordered to pay. It does not state the circumstances in which such an order would be made. Another point which could be expanded upon is the fact that s 131(3) is not limited to the types of orders listed. If the company was ordered to pay and it had few assets to meet the court's orders then it may possibly escape liability by being wound up. The section, while obviously giving the court wide discretion in this matter, does not specifically refer to orders being made against other persons such as the promoters (our four university friends). In the case of small value contracts such as stationery contracts, it is not likely that there will be protracted and costly litigation over whether there is power to go beyond the company and the 'person' when making damages orders.

You could also mention the effect of s 132 which permits parties to a pre-registration contract to release the 'person' from their liability. It may be wise for persons such as Bernard to obtain such a release before they enter into any pre-registration contract.

Keep in Mind

- Do not confuse Bernard with the other four promoters. Bernard, even though at first glance he may appear to be a promoter, will not necessarily be so classified. Persons such as solicitors and accountants who act not with a purpose of promoting a company but as part of their professional duties in performing tasks necessary for the formation of a company will not be held to be promoters.
- Similarly, you must be clear that Bernard entered the contract on behalf, or for the benefit, of the company and not the promoters. If he did so on behalf of the promoters or for their benefit then the provisions of Pt 2B.3 do not apply.

Question 9

> Kim, along with three others, is in the process of incorporating a new company called Shoppers Playground Pty Ltd. The purpose of the company is to develop a huge shopping complex. A large industrial site is for sale and Kim is of the view that it would be an ideal site for the development. She does not wish to miss the opportunity and so she negotiates a price and enters into a contract to buy the land. Kim signs the contract for sale of the land and the lease 'for and on behalf of Shoppers Playground Pty Ltd' and a deposit is paid from funds contributed by each

of the group. Luckily, Kim is able to negotiate a lengthy settlement clause in the contract. Kim and her three associates begin to make plans for the construction of their development proposal on this site. The company is finally incorporated, although its name needs to be changed to Shop and Play Pty Ltd as the other name is already reserved. The new board, which includes Kim, decides to have the land fenced even though the contract is not finalised, and the company pays for this to be done. Meanwhile, land values fall and the new board is of the view that the purchase price was too high. When it comes time to settle the contract the company refuses to do so, arguing that it was never a party to the contract.

Is the company liable to finalise the purchase?

Time allowed: 15 minutes

Answer Plan

This is a fairly simple application of the statutory code for pre-registration contracts under s 131. As this is a short answer question with limited time, there is no need for headings.

There are some basic steps to follow:

- Is it a pre-registration contract?
- Was it entered into either for the benefit, or on behalf, of the proposed company?
- Was the company ultimately registered?
- Is there a time limit for ratification?
- Was the contract ratified?
- If it is not ratified, are there grounds for an order under s 131(3)?

Answer

3-13 The code provided by s 131 is expressed in very simple terms. The contract for the purchase of the land was entered into before the company was registered. Apart from the different name, the company, 'or a company that is reasonably identifiable with it', was registered. Thus, it matters not that the company has been registered with a different name when in all other respects the company that was registered is identical to the proposed company.

That the contract was entered into before a company was registered and purportedly for the benefit or on behalf of the company is sufficient to attract the terms of s 131.

The contract to purchase land was probably a beneficial one at the time that it was entered; however, it has since emerged that it is not such a great benefit given the fall in value. 'Benefit' used in the sense of s 131 does not mean that the contract is a good bargain, so the fact that the bargain is a poor one is of no relevance. The phrase 'for the benefit of' is more likely to refer to the basis upon which the person signs the contract such as when a trustee enters a contract for the beneficiary company. Kim has specifically signed 'on behalf of' in the manner of an agent for the proposed company.

Under s 131(1), such a contract signed in this manner is governed by the section and the common law is effectively excluded: s 133. Subsection (1) permits the company to ratify the contract; something that a company was, at common law, unable to do: *Kelner v Baxter* (1866) LR 2 CP 174.

If the company does ratify the contract within either an agreed time or a reasonable time, then it will be bound under the contract: s 131(1). The question is silent as to whether there is any agreed time for ratification so it is assumed that there is no express time. The question about what is a reasonable time would depend upon the type of contract under scrutiny: *Hughes v NM Superannuation Board Pty Ltd* (1993) 29 NSWLR 653. A contract for the supply of goods such as stationery on a 14-day basis may require a shorter time for ratification than a contract for the sale of land with a lengthy settlement period. Indeed, in this situation it would appear that the settlement time has only just arrived and the contract is still in the process of performance and completion. Thus, the company would still be able to ratify the contract at this stage should it wish to do so.

The company has expressly stated that it does not wish to ratify the contract. If it does not ratify then s 131(2) applies and liability under the contract is placed upon the person who purportedly entered the contract, in this case Kim. Ratification of a contract, however, does not always need to be express and formal: *Aztech Science Pty Ltd v Atlanta Aerospace (Woy Woy) Pty Ltd* (2005) 55 ACSR 1; [2005] NSWCA 319 (ratification may be express or implied). The doctrine of unanimous assent in cases such as *Re Duomatic* [1969] 2 Ch 365 is indicative of the approach of courts in situations of small companies where all the members either agree or acquiesce in a course of action. Such situations can lead to findings that the company agreed, despite the lack of formal resolution, to that effect. In *Herrman v Simon* (1990) 4 ACSR 81, the doctrine was said to be based upon principles of estoppel. Thus, a company which acts as though the contract has been ratified may be held to have ratified it even though there may be no formal resolution to that effect. By arranging and paying for the land to be fenced, the company has acted in a manner which could only be consistent with it having ratified the contract, albeit informally. There are good grounds, therefore, to argue that the contract was ratified, which means that the company would be bound under s 131(1).

If there is no ratification because of the lack of formality then the liability would shift to Kim under s 131(2). However, if proceedings are brought to recover the purchase price from Kim under s 131(2) because the company does not ratify then the court may do whatever it thinks appropriate, including making an order that the company pay under the contract. Matters such as the action of the other incorporators in continuing to plan as though the company would complete the contract, and paying for the fencing, would all weigh heavily on the side of ordering that the company pay under the contract either because it was just and equitable or because it was appropriate.

In summary, therefore, the company would be liable either because it has impliedly ratified the contract, or because Kim would be able to seek relief from liability under s 131(3).

Examiner's Comments

3-14 Elaboration on a number of points may be warranted in this question. Section 131(1) refers to a company 'reasonably identifiable with' the proposed company. In the question, the only variation was in respect of the name of the company. It is conceivable that, between formulating a plan to incorporate and actually registering a company, many changes could occur. Additional incorporators or members may arrive in this time or others may drop out. The type of company may be different. Thus, a company limited by shares may have been proposed, but a no liability company may be registered. Changes of this nature may take a company out of being 'reasonably identifiable' with the proposed company.

You could also compare this answer with the result in *Commonwealth Bank of Australia v Australian Solar Information Pty Ltd* (1987) 5 ACLC 124. In that case, there was a change of name; however, it was a change of name in respect of a shelf company acquired for a business so the company was already in existence at the time of the contract. There was no question of the contract being a pre-registration or pre-incorporation contract.

The use of the phrase 'purports to enter a contract' begs the question of what is the difference in these situations of purporting to act and acting. The reason for the differentiation is that if the person enters the contract as an agent for the proposed company, then the person is not an agent at all as there is no principal. Therefore, the agent can only purport to be an agent and such a person only purports to enter the contract.

Keep in Mind

- Do not accept that because the company says it is not bound that is the end to the question of whether it has ratified the contract. Ratification of any pre-registration contract can take place impliedly simply by the company making a payment under the contract.

Question 10

> Bill and Ben signed a contract to purchase land from Dynamic Ltd for their company, Flowerpot Pty Ltd. They signed as directors. At the time of signing, Flowerpot had not been incorporated but Bill and Ben believed that it had because of information given to them in error by their accountant. Flowerpot's application for incorporation was rejected for technical reasons. Bill has now fallen out with Ben over this issue and he decides not to go into business with Ben. Bill and Ben had no intention of buying the land for themselves but only for their company.
>
> Are Bill and Ben liable under the contract?
>
> **Time allowed: 10–15 minutes**

Answer Plan

Again, this is a further application of the statutory code in s 131.

The following steps need to be dealt with in your answer:

- Is it a pre-registration contract?
- If the company is not formed, is s 131(2) activated?
- What would Bill and Ben be likely to pay under s 131(2)?
- Is there any way for Bill and Ben to avoid liability?

Answer

3-15 The contract described in the question bears all the hallmarks of a pre-registration contract. It was entered into prior to registration and it was probably entered into on behalf, or for the benefit, of a company by its directors.

In the event that the company is not registered, s 131(2) applies to render the persons who signed the contract liable for damages under the contract. In this case, as both Bill and Ben had signed, they would be jointly and severally liable.

The terms of the subsection are that Bill and Ben would have to pay 'damages' and the amount of damages is measured by 'the amount the company would be liable to pay to the party if the company had ratified the contract and then did not perform at all'. Under a contract for the sale of land, the usual terms are for a deposit to be paid when the contract is signed. It would be reasonable to assume that Bill and Ben would have done this. If the company had been formed, ratified the contract and then not performed it, then most commonly it would either forfeit the deposit and the vendor could sell to another party or it may be subject to an order for specific performance and be required to complete the contract by paying the balance of the purchase price. Bill and Ben would be facing these options under s 131(2).

It now appears that unless Ben continues to press ahead to register the company by overcoming the technical difficulties there will never be a company and Bill and Ben will have to pay the damages. Because they are jointly and severally liable, Dynamic Ltd could sue either of them individually and it would then be a matter for the defendant to seek a contribution from the other. Section 132 permits a party to the contract to release either Bill or Ben from liability under the contract and perhaps, in hindsight, this is a wise precaution for those who seek to enter pre-registration contracts for proposed companies. Unfortunately for Bill and Ben, they would not have necessarily sought a release from Dynamic Ltd because when they signed, they did so in the belief that the company was incorporated.

 # Examiner's Comments

3-16   This question appears to be very simple and the answer quite straightforward. However, it raises a number of issues which warrant further investigation.

First, it is interesting to note that under the common law, Bill and Ben were in a much better position than they are under s 131. At common law, pre-incorporation contracts were dealt with by an application of the law of agency. Thus, when an agent signed on behalf of a non-existent principal there was no basis upon which the principal could later ratify, as the agent could never have been an agent. Accordingly, the new company, if it wished to take advantage of the contract, was required to enter into a novation of the contract. Courts, however, took the view that where the 'agent' and the other party knew that the company was not yet in existence it was presumed that there was an intention for the contract to be valid and that someone would be liable; namely, the person who signed: *Kelner v Baxter* (see **3-1**, **3-13**); *Summergreene v Parker* (1950) 80 CLR 304.

The position was a little different, however, for the person who signed in the belief that the company existed either as an authorised agent of the company or as directors of the company when they bind the company itself, say, by affixing the common seal: *Richardson v Landecker* (1950) 50 SR (NSW) 250; *Newborne v Sensolid (Great Britain) Ltd* [1954] 1 QB 45. In these instances, it was held that there was no intention for the agent or director to be personally bound by the contract and there was no basis upon which they could be made liable. Thus, at common law, Bill and Ben would not have been liable.

Interestingly, s 131 governs two types of 'signing' of a contract: where the person enters into the contract 'on behalf of' the proposed company; and where the person does so 'for the benefit of' the proposed company. Arguably, neither situation represents the situation where a person who believes he or she is a director of an already existing company signs as an organ of the company under the terms of s 127. Under the organic theory of corporate governance, to be discussed in **Chapter 4**, directors do not sign as agents 'on behalf of' or as trustees 'for the benefit of' the company. Rather, when the directors sign in this way they are authenticating the company's assent to the contract.

If this is so, then Bill and Ben's situation may still be governed by the common law and they may not be liable to damages under s 131(2).

Keep in Mind

- If it is assumed to be a pre-registration contract for the purposes of s 131, then do not overlook the nature of the contract. The contract for the sale of land, because of the two stages of exchange and settlement, means that there are two options if there is a breach. Forfeit of the deposit or specific performance are both possible. Bill and Ben will not automatically face payment of the balance of the purchase price. Indeed, most opportunistic vendors, especially in a rising market, will opt to forfeit the deposit and sell the land to a new purchaser. In that case, Bill and Ben would lose their deposit but would not face proceedings for the balance of the purchase price.

Chapter 4

Relationships and Dealings with Others

Key Issues

4-1 Once a company is registered it becomes a separate legal entity with its own rights and capabilities: s 124. The Corporations Act attempts to fashion this legal entity as close as possible to a natural person. Like all other natural persons, it is subject to general laws that impose civil and criminal liability for acts and similarly it will be made liable in respect of any valid contracts that it executes. Corporations as legal entities are also able to appoint agents to carry out tasks on their behalf and will be bound by the acts of their agents acting within the scope of their authority.

The physical nature of a company, however, raises some complex issues for fixing liability for a tort or a crime and for determining whether a company has actually entered a contract. After all, how does an artificial entity, recognised only through law, actually engage in conduct? Liability for companies in tort and crime has been determined in a piecemeal fashion by the common law and, apart from specific statutory liability both in the Corporations Act and in other legislation, it remains largely a matter for the common law. Liability under contract, however, is subject to the common law of agency as well as significant statutory regulation under the Corporations Act.

In *H L Bolton (Engineering) Co Ltd v T J Graham & Sons Ltd* [1957] 1 QB 159, Lord Denning provided an apt allegory to explain the basis of liability in tort and crime for a company. His Honour said (at 172):

> A company may in many ways be likened to a human body. It has a brain and nerve centre which controls what it does. It also has hands which hold the tools and act in accordance with directions from the centre. Some of the people in the company are mere servants and agents who are nothing more than hands to do the work and cannot be said to represent the mind or will. Others are directors and managers who represent the directing mind and will of the company and control what it does. The state of mind of these managers is the state of mind of the company and is treated by law as such. So you will find that in cases where the law requires personal fault as a condition of liability in tort, the fault of the manager will be the personal fault of the company ... So also in the criminal law, in cases where the law requires a guilty mind as a condition of a criminal offence, the guilty mind of the directors or managers will render the company itself guilty.

Lord Denning's allegory is limited, but it is a good illustration of the inquiry that a court will undergo in order to determine whether the company itself is liable in tort or crime. A company, as a separate legal entity with the rights and powers of a natural person, may incur liability. This category of liability is called 'primary liability'.

The allegory is most often displayed in cases involving companies where the decisions can be clearly attributed to a person who strongly controls the company, such as in *Lennard's Carrying Company Ltd v Asiatic Petroleum Company Ltd* [1915] AC 705. Similarly, it would be most apt in cases involving the single member/single director companies. In such situations, it is easy to equate the state of mind of the single member as the state of mind of the company.

Attributing knowledge, intention and conduct is more difficult in two instances: in larger corporations with complex corporate relational structures and numerous levels of authority; and in situations where employees and managers of corporations change from time to time.

Lord Denning, in the above quoted passage, refers to *directors or managers*. In doing so, it was contemplated that it is not just the board of directors who will be relevant in determining the state of mind of a company. It may well be that other employees with managerial functions and discretions will constitute the directing mind and will of a company in a particular instance. This was clarified and developed in *Tesco Supermarkets Ltd v Nattras* [1972] 2 All ER 127. In *Rail Signalling Services Pty Ltd v Victorian Rail Track* [2012] VSC 452, Vickery J discussed the law of attribution of knowledge to corporations and stated (at [54]):

> ... on occasions it will be only the board of directors acting as such or an officer near the top of the corporation's organisation who will be identified with the corporation itself, such that the state of mind or the acts of the organisation will be taken to be that of the board collectively or that of the senior officer. On other occasions someone lower, and perhaps much lower, in the corporate hierarchy will suffice.

In respect of situations where more than one person has control or managerial power over a particular function then it is possible that a combination of the knowledge or states of mind of each of those persons will go to make up the directing mind and will of the company: *Brambles Holdings Ltd v Carey* (1976) 2 ACLR 176. This case was cited by the High Court in *Krakowski v Eurolynx Properties Ltd* (1995) 130 ALR 1 at 16 where the court noted: 'A division of function among officers of a corporation responsible for different aspects of the one transaction does not relieve the corporation from responsibility determined by reference to the knowledge possessed by each of them'.

Two practical limits to the liability of a corporation are whether it can be practically subjected to the penalty (obviously a corporation cannot be imprisoned) and whether it can in fact perform the necessary acts. This issue is more relevant to criminal liability (which generally requires proof of both action and intention) than to liability in contract and tort. Of course, the law may bypass the corporation altogether and find individual officers personally liable.

Most statutes provide, in express terms, that the word 'person' also includes bodies corporate, and the Interpretation Acts in each state and territory and the Commonwealth provide that unless the contrary intention appears then a statutory offence shall apply to bodies corporate. Section 24 of the Acts Interpretation Act 1901 (Cth) provides for a substitute financial penalty if the only prescribed penalty is imprisonment.

Apart from 'primary liability', a company may also be liable vicariously for the acts and omissions of its employees. This 'secondary liability' is quite different from primary liability in that there is no attempt to fix the company with any state of mind.

Vicarious or secondary liability is an example of the law attempting to redress economic imbalances in society. An example of its operation is where an employee of a building company negligently injures a member of the public. The injured person would sue the employee for damages. The employee would not have the financial resources to adequately compensate the plaintiff and the employee would argue that the accident would not have occurred had not the employer required them to carry out certain tasks from which the employer would ultimately gain financially. Courts, therefore, have long taken the view that employers will be vicariously liable for the torts committed by their employees in the course of their employment: *Lloyd v Grace Smith & Co* [1920] AC 716.

In such cases, it must merely be shown that an employment relationship existed and that the negligent act was within the course of that employment. This is because employers are not usually liable for wrongs committed by independent contractors: *Sweeney v Boylan Nominees Pty Ltd* (2006) 226 CLR 161. Proof that the worker was acting within the scope of their employment when they committed the wrong would usually render the employer/company vicariously liable for the negligence of their employee. Given this lighter evidentiary burden against employer companies, it is not surprising that the majority of claims in tort against companies are based upon secondary liability rather than primary liability. For analysis of the legal principles on vicarious liability, see the High Court decision in *Prince Alfred College Incorporated v ADC* [2016] HCA 37.

Ford, Austin and Ramsay (*Ford's Principles of Corporations Law*, looseleaf service, LexisNexis Butterworths, [16.110]) classify corporate criminal liability into three categories:

1. Crimes constituted by acts of employees of the company within the scope of their employment for which the company is penalised simply because the company is their employer. These crimes are mainly creatures of statute.
2. Crimes constituted by the company's failure to perform a duty imposed by a statute where the duty is non-delegable and the

company's liability is absolute or strict. These are also created by statute.

3. Crimes constituted by acts of directors, employees or agents which by a fiction are treated as acts of the company. These can include common law crimes as well as crimes created by statute.

Category 2 situations are often clearly expressed in the terms of the statute. Category 3 matters, as a general rule, are offences which require proof of mental element and utilise those cases which identify the directing mind and will of a company. Category 1 cases are instances of vicarious criminal liability.

Vicarious or secondary criminal liability is restricted to statutory offences, where the Corporations Act intends for the employer/company to be criminally liable for acts of employees even though the employer/company may not know of the criminal act: *Moussell Bros Ltd v London North Western Railway Co* [1917] 2 KB 836. See further the review of authorities in *Christian Youth Camps Ltd v Cobaw Community Health Services Ltd* [2014] VSCA 75; *Presidential Security Services of Australia Pty Ltd v Brilley* (2008) 67 ACSR 692.

Contractual liability is subject to a different set of rules. Assent to a contract is usually signified by a person's signature. Only from this act can it be deemed under contract law that the signatory consented to and agreed to the terms contained in the contract. Corporations cannot 'sign' in the way individuals can. Mason CJ in *Northside Developments Pty Ltd v Registrar-General* (1990) 93 ALR 385 at 392 states that the equivalent act for a corporation is the affixing of the company seal:

> The affixing of the seal to an instrument makes the instrument that of the company itself; the affixing of the seal is in that sense a corporate act, having effect similar to a signature by an individual ... Thus it may be said that a contract executed under the common seal evidences the assent of the corporation itself and such a contract is to be distinguished from one made by a director or officer on behalf of the company, that being a contract made by an agent on behalf of the company as principal.

Since the *Northside Developments* case, the Corporations Act was amended by the Company Law Review Act 1998 (Cth) on 1 July 1998. It is now optional for companies to have a common seal: s 123(1). Section 127 of the Corporations Act provides that a company can become bound by a contract either by the affixing of a common seal (if the company has one) or by the signatures of two directors (or a director and secretary). There is also specific reference to the method of signing for a single member proprietary company: s 127(1).

In addition, companies can also be bound to a contract through an agent, just as any person as principal may be bound by the acts of their agents. Section 126 of the Corporations Act echoes this common law principle. It is in this area of agency that most issues arise for corporations. A principal can only be bound by the acts of his or her agent if the agent has been authorised to act. Authority to act can be actual or apparent. Actual authority is based on the role and powers taken on by the individual person. Reference may be had to the person's contract of employment or to specific delegations of authority given to the person by the company (for example, from the board of directors). Actual authority may consist of either express or implied authority. Implied authority is derived as a necessary incident of actual express authority (that is, it must be something that the person is authorised to do having regard to the requirements of tasks coming within their actual express authority). For a review of judicial authorities on actual authority, in particular implied authority, see the judgment of Black J in *Motor Yacht Sales Australia Pty Ltd t/as The Boutique Boat Company v Cheng* [2021] NSWSC 1141.

Apparent or ostensible authority will be deemed to exist in circumstances where the principal in some way causes the third party to believe that the agent is authorised even if such is not the case. This apparent or ostensible authority will bind a principal in the same way that actual authority does. The decision in *Freeman & Lockyer (a firm) v Buckhurst Park Properties (Mangal) Ltd* [1964] 2 QB 480 considered the nature of the agent's authority and explained apparent authority in the following terms at 500–1:

> An 'apparent' or 'ostensible' authority, on the other hand, is a legal relationship between the principal and the contractor created by a representation, made by the principal to the contractor, intended to be and in fact acted upon by the contractor, that the agent has authority to enter on behalf of the principal into a contract of a kind within the scope of the 'apparent' authority, so as to render the principal liable to perform any obligations imposed upon him by such contract. To the relationship so created the agent is a stranger. He need not be (although he generally is) aware of the existence of the representation but he must not purport to make the agreement as principal himself. The representation, when acted upon by the contractor by entering into a contract with the agent, operates as an estoppel, preventing the principal from asserting that he is not bound by the contract. It is irrelevant whether the agent had actual authority to enter into the contract.

Except in circumstances where a company formally assents to a contract as provided in s 127, and as a matter of convenience, all other contractual activities of a company are carried out by agents. These agents may be specifically appointed to carry out certain activities or they may be officers or employees of the company with either actual or implied authority to carry out a range of corporate activities.

The problems in this regard are most acute for third parties dealing with agents for companies or, indeed, third parties to contracts executed under the terms of s 127(1).

Third parties need to be certain that the agent or officer with whom they are dealing has the appropriate authority — either actual or ostensible — to bind the company in the particular transaction. Unless the agent or officer carries with him or her a written and true instrument of his or her authority from the company, then the third party must investigate either the actual authority of the agent or make an assumption about his or her actual authority. The first option takes time and may mean the loss of a commercial opportunity while the second option involves a high level of risk for the third party.

The common law went some way to redress this through the doctrine of ostensible authority and also through the doctrine of indoor management: *Royal British Bank v Turquand* (1856) 119 ER 886. *Turquand's* case held that third parties, while being deemed to know the contents of the public documents, need not search further. They are entitled to assume that any technical matter required to be done to authorise the activity has been done; that is, matters of indoor management under the constitution have been complied with. For analysis of the origins and operation of the indoor management rule, see *Caratti v Mammoth Investments Pty Ltd* (2016) WASCA 84.

The Corporations Act ultimately attempted to put the rules about actual and ostensible authority along with the indoor management rule into statutory form: ss 128 and 129. These rules are expressed in terms of assumptions that third parties can make about the persons who purport to deal on behalf of companies. The Corporations Act also abolishes the doctrine of constructive notice: s 130. This was a necessary concomitant to the abolition of *ultra vires*. Sections 124 and 125 provide comfort to third parties that the company has the legal capacity to enter a contract, notwithstanding any objects or limits in its constitution. The assumptions in s 129 then provide further security for third parties in respect of persons who purport to deal on behalf of companies. However, these assumptions do not extend the authority of agents and officers of companies beyond what was afforded to them at common law.

The assumptions do make one important change to the common law. Section 128(3) provides that the assumptions may still be validly made even if the officer or agent is acting fraudulently or if there is a forgery. At common law, such acts would vitiate the company's assent but they are now valid.

Third parties may not rely on the assumptions if they know or suspect that the assumption is not true: s 128(4). This requires actual knowledge or suspicion: *Sunburst Properties Pty Ltd (in liq) v Agwater Pty Ltd* [2005] SASC 335. Constructive knowledge is not part of s 128(4): see the review of authorities in *Eden Energy Ltd v Drivetrain USA Inc* [2012] WASC 192.

Before attempting the questions below, check that you are familiar with the following:

✓ What is meant by primary liability of a corporation?

✓ What is the difference between primary liability and secondary or vicarious liability?

✓ How do you determine the directing mind and will of a company?

✓ Is the test for determining the directing mind and will the same for large and small corporations?

✓ What is the extent of a corporation's liability in crime?

✓ What ways can a company become bound under a contract?

✓ Who may act as an agent for a company?

✓ How does a third party determine whether an agent or officer of a company is acting within the scope of his or her authority?

✓ What are the powers and duties customarily performed by a director or secretary of a company?

✓ What is the meaning of the 'indoor management rule'?

✓ What factors will disentitle a third party from relying on the assumptions in s 129?

Question 11

> Bill Walsh, a director of BigBus Ltd, offered to take company documents to ASIC for lodgment on his way home. He became distracted as he was driving and talking on his mobile phone and, while distracted, knocked over and badly injured a pedestrian on a marked crossing.
>
> Is BigBus Ltd liable in tort or crime for Walsh's act?
>
> **Time allowed: 25 minutes**

Answer Plan

The question in this instance is only directed at the possible liability of BigBus Ltd and not to the question of whether Walsh will be found guilty or liable. The answer therefore can be confined to an examination of the issues that arise when considering corporate liability. It is necessary to first inquire:

• What is the nature of the wrong in this case?

The answer to this inquiry will then determine what issues need to be considered, such as:

- What is the relationship of Walsh within or to the company?
- In the case of civil liability, is this situation one in which it is necessary to establish primary liability and, if so, is it possible to establish such liability?
- Alternatively, is this more logically a matter of vicarious or secondary liability?
- In the event of there being criminal liability for these acts, will such liability attach to BigBus Ltd?

The last issue can be satisfied by an answer to the following question:

- Is the statute creating the criminal liability intended to encompass the employer?

As this is a short answer question, there is no need for headings.

 Answer

4-2 Knocking over and injuring a pedestrian in these circumstances will give rise to civil liability against Walsh for negligence at the very least and criminal liability for either negligent or culpable driving.

Civil liability involves a claim against Walsh for the tort of negligence and the pedestrian would be seeking damages. On the simple facts stated, it is highly likely that Walsh will be liable. The tort of negligence is often categorised as an unintentional tort. This is because it does not involve any positive intention or state of mind, but rather a lack of the appropriate level of care. In one sense, lack of care is also a state of mind in that it involves an omission to take into account and act according to certain risks.

On the facts, Walsh is a director of BigBus Ltd and in performing this particular task of delivering documents to ASIC he is providing a service to BigBus Ltd. As a director he would be paid some form of remuneration, although there would be no specific remuneration for this delivery service. As a director he has a relationship with BigBus Ltd, normally classified as a fiduciary relationship; however, the tasks that he performs under this appointment, namely management (or participation in management), would be similar to a relationship of service or employment. Given his position as director it is probable that his relationship would be classified as one of service, but most certainly in relation to the act of performing the delivery he would be either a servant or agent of BigBus Ltd.

Companies can be liable for the tortious acts of their servants and agents in two ways: they can be subject to either primary liability or vicarious liability.

In order to establish primary liability for a wrong it is necessary to prove that Walsh was the directing mind and will of the company when he was driving negligently: *H L Bolton (Engineering) Co Ltd v T J Graham & Sons Ltd* [1957] 1 QB 159. In this way, the acts and intentions of the agent are attributed to the company. However, whether the intention of the agent can truly be attributed to the company depends on the relative authority of the agent (in this case, a director with some degree of decision-making power), and it will also depend upon (as per Lord Denning at 172) '[t]he nature of the matter under consideration ... and the other relevant facts and circumstances of the case'.

Walsh's actions and intentions in making decisions for the company on various managerial matters can comfortably be attributed to the company. However, given the circumstances of running an errand for the company such as in this case, it does not seem possible to attribute Walsh's driving habits or attitudes as being those of the company. Indeed, it is more likely that there will be decisions or policies within the company which would dictate that servants and agents of the company should carry out their tasks with due regard for the safety of others.

In the circumstances of the type of activity, and the fact that it is an unintentional tort, it is unlikely that the company will have primary liability for these acts.

It is more likely that the company will be liable for Walsh's acts vicariously. Under vicarious liability, it is only necessary for the pedestrian to establish (as against BigBus Ltd) that Walsh was acting within the scope of his employment at the time of the negligence. The scope of one's employment is broadly interpreted. Employees can still be considered as acting within the scope of their employment even though they may be doing an act where the act or the manner of its performance is forbidden by the company. The test is focused on the degree of connection between the conduct of the servant or agent and the scope of their duties: *New South Wales v Lepore* (2003) 212 CLR 511. Under this test, employers can be held vicariously liable for employees' negligence, malice and dishonesty: *Citizens' Life Assurance Co Ltd v Brown* [1904] AC 423.

Walsh may also find himself criminally liable for negligent driving under the relevant state Act regulating traffic or, depending on the seriousness of the injuries, culpable driving, which is generally a breach of state criminal codes. Both offences, therefore, would be statutory.

For a company to be primarily liable in crime, the crime is usually statutory and liability would arise in two types of situations:

- where a statute imposes a duty directly upon a company and failure to perform the duty would incur strict liability; for example, statutes which impose absolute liability for pollution upon occupiers of land. Thus, if the land is occupied by a corporation, it will be liable under the statute for the fine;
- where the crime is one in which the intent of its directors or officers is imputed to the company: *Lloyd v David Syme & Co Ltd* [1986] AC 350.

Statutes creating offences of negligent driving or culpable driving do not by their nature impose strict liability. For the same reasons that BigBus Ltd would not be primarily liable in tort, it is not likely to be primarily liable in crime.

Companies can be vicariously liable for criminal offences: *Moussell Bros Ltd v London and North Western Railway Co* [1917] 2 KB 836. Vicarious liability is a device grounded in social policy used by courts to shift the liability or culpability from the individual to the employer. In order for criminal liability or culpability to be shifted it is necessary to examine the terms and intent of the statute which creates the offence to determine whether it was intended to cover employers.

Driving offences in general terms are expressed to apply to 'drivers' of motor vehicles, and penalties include fines, imprisonment and/or loss of licence. The exact terms of the offence with which Walsh would be charged are not included in the question. However, it is doubtful that these kinds of offences would be expressed in terms intended to cover employers. Further, it is likely that the purpose of the penalty is to promote safe driving. Punishing employers rather than drivers for unsafe driving may not achieve that purpose.

Without the actual terms of the offence that Walsh would be facing, it is only possible to conclude that it is unlikely that BigBus Ltd would be found vicariously liable in respect of the criminal offence.

Examiner's Comments

4-3 You could develop the rationale which dictates that primary liability for torts is a rarity in comparison to secondary liability. Given that most torts are unintentional, the concept of determining the directing mind and will of a company in relation to a wrong which does not really require an act of will is unreal and superfluous.

The main examples of a company's primary liability in tort are in respect of torts or acts that have a defence and the defence requires that the company's state of mind be established. Thus, defences or torts which refer to a person 'knowingly' doing the impugned act will immediately require investigation of the company's state of knowledge. *Lennard's Carrying Co Ltd v Asiatic Petroleum Co Ltd* [1915] AC 705 concerned an action for loss of cargo at sea. The loss was not malicious or deliberate and as such was unintentional. A defence against actions for loss was provided in a statute that essentially relieved the defendant shipping company of liability if they were not at fault. Establishing fault required determining whether the company knew of the state of unseaworthiness of the vessel. The requisite knowledge was proved by showing that the governing director, Lennard, knew and that he was the directing mind and will of the company. The *Tesco Supermarkets* case similarly posed potential primary liability for the corporation in crime because of the statutory defence in the United Kingdom Trade Descriptions Act 1968.

Primary liability for tortious acts may be more likely in situations where there is a statutory defence to the civil wrong or where the civil wrong itself requires a mental element.

This primary liability concept, on examination, has a fairly limited scope in comparison to secondary liability. Under secondary liability, a company can be liable *for* the acts of its servants and agents whether they hold important managerial positions or they are mere lowly paid servants. Primary liability seeks to make the acts of servants and agents the acts *of* the corporation. Therefore, under primary liability, in either tort or crime, the level of authority of the servant or agent is crucial to enable this transposition of act and intention from the individual(s) to the corporation. Primary liability in this context is clearly a natural consequence of the 'organic theory of the corporation'.

 ## Keep in Mind

- The most common error in this kind of question springs from the understandable confusion over when a corporation is either primarily or vicariously liable for an act that is done by an employee or agent. In all cases where the act is a civil wrong done by an employee or agent, that employee/agent will normally be liable personally. Primary liability may arise if the wrong is specifically aimed at persons who may also be corporations, such as occupiers of land, or if the act can truly be blamed on the corporation because that is the way it tends to or wishes to conduct its business. The tort or crime, even though done by an employee/agent, is then seen to be an act of the corporation.
- Secondary or vicarious liability, by contrast, does not attribute blame to the corporation. The employee/agent is liable, but social policy and economics dictate that the employer, who is more likely to be able to pay and who benefits from these acts, ought to be made liable for the damages or penalty. Determining whether a corporation is liable either in crime or for a civil wrong necessarily depends on the nature of the wrong. If the cause of action clearly states that corporations are liable then there is no need to investigate further. If it is not expressly provided then the intention and policy behind the relevant statute or tort is crucial to determining whether the corporation may be liable. Once this is determined you will know whether the 'directing mind and will' test needs to be applied to the corporation.

 ## Question 12

John Connell is the foreman for Cinema Constructions Pty Ltd. His role on-site is to ensure that the construction of buildings complies with the Local Government Act and any relevant building regulations.

Under the fire regulations, fire stairwells must be constructed from specified fire retardant materials. Failure to comply with the regulations is an offence. It is a further offence under the same regulations for an occupier of a building to permit members of the public to enter a building which does not comply with the fire regulations unless the occupier was unaware that the building did not comply.

There is a delay in the supply of some of these fire retardant materials and John Connell wants to meet a construction deadline. If he does, he will get a bonus. He substitutes other materials that have no fire retardant properties. Local council inspectors attend the construction site while John Connell is on sick leave. His substitute foreman shows the inspectors the site but is not aware of the substituted construction materials. He tells the council inspectors that as far as he is aware all fire regulations have been complied with.

Soon after completion of the cinema construction the cinema burns down and a number of persons are injured by fire while using the fire stairs.

Is the company liable for any breach of the fire regulations?

Time allowed: 25 minutes

Answer Plan

The question focuses upon breaches of the regulations, not the broader question of whether there is any liability generally:

- What kind of offence is created by each regulation?
- Is this a wrong which is intended to apply to corporations?
- Is there a need to identify the directing mind and will of the company in relation to each offence?
- If so, who is the directing mind and will of the company in these circumstances?

As this is a short answer question there is no need for headings.

Answer

4-4 Given that the question only asks whether the company is liable for breach of the fire regulations it is not necessary to contemplate its liability for any damages claims by patrons of the cinema.

There are two separate offences under the fire regulations. The first offence is in the nature of a strict liability offence. The High Court in *He Kaw Teh v R* (1985) CLR 523 categorised criminal offences into three areas. The relevant area for consideration in relation to this question is the category of strict or absolute liability. In this regard, Dawson J (at 594) states:

> It is generally accepted that statutes which create offences for the purpose of regulating social and industrial conditions or to protect the revenue, particularly if the penalty is monetary and not too large, may more easily be regarded as imposing absolute liability ...

An offence of this nature only requires proof of the act and no proof of the intention, and it has been established that in offences of this nature the obligation cannot be delegated. Consequently, it would not matter that an employee, an independent contractor or the board of directors itself caused the act to be done; the company would be liable: *Goodes v General Motors Holden Pty Ltd* [1972] VR 386.

The second offence provides a defence to a 'person'. In order to be guilty of the offence the corporation must be aware that the building did not comply with the fire regulations. Thus, there is a need to prove (or disprove) a mental element. To prove a mental element against a natural person the prosecution must bring evidence establishing the person's intention in doing the act. To prove the mental element and thus fix the company with primary liability requires proof that the foreman, John Connell, and/or his substitute was the directing mind and will of the company in respect of this matter: *H L Bolton (Engineering) Co Ltd v T J Graham & Sons Ltd* [1957] 1 QB 159.

Normally, the directing mind and will of a company is attributed to directors or senior managers of the company under the organic theory of corporations. It has been held, however, that the directing mind of a company can be employees of the company to whom certain managerial powers and discretions have been delegated: *Tesco Supermarkets Ltd v Nattras* [1972] AC 153. Further, in large corporations with complex organisational hierarchies it may be that more than one person will be considered to constitute the directing mind and will. This combination of states of mind was used in *Bramble Holdings Ltd v Carey* (1976) 2 ACLR 176. This case, in many ways, is highly relevant to a resolution of the current question.

The court in *Brambles* attributed the directing mind and will to a relatively junior employee (albeit a supervisor with intrinsic knowledge relevant to the facts of the offence) and in circumstances where that person was absent. It held that the substitute employee along with the knowledge of other junior employees was considered sufficient to constitute the directing mind and will of the company. The attribution of criminal liability under statute will be guided by the interpretation of the particular statutory rule, including the underlying policy of that rule: *Meridian Global Funds Management Asia Ltd v Securities Commission* [1995] 2 AC 500.

In the case of Cinema Constructions Pty Ltd there is a strong likelihood that the combined acts of the foreman and his substitute will constitute the directing mind and will of the company and render it liable under the fire regulations. The majority of the benefit of the acts goes to the corporation as it has the cinema constructed on time (although the bonus to the foreman would militate against this finding) and the subsequent commercial benefit of its operation. By delegating the control of compliance with fire regulations to the foreman the company may accept that it will bear liability for his decisions. If it did not want to be liable it perhaps should have had an alternative system to ensure compliance with such important regulations.

Furthermore, the policy behind the regulations is to ensure public safety, as in the *Brambles* case, where overloading vehicles is a matter ultimately of public safety and courts are more inclined to impose liability upon corporations directly through the doctrine of directing mind and will.

 ## Examiner's Comments

4-5 An interesting point to develop in relation to the liability of corporations for the acts and knowledge of their employees under the doctrine of directing mind and will is that corporations have been held not to have the benefit of the privilege against self-incrimination in relation to breaches of company law and regulation: *Controlled Consultants Pty Ltd v CAC (Vic)* (1985) 156 CLR 385. Prosecutions of corporations for breaches of statute generally involve the company being required to produce all documents in relation to the matter and without the benefit, as a natural person, of claiming the privilege. The High Court confirmed the position in *EPA v Caltex Refining Co Pty Ltd* (1993) 12 ACSR 452; however, there are some compelling remarks in the dissenting judgments to the contrary.

 ## Keep in Mind

- There is no need to consider secondary or vicarious liability for civil action by patrons of the cinema because the question focuses upon breaches of regulations. Do not treat both offences identically, even though they are referred to as 'fire regulations'. They are clearly different and only the latter regulation requires proof of a mental element.
- Avoid becoming entangled in the notion of vicarious liability for criminal acts under the principle established in *Moussell Bros Ltd v London and North Western Railway Co* [1917] 2 KB 836. These situations are rare and there is no need. In respect of the first regulation, the offence creates absolute liability and the company is primarily liable. In the second, the act of admitting members of the public to the building is obviously an act of the company and there is no need to resort to the fiction available under vicarious liability.

Question 13

In a company with a constitution containing an express prohibition on futures trading and financial speculation what happens to contracts in which the company engages in these activities?

> What happens to the officers of the company who conduct these transactions on behalf of the company?
>
> **Time allowed: 20 minutes**

Answer Plan

- What is the effect of provisions in a constitution which restrict or prohibit activities?
- Are these matters provided for in the Corporations Act or are they matters arising from the contractual nature of the constitution?
- What are the contractual consequences of a breach of the constitution?
- What are the statutory consequences of a breach of the constitution?

As this is a short answer question there is no need for headings.

Answer

4-6 The constitution of a corporation is a statutory contract between the officers and the corporation, between members and the corporation and between each of the members: s 140.

Section 125(1) of the Corporations Act permits a company to have express restrictions or prohibitions on the exercise of any of the company's powers in a constitution. Such a provision exists in the light of the terms of s 124 in which a company's powers are stated in an unrestricted fashion. A company would normally have the power to enter into contracts which involve futures trading and other forms of financial speculation under s 124.

Section 125(1), however, further provides that if a company does exercise a power contrary to an express restriction or prohibition then that act is not invalid simply because it is contrary to the constitution — a case of giving and then taking away!

There may be other factors, however, that will render the act invalid and this will be dealt with later.

The Corporations Act makes no express reference to the effect of a contravention of the constitution — the effect must be deduced from other provisions. Principally, the effect of a contravention of the constitution is contractual. As stated above, the constitution determines the civil relationship concerning persons within the company and the company itself, and a breach of that relationship has civil consequences.

The purpose of removing any former penalties for constitutional breaches is to relegate these matters to the realm of internal administration and compliance rather than to compromise a company's relationship with those who deal with the company.

Accordingly, third parties may now enter into transactions with companies on the basis that the company has the same power of a natural person, and that any objects or restrictions in the constitution will not invalidate those transactions. The exception to this general rule is contained in s 128(4). Under s 128(1), third parties are entitled to assume that, inter alia, a company's constitution has been complied with: s 129(1). This means they can assume that internal procedures have been complied with correctly (indoor management rule as in *Royal British Bank v Turquand* (1856) 119 ER 886) and that the objects or restrictions have been obeyed. The company cannot later assert that this was not the case even though there was in fact a breach of the procedures or objects. It sets up a fiction of compliance.

Third parties will lose that protection or the benefit of the fiction if they knew or suspected that the assumption was incorrect: s 128(4).

The extent of the knowledge required under this section is as yet unsettled. While actual knowledge will disentitle the third party to the benefit of the fiction, with a resulting invalid transaction, what amounts to suspicion is not clear. It will very much depend upon the parties involved and their expertise as well as any past dealings with the company. At common law, in *Turquand's* case, if facts existed which would have put a normal person on inquiry and that person did not make inquiry then they were not entitled to the benefit of the indoor management rule. The predecessor to s 128(4) was expressed quite differently as it contemplated situations where the third party was in such a relationship or connection with the company that they ought to know that the assumption was not correct. Section 128(4) is expressed a little more objectively which suggests that the third party would actually have to form a suspicion before they would be disentitled to rely on the assumption.

There is certainly debate about whether suspicion includes the common law concept of being 'put on inquiry', with strong judicial authority in support of either conclusion. The Explanatory Memorandum in respect of the Company Law Review Bill 1997 (Cth), which introduced these changes, indicates that the concept of 'put on inquiry' is no longer applicable. The South Australian Supreme Court has held that actual knowledge or suspicion is needed and being put on inquiry is not sufficient: *Sunburst Properties Pty Ltd (in liq) v Agwater Pty Ltd* [2005] SASC 335 (applied in *Eden Energy Ltd v Drivetrain USA Inc* [2012] WASC 192; *Correa v Whittingham (No 3)* [2012] NSWSC 526).

Consequences for the officers of the corporation, again, are not expressly provided for in the Corporations Act.

Constitutional breaches, however, may give rise to actions either by or on behalf of the corporation for a breach of duty. The duties owed by directors and officers are set out in ss 180–184, as well as general duties. Acting in breach of the constitution would tend to suggest that the director or officers were not acting in the best interests of the company. Statutory consequences for a breach of the duties under the Corporations Act would include the civil penalty orders under ss 1317E, 1317G and 1317H and possibly an order that the person be disqualified from managing a corporation under s 206C.

Apart from any orders that may be made against the director or officer as a result of any civil suit for breach of the statutory contract (the constitution) or for breach of any fiduciary duty, the practical consequences for such a person may well be that they will be removed as a director or their services otherwise terminated as an officer of the company.

The consequences for the corporation are that unless the corporation can make out that the third party either knew or suspected that the constitution was contravened (s 128(4)), the corporation will be bound by any obligations created by the exercise of its power (s 125(1)).

Examiner's Comments

4-7 This question raises some interesting policy arguments which surrounded the abolition of the doctrine of *ultra vires*.

Prior to 1984, limits to the power of a company contained in a constitution, either through the statement of objects or through an express prohibition, had certain consequences. Acts which were not permitted because they were not authorised in the constitution were without power and void. Thus, if a company did not have power to lease property, then any lease that it purported to enter would be *void ab initio*.

Objects in a constitution were a means of limiting or controlling the activities of directors for the protection of shareholders. Thus, persons who invested in a company because it was limited by its objects to low-risk activity were comforted in the knowledge that activities outside the objects which presented a different risk were void under the doctrine of *ultra vires*. The scheme was completed by the doctrine of constructive notice which meant that all third parties were deemed to know the contents (and therefore restrictions) of a company's memorandum if it was lodged on the relevant public register.

The regulatory policy was focused upon the protection of members of the company. The changes in 1984 and 1998 demonstrate a dramatic shift in policy. It would be interesting to note that this shift occurred at the same time that the corporate veil was seen as not necessarily impervious.

The first move to abolish this policy occurred in 1984 when the Act expressly abolished *ultra vires* and stated that all companies under the Act had the power of natural persons. Objects and their effect were relegated to internal administrative rules. However, exceeding objects could still lead to contravention of the Act. In July 1998, the last external vestige of objects was removed in the newly drafted s 125.

It is probably worth noting that despite the express abolition of *ultra vires* in the 1984 amendments, this section was omitted in the July amendments. Perhaps it is warranted in this context to elaborate on *ultra vires* in the wide sense as where directors act in abuse of their power as opposed to the narrow sense where they act without power: *ANZ Executors & Trustee Co Ltd v Qintex Australia Ltd* [1991] 2 Qd R 360.

Cases on the former legislation could be canvassed in this answer; however, they may not in the end be all that useful given the different wording of the new section. The effect of the new wording is referred to in the Explanatory Memorandum to the amending Act of 1 July 1998.

Keep in Mind

- Do not assume that because *ultra vires* is abolished, third parties are now protected in their dealings in all cases with companies. The directors of companies are still expected to comply with the constitution, and the assumption about compliance is only as good as the lack of knowledge or suspicion under s 128(4). In this sense, *ultra vires* can 'revive'.

Question 14

Steptoe Pty Ltd operates a small chain of retail shoe stores. James was appointed as managing director for a period of three years from 1 December 2017. The company, when incorporated, simply adopted the old Table A articles. James was also appointed subject to a contract. One of the terms of the contract restricted James from borrowing more than $10,000 on behalf of the company.

James was not formally reappointed at the end of three years but he continued to carry out the duties of managing director. No new document of appointment was lodged with ASIC.

On 1 April 2021, James went to the Willis Bank and asked to borrow $100,000 on behalf of Steptoe Pty Ltd. Willis Bank had been the banker for Steptoe for many years. James told the bank that the money was needed to purchase an interest in a pine plantation which would give the company substantial tax benefits.

James executed the loan contract on behalf of Steptoe. The bank advanced the money by a cheque payment to Steptoe. James misappropriated this money by diverting it into a similarly named account at another bank. He is now living in Majorca.

Is Steptoe bound under the loan contract?

Time allowed: 25 minutes

Answer Plan

This question only asks whether the company is liable to repay the loan. It can only be liable under the loan contract if it has executed the contract. Companies execute contracts in two possible ways:

- the board, as an organ of the company, can sign: s 127; or
- an agent may sign on behalf of the company: s 126.

Agents may be expressly or impliedly appointed (for example, being held out by the company as an agent).

Agents may have actual, implied or ostensible authority.

As this is a short answer question there is no need for headings.

Answer

4-8 The contract with Willis Bank was not signed by the company under the terms of s 127. This section provides that the company itself is signing when the common seal is affixed and witnessed by either two directors or the director and secretary: s 127(2)(a) and (b). Companies are no longer required to have a common seal: s 123. Thus, it is now also possible for a company to sign a document by the signature of either two directors or a director and secretary: s 127(1)(a) and (b).

In this question, only James has signed the contract. Thus, in order for the company to be bound by the contract, the bank must show that James was acting as an agent for the company so that the company will be bound under s 126.

An agency may be either actual or ostensible. Actual agency arises because of an express or implied grant of authority by the company. There are two possible sources of authority for James. Under his service contract it would seem that he is entitled to borrow money on behalf of the company up to $10,000. This express grant of authority, however, is insufficient for this borrowing.

By virtue of his appointment as managing director, James has an implied grant of authority to do all things that commonly fall within the scope of that office: *Hely-Hutchinson v Brayhead Ltd* [1968] 1 QB 549. The level of his authority is determined by reference to what is commonly within the scope of the duties attaching to the office of a managing director. In general, the managing director runs the day-to-day business of the company and therefore has the implied authority to enter into contracts on behalf of the company in that context: *Entwells Pty Ltd v National & General Insurance Co Ltd* (1991) 6 WAR 68.

Determining what the usual day-to-day business of a company is will depend upon the actual nature and scale of the business. The manager of a small trading company will have authority to execute contracts commensurate with the activities of that business, while the manager of a large financial institution may have authority to commit the company to much larger obligations. At common law, a managing director has been held to have authority to engage employees or subcontractors for the company: *Freeman & Lockyer (a firm) v Buckhurst Park Properties (Mangal) Ltd* [1964] 2 QB 480. However, the managing director cannot be said to have implied authority to enter into contracts which are outside that company's normal trading transactions: *Corpers (No 664) Pty Ltd v NZI Securities Australia* (1989) ASC 55–714. Thus, borrowing or granting security for a borrowing in respect of a transaction outside the company's normal day-to-day business would not be part of the implied authority of a managing director: *Re Tummon Investments Pty Ltd (in liq)* (1993) 11 ACSR 637.

Much of the common law regarding usual authority of officers of a company has been encapsulated in s 129. This section sets out what assumptions a third party may make about the level of authority of certain officers of companies. In subs (2) there is a reference to the authority of a director or secretary of a company. That a person holds such an office can be determined by the existence of their appointment as notified in documents held by ASIC. Companies are only required to lodge notices of appointment of directors and secretaries, not of managing directors. James may appear on the records of ASIC as a director but there is no form of notification of a managing director. The implied authority of a director is far less than the implied authority of a managing director because the managerial authority of the corporation is typically vested in the board of directors as an organ of the company and not in a single director unless the board delegates part of that authority to that director (typically designated as a 'managing director'): see ss 198A, 198C; *Northside Developments Pty Ltd v Registrar-General* (1990) 170 CLR 146.

Usually, the appointment of a managing director by a company would mean that the company would provide the appointee with certain trappings to indicate the appointment. Company cards, an office or a history of honouring agreements or transactions made by that person as a managing director would all go towards a representation or holding out that the person was appointed to that position with the requisite authority. Thus, the position of a managing director would have its implied authority as a result of the principle of ostensible authority set out in s 129(3). The words of that subsection encapsulate the common law by limiting the authority of the person to the authority 'customarily exercised ... by that kind of officer or agent of a similar company'.

James is in the position where his formal appointment as managing director has expired; however, he has continued to act in the position. It is assumed that this continuation would be with company approval and probable payment, otherwise James would not do the work. If this is the case then the expiration of his appointment makes no difference, for the company would be continuing its representation that James was the managing director by allowing him to remain in the position. This position bears some similarity to the case of *Freeman & Lockyer (a firm) v Buckhurst Park Properties (Mangal) Ltd* [1964] 2 QB 480, where the company's constitution provided for the appointment of a managing director. However, none was ever appointed, but Kapoor acted as de facto managing director with the knowledge and acquiescence of the board which then bound the company to contracts entered into by him.

Accordingly, Willis Bank can assume, as a result of s 129(3), that James was both duly appointed as managing director and that he has the customary authority of a managing director of a company which conducts retail shoe sales.

The customary authority of such a person is unlikely to include the authority to borrow a large sum of money to invest in a pine plantation even if it did deliver tax advantages. Thus, James would not have authority to enter this transaction and Willis Bank cannot assume that James had authority to do so under s 129. Therefore, the company would not be bound by the contract.

 ## Examiner's Comments

4-9 The authority of the managing director derives from the power of the board to delegate its authority as a board to a managing director: currently s 198C. The usual delegation is to manage the day-to-day affairs of the business of the company. To find a higher or a different level of authority there would be a need to examine the exact terms of the delegation to determine the extent of the actual authority given to the managing director.

 ## Keep in Mind

- Avoid getting caught up in describing any breaches of duty by James. While it is true that there is a serious breach of duty and criminal activity on his part, the immediate problem is whether the company has to pay. James may never return to face any proceedings and it is apparent from past extradition failures by Australian authorities that Majorca is probably a relatively safe haven!
- Do not think that because James is the managing director, he has power and authority to bind the company in any transaction. His authority is still limited by the customary authority of managing directors as determined at common law.
- Section 129(2) does *not* refer expressly to the managing director: this section relates only to directors and secretaries. The position of managing director is one which attracts s 129(3) because there would be a holding out by the company. It is irrelevant then that his appointment formally expired. If the holding out continues then the ostensible authority and the assumption under s 129(3) still operates.

As to the distinction between executive and non-executive directors, see discussion in *AIG Australia Ltd v Jaques* [2014] VSCA 332.

 Question 15

> Mr and Mrs Kimble operate a small tourism business. The main activities of the business are to take small groups of tourists on ecological awareness walks in the wilderness areas of New South Wales. The business is conducted through a corporate structure called ECO-TOURS Pty Ltd. Mrs Kimble is a director of the company and Mr Kimble is a director and secretary. Mrs Kimble goes to the bank where ECO-TOURS has its accounts and she says that the company needs to borrow $150,000 for a new off-road vehicle. The bank agrees to lend so long as it can take security over the major asset of the company which is the building from which ECO-TOURS Pty Ltd operates and in which Mr and Mrs Kimble live. Mrs Kimble intends to use the money to run away with someone that she has met on a tour. Mr Kimble has no knowledge of her activity. Mrs Kimble obtains the loan and mortgage documents from the bank. She affixes the common seal of ECO-TOURS and forges her husband's signature as secretary. The bank advances the money and Mrs Kimble absconds with it.
>
> Is ECO-TOURS Pty Ltd liable under the loan contract and mortgage?
>
> **Time allowed: 20 minutes**

 Answer Plan

Similarly to Question 14, this question only asks whether the company is liable to pay under the loan contract with the bank. The following points need to be discussed:

- A company can execute a contract either under s 126 or s 127.
- This contract was purportedly executed under s 127.
- What assumptions can be made under s 129 for such an execution?
- What is the effect of fraud or forgery on such an execution?

As this is a short answer question there is no need for the use of headings.

 Answer

4-10 Under the Corporations Act, there are only two methods by which a company may execute a contract. The methods are set out in ss 126 and 127. Section 126 refers to contracts signed by agents on behalf of companies and is not relevant to this situation. Section 127 refers, inter alia, to the more formal method for a company to sign a contract, namely the affixing of the company seal: s 127(2).

By affixing the common seal and employing the method used in s 127(2), the company is deemed to have signed the document itself.

For a third party entering into a contract with a company under s 127(2), the Corporations Act provides that certain assumptions can be made in relation to the affixing of the common seal. Thus, s 129(6) provides that a third party may assume that the contract is duly sealed if it appears to have the company seal on it and it appears to have been witnessed either by two directors or a director and the secretary. In making the assumption about the witnessing of the seal, third parties may make an assumption about the authority of those signatories under s 129(2); namely, that the director and secretary were duly appointed and that they had the authority to witness the affixing of the common seal of the company.

Basically, for a third party, having the company's seal affixed and witnessed by a director and secretary, especially by a director and secretary whose appointment has been notified to ASIC, is the most secure means of ensuring that the company is bound.

The certainty that accompanies such a form of signature is enhanced by the terms of s 128(3) which permit third parties to make the assumptions even if the director or secretary is acting fraudulently or if the document or signature is forged.

This provision of the Corporations Act significantly modifies the common law with respect to forgeries: *Story v Advance Bank Australia Ltd* (1993) 31 NSWLR 722. At common law, a forged document was a nullity (*Ruben v Great Fingall Consolidated* [1906] AC 439) and even the indoor management rule could not overcome the effect of a forgery: *Northside Developments Pty Ltd v Registrar-General* (1990) 170 CLR 146.

Care must be taken, however, in relation to s 128(4) which prevents a third party relying on the statutory assumptions in s 129 if they know or suspect the assumption to be untrue. Thus, if the bank knew, or if there is any evidence that the bank suspected, that Mr Kimble's signature was a forgery then it could not assume that the loan contract was duly sealed and therefore executed by the company. In the absence of such evidence, it would appear that ECO-TOURS Pty Ltd would be bound under the contract.

Examiner's Comments

4-11 Despite the general statement that there are only the methods described in ss 126 and 127 available for companies to sign documents, for completeness you may indicate that these methods are not exclusive: s 127(4). Indeed, other laws may require different processes for the execution of certain deeds or instruments; for example, negotiable instruments and deeds of company administration.

An interesting point is raised by the new version of the assumptions that third parties may make regarding the execution of documents by a company. Formerly, s 166 of the Corporations Law (repealed) was the provision that dealt with the effect of fraud or forgery upon the execution of a document. As noted in the answer, at common law a forged document was a nullity. The former s 166 modified the common law to the extent that third parties could still assume the validity of the document, notwithstanding that there was a forgery or fraud, unless they had *actual knowledge* of the forgery or fraud. This was the law (then ss 68A and 68D of the Companies Code) at the time of the decision in *Story v Advance Bank Ltd* (above). The court held in that case that there was no actual knowledge on the part of the bank's officers of the forgery.

As a result of the amendments on 1 July 1998, s 166 was repealed and replaced by a much simpler and shorter version in s 128(3). This provision is then followed by s 128(4) which provides that '[a] person is not entitled to make the assumption in s 129 if at the time of the dealings they *knew or suspected* that the assumption was incorrect' (emphasis added).

This change brings the effect of fraud or forgery in line with other defects in the authority of officers of companies, although it still represents a modification to the common law. A third party therefore can make the s 129 assumptions, including an assumption that officers are properly performing their duties (s 129(4)), unless the third party knows of or suspects a forgery: see the review of the relevant law in *Eden Energy Ltd v Drivetrain USA Inc* [2012] WASC 192; *Correa v Whittingham (No 3)* [2012] NSWSC 526; *Australia and New Zealand Banking Group Ltd v Adventure Quest Paintball-Skirmish Pty Ltd; Woollard v Hodgson; Hodgson v Woollard* [2016] NSWSC 188.

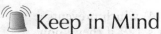 Keep in Mind

- This is not a question about breaches of directors' duties, despite the existence of clear wrongdoing by Mrs Kimble. The only issue is whether the company is bound by its 'signature' despite the forgery. Avoid discussions of directors' duties.
- There is no need to examine the assumptions under s 129 to establish any implied or ostensible authority for Mrs Kimble to bind the company. Simply because it is a situation where the company itself signs (by affixing the common seal) the issue of agency does not arise. The concern is only whether the seal is apparently fixed in the requisite manner which includes witnessing signatures.

Chapter 5

Internal Management Rules and Meetings

Key Issues

5-1 Throughout the regulatory history of corporations, a major issue for parliaments has been the regulation of the relationship between individual participants in a corporation. Due to the variability of the size and type of corporations as commercial ventures, the participation of each member of the corporation is not always feasible and, indeed, the attractiveness for individuals of corporate investment was the possibility of distancing capital contribution from participation or management of the enterprise. Functions of management are now, under corporate theory and regulation, quite separate from capital contribution, at least for companies with dispersed shareholders. For small, closely held companies, it is typical for the major shareholders to also sit on the board of directors.

Given this distinction, there was a need to ensure responsibility and accountability within the corporation as between the managers and those who merely contributed the capital.

Under common law, there are two main organs of a company in which managerial powers are vested. They are the members in general meeting and the board of directors. Each organ has full power or authority to perform the acts which are specifically allocated to it, either by the company's constitution or the Corporations Act. As a general rule, neither organ can override the power or authority of the other: *John Shaw & Sons (Salford) v Shaw* [1935] 2 KB 113. As a further general rule, most corporations vest all managerial power of the company in the board of directors: s 198A (replaceable rule). The allocation of power between the two organs is done by both the Corporations Act (which requires certain decisions to be made or approved by the general meeting, with the remaining decisions left to the board of directors) and the company's internal rules (the corporate constitution).

All companies must have internal rules of administration and management, dealing with matters such as how to call a members' meeting to the appointment and removal of company directors. This is achieved by permitting companies to choose the mix of internal rules that are most appropriate. Subject to limited exceptions, companies may choose to have their own written constitution or to simply be governed by the replaceable rules that are included within the Corporations Act (see the list in s 141), or to use a combination of both: s 134. The replaceable rules listed in s 141 are replaceable because a company may choose to adopt a different rule in its written constitution which thereby 'replaces' the default rule in the Corporations Act.

The constitution or replaceable rules are the principal source of members' rights and how the company is to function. They form a binding statutory contract (s 140), and there are special rules and common law restrictions governing alterations to these rules: s 136.

While under organic theory neither organ of the company has the authority to override or usurp the authority of the other, in reality members in general meeting will, with their voting power, have control over the composition and, therefore, decisions of the board of directors. Further, directors owe duties to the company but members owe no corresponding duty to the company, and directors cannot expel a member but members can either expel (ss 203C and 203D) or not re-elect a director. Both these considerations mean that control of the voting power at a general meeting will no doubt also mean control of the company despite the legal fact that only directors have control of the business of the company: *Mendes v Commissioner of Probate Duties (Vic)* (1967) 122 CLR 152.

Despite there being no duty upon members towards a company, the common law doctrine of fraud on the minority and the decision of the High Court in *Gambotto v WCP Ltd* (1995) 182 CLR 432 places a restriction on the alteration of a company's constitution where the alteration affects rights of members and property rights in shares. These restrictions control the power of the majority to change the rules to suit themselves but still give appropriate weight to the principle of majority rule. The rights of members are discussed further in **Chapter 8**.

Meetings of a company, in particular in meetings of directors, are where decisions about the affairs of the company are made. They are governed either by the constitution or by the Corporations Act — in particular, Ch 2G. Notice, procedure and voting at meetings are all the subject of regulation as these are all critical elements in the process of management or governance of corporations.

Before attempting the questions below, check that you are familiar with the following issues or terms:

✓ What is the organic theory?

✓ Who has the power to manage the affairs of a corporation?

✓ What powers are exclusive to or subject to the approval of the company in general meeting?

✓	What is a constitution and what does it contain?
✓	What are the replaceable rules?
✓	What is the effect of a company's constitution and who may enforce it?
✓	What procedure is there under the Corporations Act for the alteration of the constitution?
✓	What is fraud on the minority?
✓	How do companies make decisions about their affairs?
✓	What kinds of meetings occur within a company?
✓	Who may call meetings of company members?
✓	What degree of informality is now permitted for meetings under the Corporations Act and the doctrine of unanimous assent?

Question 16

Maxwell and Smart are directors of a successful publishing company called Get Smart Pty Ltd. The company has as its constitution a simple rule that only holders of 'A' class shares may be directors of the company. Apart from this, the replaceable rules apply. Only Maxwell and Smart have 'A' class shares. The company has been managed smoothly since its commencement. The two directors, along with members of their respective families, are shareholders in the company. Smart succumbs to the Covid-19 virus and is deceased. Under his will, he leaves his 'A' class shares to his sister Eileen and so she replaces him as director of the company.

At the first meeting of the new board of directors there is outright resentment between Eileen and Maxwell and after only a short time each meeting of the board ends in deadlock. No managerial decisions can be made.

Maxwell seeks your advice on how to proceed.

Time allowed: 15 minutes

Answer Plan

The question raises the issue of what can be done when a company's board cannot make decisions. The logical sequence would be to primarily identify that the organ of the company which can make decisions is the board. Given that the two-member board is deadlocked, you need to examine options for a resolution:

- Can a 'recalcitrant' director be removed?
- Can any other organ of the company act when the board is deadlocked?
- Can the board's power be altered?
- If none of these options are likely to succeed, then Maxwell may have to consider dissolving the company under s 461.

 Answer

5-2   Under the organic theory of corporate governance, the power to act as the company (as opposed to acting as agent for a company) is vested in the two organs of the company:

- the board of directors; and
- the company in general meeting.

The degree of power vested in each organ is dependent upon the company's constitution and the Corporations Act. This company relevantly has the replaceable rules and s 198A clearly places managerial power in the hands of the board. The effect of this section and common law decisions on the organic theory of corporate management is that decisions which are characterised as managerial can only be made by the board of directors. The members in general meeting have no overriding power over the board: *Automatic Self-Cleansing Filter Syndicate Company Ltd v Cuninghame* [1906] 2 Ch 34; *John Shaw & Sons (Salford) v Shaw* [1935] 2 KB 113; *Australasian Centre for Corporate Responsibility v Commonwealth Bank of Australia* [2016] FCAFC 80.

The members in general meeting, apart from anything stated in the constitution, have certain powers reserved under the Corporations Act, including the power to alter the constitution (s 136) or to resolve to wind up the company (s 491).

In addition to these powers, the members in general meeting of a public company can remove a director: s 203D. A proprietary company may have a similar power under s 203C which is a replaceable rule.

Short of a motion at a general meeting to remove Eileen as a director, under the organic theory Maxwell has a problem at first instance. However, there is an exception to the general rule regarding the board's sovereign power on issues of management. *Barron v Potter* [1914] 1 Ch 895 provides that, where the board is deadlocked and unable to make decisions, then the members in general meeting have a reserve power to make decisions in such a case. However, this reserve power will not be triggered where the company's constitution allows the members to elect further directors: *Massey v Wales* (2003) 57 NSWLR 718.

In order to avert future problems of the board becoming deadlocked, Maxwell should consider altering the company's constitution so as to overcome the problem. A simple alteration may be to make provision for the appointment of a third director so that there can never be a split decision. A further alteration may be to provide specifically for an alternative means of decision-making in the event of a deadlock.

Alteration of the company's constitution is provided for under s 136 of the Corporations Act. As noted earlier, this power is a power to be exercised by the members in general meeting wherein there must be a special resolution to amend the articles. A special resolution is one that requires at least a 75 per cent majority vote at a meeting of which there has been 21 days' notice: ss 9 and 249H (note also the requirement of notice of the special resolution in s 249L).

Each of Maxwell's options requires a general meeting of the members and an ordinary resolution of the members, although the alteration of the constitution would require a special resolution. If Eileen can command a majority of the votes at a general meeting, either through ownership or persuasion, then Maxwell's attempts to overcome the deadlock will be thwarted.

A final option for him may be to apply to the court for the company to be wound up under s 461(1)(k); that is, 'that it is just and equitable that the company be wound up'.

One of the bases upon which a court will order that a company be wound up is when there is a deadlock amongst the members so that the company's activities or purpose cannot be pursued: *Re Westbourne Galleries Ltd* [1973] AC 360. This will commonly occur in small, closely held companies which are probably not much more than corporate forms for what is essentially a partnership. A winding up order will be available under this ground (provided that there is proof of a deadlock) to Maxwell as he has standing under s 462 to make an application himself.

Examiner's Comments

5-3 Further areas to develop in this answer may be the 'power' of the general meeting, or the board in some companies, to dismiss or remove a director. These provisions (ss 203C and 203D) require only an ordinary resolution, although the right to remove under s 203D (for public companies) requires special notice of two months: s 203D(2). Interestingly, this rule cannot be supplanted by some other procedure for removal in the constitution and certainly cannot be replaced by a power in the board to remove other directors. By contrast, the right to remove for proprietary companies may be replaced by some other power of removal, perhaps even a power of removal vested in the board itself. It is worth developing the reasoning for this difference in regulation between these two types of company.

You could also discuss, in relation to winding up on the just and equitable ground, what it is that constitutes a deadlock. It has to be more than dissatisfaction at being outvoted or merely a quarrel between directors or shareholders: *Loch v John Blackwood Ltd* [1924] AC 783. For a summary of the legal principles underpinning s 461(k), see *Re TM Fresh Pty Ltd* [2019] VSC 383.

You may also want to comment on the ability, if Maxwell wanted to call a general meeting, of a member to requisition a general meeting: s 249F. Generally, it would be a board decision to call a general meeting, and if the board is so deadlocked that it cannot resolve to call a meeting then Maxwell must utilise his power as a member to call a meeting.

Keep in Mind

- Do not overlook that it is a proprietary company and not a public company, so the source of the power to remove a director is in s 203C and not s 203D.
- You must be certain that you understand that the relationship between the board and the general meeting is one of sovereign power to decide within their own areas of decision-making. Just because there may be more members than directors does not mean they can control or override the board, no matter how unhappy they are with the board's decision (or indecision): *Automatic Self-Cleansing Filter Syndicate Co Ltd v Cuninghame* [1906] 2 Ch 34. The general meeting's power to override the board is truly a reserve power; that is, it only comes into play in extraordinary circumstances such as where the board is truly unable to act.
- A justifiable lack of confidence in the management of the company's affairs falls within the scope of the 'just and equitable' ground for winding up in s 461(K). For a collection of authorities on this point, see *ASIC v Gognos Holdings Ltd* [2017] QSC 207; *Gognos Holdings Ltd v Australian Securities and Investments Commission* [2018] QCA 181.

Question 17

> Mr Rebel and Mr Penfold are the majority shareholders of Hunger Wines Pty Ltd, owning 98 per cent of the issued shares between them. The remaining 2 per cent are held by a small group of employees. The company needs more capital for expansion; Rebel and Penfold are willing to lend to the company, provided that the 2 per cent minority shareholding is eliminated.
>
> Rebel and Penfold approach you for advice about altering the constitution so that they may compulsorily acquire the minority shares.
>
> **Time allowed: 25 minutes**

Answer Plan

You will need to deal with the following points:

- The procedure under the Corporations Act for altering the articles contained in s 136.
- Subject to there being any restrictions on changing the constitution, Rebel and Penfold will normally only need to command a 75 per cent majority at a general meeting to change the articles.
- Would the alteration impose a restriction on share transfer within the meaning of s 140(2) and, if so, what is required to overcome this provision?
- Are the shares issued under an employee share incentive scheme and, if so, what are the terms of the issue and how can they be redeemed?
- Apart from the limitation contained in s 140(2) of the Corporations Act, at common law there is a limitation to alterations which would constitute a fraud on the minority: *Gambotto v WCP Ltd* (1995) 182 CLR 432.

Answer

5-4 A company may alter its constitution and cannot deprive itself of this power: *Peters' American Delicacy Co v Heath* (1939) 61 CLR 457. Section 136 of the Corporations Act permits alterations after there has been a special resolution by the company. Alterations to the constitution may be limited by additional requirements within the constitution (s 136(3)) so it would be necessary to examine the constitution of Hunger Wines Pty Ltd to determine what exact procedure, apart from a special resolution, may be required to amend the constitution.

If there are no additional requirements then all that is required is a special resolution. A special resolution is described in s 9 as a resolution passed by a 75 per cent majority at a general meeting, notified under s 249L(1)(c). Such meetings require 21 days' notice including notice of the motion to alter the constitution.

There is only one other relevant limitation to altering the constitution under the Corporations Act — the restriction contained in s 140(2). Amendments to the constitution which are duly passed are then binding upon all members, whether they voted in favour of the amendment or not, except when the amendments are of a particular type as set out in s 140(2). Under this subsection, amendments which increase or impose restrictions on the right to transfer shares held by existing members shall not be binding on those existing members unless the member agrees in writing to be bound by that alteration: see, for example, *Ding v Sylvania Waterways Ltd* (1999) 46 NSWLR 424.

Of course, Hunger Wines is a proprietary company and, while it is now not a requirement, many proprietary companies have restrictions on the transfer of shares anyway. Directors of proprietary companies have a complete discretion as to whether to register share transfers: see s 1072G. A common restriction is that shareholders who wish to sell can only sell to existing shareholders or by offering to existing shareholders first. These are rights of pre-emption and they are contained, if they exist, in the company's constitution.

If the proposed alteration imposed a further restriction upon the transfer of these shares then Rebel and Penfold would need to obtain the written consent of each employee shareholder before their amendment would be effective.

As well as pre-emption rights, if the shares were issued under an employee incentive scheme then the terms of issue would also need to be examined. Most share incentive schemes contain a provision for the redemption of these shares by the company. If this is so then Rebel and Penfold need only to follow the procedure for a buy-back of these shares under s 257B.

The other restriction on the power to alter the constitution arises from the common law doctrine of fraud on the minority. The operation of this doctrine was examined very closely by the High Court in *Gambotto v WCP Pty Ltd* (1995) 182 CLR 432 in relation to a proposal to alter a company's articles so as to acquire the shares of a minority.

The High Court accepted that some companies when incorporated had included the power to expropriate shares in their original articles of association, and members in subscribing for shares or acquiring them in some way did so in the knowledge that the power existed. But when a company seeks to alter its articles so as to include such a power it requires the application of rules arising from the equitable doctrine of fraud on the minority. This doctrine is used to prevent majority shareholders from using their voting power in an abusive way such that minority shareholders will be oppressed.

In some respects, the facts of the *Gambotto* case are similar to the facts in the question. In *Gambotto*, the majority shareholder owned 99.7 per cent of the shares. The amendment proposed was to permit the majority to acquire the remaining issued shares before a particular date and at a stated price. The stated price was higher than a valuation of the shares which was obtained by the directors (no doubt on behalf of the majority).

Essentially, the High Court said that expropriating shares was not wrong in itself even though they are a class of property, but it would be an abuse of the majority's voting power if:

- it was not done for a proper purpose; and
- its use would operate oppressively towards the minority; that is, the expropriation must be 'fair in the circumstances'.

The court identified a number of proper and improper purposes. If the power to alter the articles was used only for the purpose of aggrandising the majority then that would be an improper purpose: *Re Bugle Press Ltd* [1961] Ch 270. However, if the power was used to eliminate a minority shareholding which is detrimental to the company or the company's business then using the power to alter the articles to expropriate the minority shares would be a proper purpose. An example of this would be where the minority shareholder was in competition with the company (*Sidebottom v Kershaw, Leese and Co Ltd* [1920] 1 Ch 154) or where it is necessary to ensure that the company complies with certain regulations such as 100 per cent Australian ownership for the issue of a licence to continue its principal business activity and the minority was not Australian.

In relation to the second requirement that the alteration must be fair in the circumstances, this means that there must be both procedural and substantive fairness. By procedural fairness, the court said that there would be a need to have full disclosure of all material information leading to the alteration and an independent expert valuation of the shares. Substantive fairness is essentially the need to offer a fair market price for the expropriated shares and that market value along with assessing the assets of the company, dividends, type of company and the company's future would all be relevant to ensuring substantive fairness. In the case of Hunger Wines, it would also be relevant to acknowledge that the shares were acquired under an employee incentive scheme and consider whether there are any existing arrangements for the acquisition or resale of those shares.

For Messrs Rebel and Penfold, satisfying the procedural and substantive fairness requirements is possible by giving the appropriate notice and valuations. But the proposal to alter the articles may well be categorised as being for an improper purpose. In *Gambotto's* case, the purpose stated was to reduce administrative costs (maintenance of share register, etc.) and to gain certain tax advantages. This, by a majority, was held not to be a proper purpose. It would be difficult to argue that Messrs Rebel and Penfold were motivated by altruistic considerations which were for the benefit of the company and not for some commercial gain or control for themselves.

The key to the problem may well be in the terms of the original share offer scheme to employees; that is, if the employee–shareholders do not wish to take up the offer of a 'fair market price' on the shares anyway.

Examiner's Comments

5-5 There is an interesting point of distinction regarding share transfer restrictions for the purposes of s 140(2). When there is a pre-emption right which dictates that a share can only be sold to another shareholder, such as Rebel or Penfold, is it a further restriction requiring written consent if the constitution is altered to require a sale to the same people? Arguably it is not a further restriction upon share transfer; rather, it is a provision of a completely different character — namely, a compulsory acquisition which forces a transfer. It would then follow that written consent is not relevant.

Apart from an alteration of the constitution, you may wish to explore the general compulsory acquisition provisions of Pt 6A.2 of the Corporations Act. This power to compulsorily acquire shares was added to the legislation in 2000 and is not dependent upon a preceding takeover (these acquisitions are dealt with in Pt 6A.1). General compulsory acquisitions are now available where a person holds 90 per cent of the securities in a company. Of course, in this problem no one person holds 90 per cent and the power to acquire can only be exercised by a person who holds the 90 per cent either alone or with another body corporate.

In *Re Bugle Press Ltd* [1960] 3 All ER 791, a number of shareholders of a 'target' company formed a company which then made a takeover bid and acquired 90 per cent of the shares in a target company. The shareholders concerned, of course, sold their shares to the newly formed bidder. This was done so that the remaining 10 per cent of the shares could be compulsorily acquired under the equivalent of Pt 6A.1. The acquisition was disallowed, with the court lifting the corporate veil and deciding that this was an improper use of the takeover provisions. This decision tends to discourage a plan by Rebel and Penfold to combine their shareholding and form a company which would hold their combined 90 per cent. However, the general compulsory acquisition power in Australian corporate regulation is not dependent upon a takeover. Its purpose is to recognise the economic benefit and administrative saving that flows from holding companies owning all the shares in a subsidiary. In one sense, it is a response to the *Gambotto* case and a recognition of the pragmatism contained in the opinion of McHugh J in his dicta in that case. It is notable that it contains protection of the type envisaged by the High Court in *Gambotto*; namely, the provision of independent expert valuation of the securities.

You may also like to refer to the provisions of s 232 which relate to oppressive conduct. This section is dealt with in more detail in **Chapter 8**.

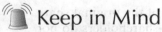 Keep in Mind

- Alterations of a company's constitution are governed by the Corporations Act only. The most important restriction on this power of the members in general meeting arises from the equitable doctrine of fraud on the minority. By fraud on the minority, we do not mean that there is some actual fraud or trick upon the minority but rather an abuse of voting power by the more powerful majority shareholders. This limitation is much more significant than any of the procedural requirements for voting and notice under the Corporations Act.

- When referring to possible existing restrictions on the transfer of shares (either in the articles or under the employee incentive scheme), avoid assuming that rights of pre-emption in favour of Rebel and Penfold give an entitlement to compulsory acquisition. A right of pre-emption is like a right of first refusal and it is not a right to compel a sale.

Question 18

> Australian Forest Conservation Pty Ltd is a company formed by environmental scientists. In its constitution it provides that the company's aims are to promote the conservation of forests and the environment.
>
> Smith, Jones and Brown set up a land development company called Hopscotch Pty Ltd. Brown is a solicitor and the constitution of Hopscotch Pty Ltd nominates that Brown will be the solicitor for any land purchases or sales made by the company. The articles also provide that any disputes which arise between the company and its members should be first referred to an arbitrator before there are any court proceedings.
>
> After a number of years, Smith and Jones meet another solicitor who they think is more efficient than Brown and they appoint him as solicitor for Hopscotch Pty Ltd.
>
> Brown brings legal action against Hopscotch Pty Ltd over the matter.
>
> Advise the company as to its legal position.
>
> **Time allowed: 20 minutes**

Answer Plan

This question deals with issues of the enforcement of the constitution both by the company and an individual:

- Explore the fact that it is a statutory contract under s 140.
- What enforcement rights does a member have? (Refer to *Eley v Positive Government Security Life Assurance Co Ltd* (1875) 1 Ex D 20; and *Bailey v New South Wales Medical Defence Union Ltd* (1995) 132 ALR 1.)
- What enforcement rights does the company have? (Refer to *Hickman v Kent or Romney Marsh Sheepbreeders' Association* [1915] 1 Ch 881.)

Answer

5-6 Section 140 of the Corporations Act provides that the constitution of a company and any replaceable rules that apply:

- have effect as a contract:
  - between the company and each member;

- between the company and each director and company secretary; and
- between a member and each other member,

- under which each person agrees to observe and perform the constitution and rules so far as they apply to that person.

There are two particular terms of this statutory contract for Hopscotch Pty Ltd. The first is the provision appointing Brown as the solicitor, this being a term which Brown would no doubt wish to enforce. The second is the arbitration provision.

As a matter of privity of contract, the terms of the statutory contract can only be enforceable by the company or the members. The contract cannot confer enforceable rights or benefits on third parties. This was established in *Eley v Positive Government Security Life Assurance Co Ltd* (1875) 1 Ex D 20. The facts in *Eley's* case are in many respects similar to the question but with one important difference. Eley, the solicitor appointed under the articles, was not a member of the company and he could not enforce the contract contained in the articles of that company. Brown, however, is a member and thus would have standing to enforce the contract. However, there is a limitation at common law which permitted enforcement of rights or duties under the contract which were properly described as rights or duties attaching to the person in his or her capacity as a member generally. Thus, if a term of the constitution purported to appoint a person as a solicitor for the company, then that was not something which normally was a member's right. Dicta in *Eley's* case and the court in *Hickman v Kent or Romney Marsh Sheepbreeders' Association* [1915] 1 Ch 881 made the distinction between rights in a capacity as a member and other rights conferred by the constitution.

Examples of rights enforceable by a member are rights which, generally, are rights available to all members equally such as the right to proper notice of meetings, rights to vote at meetings and rights to receive dividends within classes of shares. Membership rights were clarified even further in *Bailey v New South Wales Medical Defence Union Ltd* (1995) 132 ALR 1, where it was held that even when a company is formed to provide insurance for members and where the insurance for professional indemnity was included as part of the constitution, such a term did not confer a membership right. *Bailey's* case made a distinction between a person's capacity as a member of a company and the existence of separate rights arising from the existence of another contract between a member and the same company. In *Bailey's* case, the separate contract was a contract of indemnity.

The common law distinction between rights in the capacity of members and other rights is consistent with the wording of s 140 and certainly the reasoning in *Bailey's* case was based upon the wording of the predecessor of s 140.

Thus, Brown would have the right to enforce the statutory contract but the term which purported to appoint him as solicitor does not confer a membership right and as such it would not be an enforceable right under s 140. For Brown to succeed against Hopscotch he would need to be able to establish a separate contract outside the constitution wherein he was appointed a solicitor by the company.

The second relevant term, being the arbitration clause, would be a right available to all members and to the company. The company has the capacity to enforce the statutory contract under s 140 and, based on the reasoning in *Hickman's* case which was a suit over the enforcement of an arbitration clause in articles, the company would be likely to succeed. However, given that it is unlikely that Brown would have any enforceable right under the constitution to reinstatement as the solicitor, it would be unnecessary for the company to have the arbitration clause enforced. If Brown sued under the terms of a separate contract of appointment, then unless that contract also contained an arbitration clause the company could not enforce the constitutional arbitration clause as the suit would not be a suit over the constitution.

Examiner's Comments

5-7   A further matter that could be added to this answer would be the types of remedy available under a suit to enforce the statutory contract. It is to be noted that if a member sues to enforce a membership right then damages are not normally available. The remedy is usually a declaration and/or injunction. To permit damages to be awarded to a member may possibly defeat claims of creditors in a winding up: *Houldsworth v City of Glasgow Bank* (1880) 5 App Cas 317; *Webb Distributors (Aust) Pty Ltd v Victoria* (1993) 179 CLR 15. See also s 563A which provides for the order of priority of payments and places claims by members in their capacity as members after claims by creditors (first, simple creditors and then claims by members as creditors). However, it should be noted that the rationale of *Houldsworth's* case has been doubted by the High Court in *Sons of Gwalia Ltd v Margaretic* (2007) 231 CLR 160, although in a different context dealing with s 563A. The New South Wales Court of Appeal has granted an award of damages for a breach of the constitution (albeit in a 'company title' company) without citing *Houldsworth* or *Sons of Gwalia*: *Dungowan Manly Pty Ltd v McLaughlin* (2012) 90 ACSR 62; [2012] NSWCA 180.

Keep in Mind

- It is necessary to understand the concept of a member's right as opposed to some other term or 'promise' in the constitution. The enforceability of the statutory contract by a member turns on whether the right is one which is enjoyed in the member's capacity as a member of the company and not whether it merely appears in the constitution.

- Do not presume that because the company's constitution is deemed to be a contract it is just like any other contract. It is deemed as a contract because that is one way of ensuring that internal rules for the management of a company are followed, because they are enforceable as a contract.

Question 19

Shareholders in Coldstream Ltd have requested that the directors call a meeting of the company in order to discuss the performance of the directors in relation to certain contracts. The directors refuse to do so.

What action should or could the members now take?

Time allowed: 20 minutes

Answer Plan

The shareholders have embarked on a process of calling a meeting. The process is provided by Pt 2G.2 Div 2 of the Corporations Act. It is necessary to look at the process of requisitioning a meeting and to resolve the following issues:

- Can the board of directors refuse to call a meeting requested under s 249D?
- If so, on what grounds?
- If directors do not call a meeting, then what further action is available to members?
- Can the members call a meeting independently of the directors?
- What business can be dealt with at meetings that are requisitioned or called by members?

As this is a short answer question there is no need for headings.

Answer

5-8 The process whereby members may requisition or call a meeting themselves is an important adjunct of corporate governance in ensuring accountability of the board.

Under s 249D, members entitled to vote or members holding at least five per cent of the total votes may requisition a meeting. The question refers to the request having already been made and accordingly it is assumed that it complies with the requirements of form in s 249D. In particular, it is assumed that the shareholders have five per cent of the vote as at midnight before they requested the meeting: s 249D(4).

The Corporations Act does not state on what grounds the directors may refuse to comply with a request. It only provides a further procedure in the event that the directors fail to call a meeting: s 249E.

It would be inconsistent with the organic theory if members were able to call a meeting on any matter. For example, if the members called a meeting to propose a matter for decision which is clearly a managerial matter, then directors ought not be forced to call the meeting to permit their power to be usurped: *Turner v Berner* [1978] 1 NSWLR 66; *NRMA v Parker* (1986) 6 NSWLR 517; *Australasian Centre for Corporate Responsibility v Commonwealth Bank of Australia* [2016] FCAFC 80.

Further, if the object of the requisition is to harass the company and its directors then the directors may be justified in refusing to call the meeting: *Australian Innovation Ltd v Petrovsky* (1996) 14 ACLC 1257. A requisition to call a meeting will be invalid if the purpose of calling the meeting is collateral to voting on the resolutions: *Re Australian Style Investments Pty Ltd* (2009) 71 ACSR 186. Similarly, a company need not put a proposed resolution to the meeting if its purpose is to seek to usurp management powers: *NRMA v Parker* (1986) 6 NSWLR 517; *Australasian Centre for Corporate Responsibility v Commonwealth Bank of Australia* [2016] FCAFC 80.

For example, in *Capricornia Credit Union Ltd v ASIC* (2007) 159 FCR 69, the court held that the members' meeting could not vote to change the company's constitution to install directors who would follow members' instructions as such conduct would breach their directors' duties to act in the best interests of the company (which may or may not be in the best interests of the majority of members).

In Coldstream's situation, the purpose of the meeting appears to be legitimate. The shareholders would need to formulate the motions for resolution carefully so as to evoke a response. Members can put resolutions to a meeting (s 249N) and the form of request for the meeting must state the resolutions to be moved: s 249D(2)(b). Failure to state the resolutions may lead to a finding that the requisition is no more than harassment: *Humes Ltd v Unity APA Ltd* (1987) 5 ACLC 15.

If the purpose of the requisition is legitimate, and there is no defect in the form of request, then the members can resort to s 249E if the directors fail to call the meeting: see, for example, *NSX Ltd v Pritchard* (2009) 72 ACSR 122 (where the directors failed to provide notice of the meeting within 21 days). This allows the members (at least those with 50 per cent of the votes for the original requisitioning members) to call the meeting anyway. The company must provide them with the register of members and the company will be liable to pay the reasonable expenses of the members in calling the meeting. These expenses are recoverable from the directors who refused or failed to call the meeting after the request.

The procedure under s 249E is useful for members with legitimate issues to raise as they will not be liable to pay the expenses of calling the meeting.

Quite apart from the right to requisition a meeting, the members have an independent statutory right to call a meeting under s 249F. This procedure is at the expense of the members calling the meeting. These expenses could be substantial if Coldstream has a large number of shareholders.

Once the meeting has been called then the same procedure applies to a meeting called or requisitioned by members as applies to any other members' meeting. There is no special limit upon the nature of the business that can be done at the meeting; thus, other resolutions may be moved so long as there has been the appropriate notice: *Holmes v Life Funds of Australia Ltd* [1971] 1 NSWLR 860. Shareholders who requisition a meeting under s 249E may initiate the process in their own interests (*Humes Ltd v Unity APA Ltd*, above); however, during the meeting they are then required to act in the interests of the company as a whole (*Re Ariadne Australia Ltd* (1990) 8 ACLC 1000 at 1003 per Cooper J):

> Such a power must be used reasonably in the interests of the company, the shareholders and in certain circumstances the creditors of the company. The essential feature of s 246 [predecessor of s 249D] is to cloak the requisitionists with the power to act in place of the directors where the directors are refusing to call a meeting of shareholders which they are obliged to call.

In this way, the shareholders are subject to a similar duty as that borne by directors in the conduct of the meeting, while, normally, shareholders are entitled to act in their own interests, limited only by the doctrine of fraud on the minority.

🔎 Examiner's Comments

5-9 In interpreting or applying s 249D or s 249F it could usefully be noted that despite the use of the phrase 'members with at least five per cent of the vote' the section would also include a single member with at least five per cent of the vote.

Whether a shareholder's insistence that a meeting be called is harassment is not always easily answered. What a director terms harassment may not objectively be harassment. In *Humes Ltd v Unity APA Ltd* (above), the shareholder requisitioned a meeting for the purpose of putting motions to remove the directors. Similar motions were put and defeated at the annual general meeting (AGM). The directors tried to prevent the shareholder from proceeding with the requisition, arguing that it was harassment because the motions were likely to be defeated again. The shareholder was permitted to continue with the requisition because the statutory right conferred upon members ought not be lightly interfered with even though to permit the meeting to go ahead would be inconvenient and expensive. The court would not 'guess' what the outcome of the motion would be.

The right of members to call a meeting independently of the directors was clarified in the changes to the law in July 1998. Prior to then, members had a right under the former Corporations Law (repealed) to call a meeting 'so far as the articles do not make provision'. This has been interpreted to mean that a company can restrict the members' right to convene a meeting in its constitution by adding further requirements such as a higher percentage of voting rights or higher number of members: *Favretto v Eagland* (1995) 18 ACSR 196; and see also *Re Totex-Adon Pty Ltd* (1980) 4 ACLR 769.

Keep in Mind

- Do not assume that members have an unfettered power to requisition meetings.
- Be careful to distinguish between public and proprietary companies.
- Ensure that you identify what type of meeting is being requisitioned (general meeting or an AGM).
- Be aware of the limits of membership rights.

As Davies J said in *Australian Centre for Corporate Responsibility v Commonwealth Bank of Australia* [2015] FCA 785 at [16] (upheld on appeal):

> ... if the company's constitution gives to the board the power to manage the company's business the directors are exclusively responsible for the management of the company and the shareholders cannot control the directors in the exercise of that power or direct the board by resolution to exercise that power in a particular way (save for any matters that are within the power of the company in general meeting).

Question 20

Mr Brown, a retired family law solicitor, is a director in Family Matters Pty Ltd. This is a small company with only five members and three directors. Meetings for directors are often called without notice and with insufficient information about motions, and general meetings are very informal and often take place in a nearby restaurant.

Mr Brown feels that motions are not thoroughly discussed and resolutions are made without adequate consideration. He tells the other members that the irregularities mean that all the company's activities are void and that each meeting has to be reconvened and the resolutions decided properly.

Is he right in the legal opinions expressed?

Time allowed: 20 minutes

Answer Plan

Mr Brown's complaints are in respect of two different types of meetings: directors' meetings and members' meetings. It is best to separate the complaints and deal with them individually.

- In respect of the directors' meetings there are two problems:
  - no notice; and
  - insufficient information.
- Do these irregularities render the resolutions void or may they be validated under s 1322?
- In respect of members' meetings there are three problems:
  - informality;
  - inappropriate venue; and
  - insufficient discussion or consideration of resolutions.
- Do these irregularities render the resolutions from members' meetings void?
- Does the doctrine of unanimous assent apply to these resolutions?
- Does s 1322 provide a remedy to validate these resolutions?

As this is a short answer question there is no need to use headings.

Answer

5-10 Changes to corporate practice and responsive changes by the Corporations Act have meant that directors' meetings no longer have the same degree of formality that they traditionally had. It is no longer necessary for all directors to be present around the ubiquitous boardroom table; indeed, the Corporations Act permits directors' meetings to take place using modern means of telecommunication (s 248D) and it also permits directors to pass resolutions without a meeting by utilising a circulating resolution (s 248A). However, there are some minimum requirements.

Under s 248C, there must be reasonable notice of a directors' meeting. Reasonable notice is obviously less exacting than the 21 days required for a members' meeting; however, whether the notice is reasonable will depend on the way in which the company has conducted its affairs: *Toole v Flexihire Pty Ltd* (1991) 10 ACLC 190; *Summerdowns Rail Ltd v Stevens* [2015] NSWSC 321 at [175]–[176] per Robb J.

For small companies with only a few directors, especially when those directors are involved on a regular or daily basis with the business of the company, then reasonable notice may be a very short period of time. It has been held that notice given to a director only minutes before the start of the meeting can be reasonable (particularly where the director had made it clear he or she would not attend a meeting if held): *McMaster v Eznut Pty Ltd* (2006) 58 ACSR 199.

Notwithstanding the flexibility of the phrase 'reasonable notice', there must be some kind of notice. In *Petsch v Kennedy* [1971] 1 NSWLR 494, it was held that informal discussions between directors will not constitute a valid directors' meeting unless the directors are aware before they begin that the discussion is to be a directors' meeting. Thus, a meeting of which there is no notice is likely to be held to be invalid and any purported resolution from such a meeting would be void.

Notice, as well as being reasonable, would have to be given to all directors: s 248C; *Mitropoulos v Greek Orthodox Church* (1993) 11 ACLC 277. If Mr Brown's assertions about there being no notice are true then it would seem that this matter alone would serve to make the resolutions void.

As for the lack of information, if there is no notice then clearly there is no notification of the business to be dealt with. Notice of the business for consideration is essential to enable directors to decide whether or not they will attend the meeting, and the absence of a notice with a summary of the business for consideration may further render the resolutions void: *Jenashare Pty Ltd v Lemrib Pty Ltd* (1993) 11 ACLC 768. However, compare *Wilson v Manna Hill Mining Co Pty Ltd* [2004] FCA 912 at [26], where Lander J said: 'It is not essential that a director be given notice of the business to be conducted at the meeting, although it may be preferable and prudent to give notice of any special business'. This is because directors are expected to attend all board meetings.

Of course, if all of the directors agree to forgo notice, or they effectively waive the requirement of notice when they are together, then it is less likely that lack of notice will invalidate the meeting and its proceedings. Principles of estoppel or the doctrine of unanimous assent would serve to validate such proceedings: *Swiss Screens (Aust) Pty Ltd v Burgess* (1987) 11 ACLR 756; *Herrman v Simon* (1990) 4 ACSR 81. Each of these cases requires unanimity and it seems Mr Brown may represent the dissenter in these proceedings. Unless Mr Brown voiced his dissent at the time then he may be estopped from asserting the irregularity later. It is assumed that he did.

Lack of notice and insufficient information are serious irregularities for a directors' meeting. These problems severely compromise a director's ability to give full consideration to the business of the company. Section 1322(2) provides automatic validation of resolutions which are tainted by a procedural irregularity or by other matters such as the accidental failure to give notice or where certain persons did not receive notice: s 1322(3), (3A) and (3B). The court may invalidate such proceedings if certain persons apply to the court for the meeting to be invalidated. Courts, in making such orders, are motivated by whether or not substantial injustice will arise.

The meetings for Family Matters Pty Ltd are claimed to be irregular not because of an accidental omission to give notice or because not everyone was notified, but because habitually and deliberately there is no notice and there is insufficient information. Therefore, there can be no automatic validation under s 1322. All other irregularities would clearly render the resolutions void. In this respect, Mr Brown is probably correct. However, s 1322 does provide a means of obtaining a court order to validate otherwise invalid resolutions under subs (4) and in doing so it must be established that the omission is essentially of a procedural nature, that the persons concerned acted honestly or that it is in the public interest to make the order: s 1322(6)(a). In *Beck v Weinstock* (2013) 251 CLR 425, the High Court held that the irregular appointment of a director who ceased to be officially appointed to the board, but continued to act for many years in that capacity, was capable of validation under s 1322(4).

There is a danger in seeking a validating order. It may be that the failure to give notice can be characterised as procedural, but the consistent failure to give notice coupled with the insufficient information will reflect on the honesty of the directors involved and will certainly give rise to the issue of whether sufficient consideration was given to the matters for decision by the board. Such matters may constitute a breach of duty by the directors.

There is a risk therefore that the court will refuse to validate the resolutions and the directors will find themselves possibly exposed to action for breach of duty.

Mr Brown's suggestion that the meetings be reconvened and resolutions made again is probably the safest option.

Regarding the members' meetings, changes in company practice, especially in small proprietary companies, as well as changes to the Corporations Act seem to recognise that informality is not a bar to a valid meeting. Section 249A permits resolutions of members' meetings to be made without a formal meeting so long as the circulating resolution is unanimously agreed upon. The principle in *Re Duomatic Ltd* [1969] 2 Ch 365 would also appear to validate informal meetings where there is unanimous assent to the resolution. However, as for the directors' meetings, Mr Brown seems to be in dissent and there has been insufficient consideration of the issues for decision. Neither s 249A nor the doctrine of unanimous assent would appear to assist in this situation.

The claim of informality is not very specific and the place for the meeting only has to be reasonable: s 249R. Lack of formality alone is probably not sufficient to invalidate the meeting. The lack of consideration of matters may present a problem if this is as a result of the lack of information given to the members by directors.

Directors are under a duty to provide full and true disclosure of all relevant information relating to the matters for decision. If the information is misleading or incomplete then the meeting may be subject to an injunction and any decision may be voidable: *Chequepoint Securities Ltd v Claremont Petroleum NL* (1986) 4 ACLC 711. A voidable resolution is valid until it is overturned by a court. Thus, Mr Brown would probably need to seek an order under s 1322(2) that the resolutions of the members' meetings were invalid. In such a case, the court will apply the substantial injustice test as set out in the section.

🔍 Examiner's Comments

5-11 If the directors of Family Matters Pty Ltd are purporting to make decisions without sufficient information, then apart from any question about the validity of the resolution there is the strong possibility that they will have breached their duty of care, skill and diligence and will be liable to the company under a breach of the statutory duties: see **Chapter 6**.

Lack of notice will not automatically invalidate a directors' meeting. There are conflicting decisions about whether an informal meeting will constitute a directors' meeting: *Swiss Screens (Aust) Pty Ltd v Burgess* (1987) 11 ACLR 756; *Poliwka v Heven Holdings Pty Ltd (No 2)* (1992) 10 ACLC 641. What seems to be clear from the decisions is that where there is at least some clear recognition that the directors are exercising their directorial powers and that the decision is clearly identifiable as a resolution then the lack of formality and possibly lack of formal notice will not affect the validity of the resolution: *MYT Engineering Pty Ltd v Mulcon Pty Ltd* (1997) 25 ACSR 78. For a collection of legal authorities on the operation of s 248C, see *Career Employment Australia Ltd v Shepley* [2021] QSC 235.

The meaning of procedural irregularity is not clear. There have been some cases involving procedural irregularities and it is noted that the court will examine whether any prejudice is suffered as a result of the irregularity under s 1322(2). However, it is difficult to reconcile this with an application for validation under s 1322(4) where, again, the irregularity must be essentially procedural but the grounds for making the order are different: s 1322(6).

🔔 Keep in Mind

- Do not overlook the two types of meetings here, and the fact that they are each subject to different regulations under the Corporations Act as to notice and other procedural requirements.
- Remember that the procedures under ss 248A and 249A for resolutions without meetings only work if there is unanimous agreement to the resolution, consistent with the common law doctrine of unanimous assent.
- Ordinarily, less formality is required for a directors' meeting than a meeting of members of a corporation: *Bentley Capital Ltd v Keybridge Capital Ltd* [2019] FCA 1675.
- For consideration of authorities on urgency as a factor informing what period of notice is reasonable for directors' meetings, see *Re Keneally* [2015] NSWSC 937; *Career Employment Australia Ltd v Shepley* [2021] QSC 235.

- In *Bentley Capital Ltd v Keybridge Capital Ltd* [2019] FCA 1675, Banks-Smith J stated at [38] that '[w]hat is required by way of notice [for a directors' meeting] may ultimately need to be resolved by reference to the nature of the business to be dealt with at a particular meeting'.
- Remember that s 1322 is a procedure for validating resolutions or meetings which suffer from procedural deficiencies. While the exact nature of a procedural irregularity may be unclear, it should be recognised that more substantial deficiencies, such as lack of information before the meeting, will not be remedied under this section.
- The guidance on the scope and application of s 1322(4) is given in *Weinstock v Beck* [2013] HCA 14. Although the High Court held that s 1322(4) is to be construed broadly and applied pragmatically, it also cautioned that the dispensing power in this section is not in the nature of a general absolution for all past errors.

Chapter 6

Directors and Their Duties

Key Issues

6-1 For most companies, the power to make managerial decisions and to exercise other corporate functions, such as the allotment of shares, is a power vested in the board of directors: s 198A. With this power comes the responsibility of duties imposed on directors to exercise their powers to act in the best interests of the company, to act for a proper purpose, to act in good faith and to act with the degree of care and diligence that a reasonable person would use if they were a director of the company in similar circumstances.

Section 201A of the Corporations Act requires that proprietary companies have at least one director (two for crowd-sourced funded proprietary companies) and public companies have at least three directors. These are minimum requirements only and companies can prescribe larger minimum numbers by their constitution.

Once the company is registered, new directors are normally appointed by the members in general meeting after an election (s 201G) although directors will usually also have power to appoint directors who must then be confirmed by the members' meeting: s 201H. Section 201H provides that a failure to have the appointment confirmed will mean that the person ceases to be a director at the end of two months (for proprietary companies) or at the end of the next AGM (for public companies). Section 201H is, however, a replaceable rule and may be varied by a particular company's constitution.

Some constitutions will provide for the appointment of directors either by a particular group of shareholders or to represent a particular interest such as a financier or, occasionally, the employees. It is common for the constitution of a non-profit corporation to provide for the appointment of directors from government authorities, particularly where there is an element of public funding.

The Corporations Act insists that only natural persons over 18 years of age can be directors (s 201B), although the definition of director under s 9 is broad enough to cover a corporation which directs or instructs directors on how they are to exercise their discretions within the company: *Standard Chartered Bank of Australia Ltd v Antico*

(1995) 18 ACSR 1. This type of person is not formally appointed as a director but is commonly referred to as a 'shadow director'. The s 9 definition also covers 'de facto' directors who act in the position of directors but are not formally appointed (usually because of a defect in the process of appointment). The broad definition is relevant in attaching responsibility and accountability for the management of the company to persons, including corporations, who control the activities of a company: see further *Grimaldi v Chameleon Mining NL (No 2)* [2012] FCAFC 6; *Buzzle Operations Pty Ltd (in liq) v Apple Computer Australia Pty Ltd* [2011] NSWCA 109. For a useful summary of the factors relevant for determining whether a person is a de facto director, see *Re Swan Services Pty Ltd (in liq)* [2016] NSWSC 1724; for shadow director, see *Re Akron Roads Pty Ltd (in liq) (No 3)* [2016] VSC 657.

In *ASIC v King* [2020] HCA 4, the High Court considered the scope of the definition of 'officer' in s 9(b)(ii) of the Corporations Act which references a person 'who has the capacity to affect significantly the corporation's financial standing'. Applying this definition, Mr King, the former CEO and executive director of MFS Ltd, but who was not a director of its subsidiary, was held to be an officer of the subsidiary although he did not hold a designed office within the subsidiary, nor was he named as an office holder. The case illustrates the broad reach of the s 9 definition and affirms that anyone in the company, regardless of title and office, who can affect significantly the company's financial affairs can be held to be an officer, and can therefore be subject to the officers' duties in ss 180–184 of the Corporations Act. The High Court also recognised that the definition of 'officer' can extend to third parties such as lenders, particularly where a company was in financial difficulty and the lender did more than give advice to the company.

The retirement, resignation and removal of directors is dealt with in Pt 2D.3 Div 3 and of special note is the restriction of removal powers in a public company to members in general meeting: s 203D. The replaceable rules or constitution for a proprietary company usually governs these matters. In addition, the Corporations Act makes provision for certain people, usually insolvents, persons convicted of fraud and persons who have managed failed companies previously, to be prevented from becoming directors: Pt 2D.6.

Terms such as governing director, executive and non-executive directors, associate directors and nominee directors are not used in the Corporations Act. They are all descriptive of the types of function or level of power of a particular director on the board. These functions or powers are usually set out in the particular company's constitution. For an analysis of the powers of a governing director, see *Ngurli Ltd v McCann* (1953) 90 CLR 425; *Whitehouse v Carlton Hotel Pty Ltd* (1987) 162 CLR 285. For a compendious view on the power, authority and responsibility of the chair (which goes far beyond procedural duties), see the analysis in *ASIC v Mitchell (No 2)* [2020] FCA 1098.

While the managerial power of the corporation is typically given to the board of directors under s 198A (a replaceable rule), the board of directors may delegate particular functions to a specific director or officer of the company such as a managing director or chief executive officer: s 198D. The board of directors remains ultimately responsible for the conduct of its delegates: s 190.

It should be noted that matters of high importance require some degree of board oversight and cannot be completely delegated to subordinates: *ASIC v Macdonald (No 11)* [2009] NSWSC 287 (the *James Hardie* case; non-executive directors could not delegate their responsibility to consider the accuracy of an important press release that contained critically vital information about the company's future); *ASIC v Healey* [2011] FCA 717 (the *Centro* case, where directors could not delegate the task of ensuring the accuracy of financial reports where they had a statutory obligation to ensure that they were a true and fair view of the company's position).

A director cannot rely on advice where the circumstances are such as to give rise to a duty to inquire into a matter: *ASIC v Flugge* [2016] VSC 779 at [1874] (*AWB* case). Greater vigilance is required by a director to critically assess and verify information supplied by senior management when put on notice that reasons exist to doubt the reliability of that information. In *ASIC v Vocation Ltd (in liq)* [2019] FCA 807, a non-executive chair of the company was held to have breached the duty of care and diligence when he continued to accept and act upon information provided to the board by the CEO uncritically, without making any sufficient attempt to analyse or evaluate that information in light of new information that became available. A director cannot rely exclusively on other directors and professional advisers to discharge their legal duties and the disclosure obligations imposed on ASX publicly listed companies without making an effort to understand their legal obligations as a director. Failure to do so will result in a breach of the duty of care and diligence: *ASIC v Sino Australia Oil and Gas Ltd (in liq)* [2016] FCA 934.

Directors in control of a company, whether a proprietary or public company, have a duty to ensure that they do not cause the company to break the law. The *Storm Financial* litigation affirms that the foreseeable risk of harm to the company, for purposes of the duty of care and diligence, is not confined to financial harm, but includes harm to all the interests of the company, including its reputation, and interests which relate to compliance with the law: *ASIC v Cassimatis (No 8)* [2016] FCA 1023; affirmed on appeal in *Cassimatis v ASIC* [2020] FCAFC 52.

Under the organic theory (discussed in **Chapter 5**), directors and other officers involved in the management of companies have extensive powers to control the activities of the company and to commit the company to transactions or obligations. Because the organic theory delivers this power to the directors without any systematic review over its exercise by other members of the company, the law imposes wide duties upon directors to ensure that there is no abuse or dishonesty in the exercise of those powers. The duties were imposed first under the general law and later by the Corporations Act. Notably, when a person is appointed as a director, his or her appointment must be preceded by a consent to act as a director: s 201D. This is some acknowledgment by the person that they will, once appointed, be subject to responsibilities and duties attaching to that position.

The source of the general law duties is predominantly equity, with common law duties imposed upon directors and some senior officers by virtue of their proximity to decision-making. Some duties will arise as a matter of contract.

The Corporations Act in some part replicates these duties by setting them out in Pt 2D.1 and imposing them upon 'officers' of a corporation. The general law duties and the statutory duties coexist (s 185), but they give rise to different remedies and have different enforcement mechanisms.

Under the law of equity, the relationship between a director and company is said to be a 'fiduciary relationship' because it is a relationship where one party (the director) is appointed or has the power to direct the affairs of the other (the company). The director under this relationship can only act for the benefit of the company and is subject to high standards of loyalty and honesty: *Hospital Products Ltd v United States Surgical Corporation* (1984) 156 CLR 41; *Howard v Commissioner of Taxation* (2014) 253 CLR 83. The content of these standards is expressed in terms of separate duties:

- the duty to act in good faith for the benefit of the company as a whole: *Re Smith & Fawcett Ltd* [1942] Ch 304;
- the duty to keep discretions unfettered: *Russell v Northern Bank Development Corp Ltd* [1992] BCLC 1016;
- the duty to exercise powers only for the proper purposes of seeking to benefit the corporation: *Howard Smith Ltd v Ampol Petroleum Ltd* [1974] AC 821; *Whitehouse v Carlton Hotel Pty Ltd* (1987) 70 ALR 251; and
- the duty to avoid conflicts of interest: *Aberdeen Railway Co v Blaikie Bros* (1854) 1 Macq 461; *Cook v Deeks* [1916] 1 AC 554; *Furs Ltd v Tomkies* (1936) 54 CLR 583; *Regal Hastings v Gulliver* [1967] 2 AC 134; *Chan v Zacharia* (1984) 154 CLR 178; *Warman International Ltd v Dwyer* (1995) 182 CLR 544; *Coope v LCM Litigation Fund Pty Ltd* [2016] NSWCA 37.

A detailed review of directors' fiduciary duties was undertaken in the *Bell* litigation: *Bell Group Ltd (in liq) v Westpac Banking Corp (No 9)* [2008] WASC 239 (trial decision upheld in part; appeal allowed in part: *Westpac Banking Corporation v Bell Group Ltd (in liq) (No 3)* [2012] WASCA 157).

Where an equitable duty (including fiduciary duties) is contravened by a company director, the company may seek a range of remedies, including:

- rescission of contract;
- account of profits;
- injunction; and
- constructive trust.

In addition to the equitable and fiduciary duties there is a common law duty to exercise care, skill and diligence. The content of this duty is now well established in the decision of the New South Wales Supreme Court in *AWA Ltd v Daniels t/as Deloitte, Haskins & Sells* (1992) 7 ACSR 759. This decision was confirmed on appeal in *Daniels v Anderson* (1995) 16 ACSR 607. (These cases are collectively referred to as the *AWA* cases.) A summary of the principles for the duty of care and diligence can be found in many subsequent cases; for example, see *Re HIH Insurance Ltd (in liq); ASIC v Adler* [2002] NSWSC 171 at [372] (the *Adler* case); *ASIC v Healey* (the *Centro* case) at [119]–[124].

The common law duty differs in some respects from the normal fiduciary duty of care and diligence imposed on, say, a trustee. A director, because he or she is involved in the management of a commercial venture with its associated risks and uncertainty, is entitled to some flexibility in terms of making speculative decisions. This is now recognised by a statutory defence in s 180(2), referred to as the 'business judgment rule'. The defence is available in respect of a breach of either the statutory or general law *duties of care and diligence only* and does not apply to other duties such as insolvent trading or acting for proper purposes. The elements of the statutory business judgment rule were explained in *ASIC v Rich* [2009] NSWSC 1229, Ch 23 (the case is divided into chapters).

The duty of care, skill and diligence may also be either an express or implied term in a contract of employment for an officer of a corporation.

The statutory duties imposed on directors and officers are principally contained in ss 180–184.

In addition to ss 180–184, the Corporations Act imposes duties to disclose interests (ss 191–195) and prevents certain benefits being given to related parties of public companies and crowd-sourced funded proprietary companies (Ch 2E). These additional statutory requirements go some way to corresponding more fully with the fiduciary duty to avoid conflicts of interest.

Corporate regulation has had to deal with numerous situations where, as a result of actions taken by managers of a corporation, the corporation becomes insolvent and third parties and employees are left with little or no satisfaction in respect of money owed to them. Section 588G is a most powerful weapon, available principally to a liquidator to recover debts incurred while a company is insolvent. The recovery is made against the directors personally. While this section is most commonly pursued by a liquidator after a corporate collapse, it is often referred to as the duty to prevent insolvent trading. It is the most spectacular statutory breach of the corporate veil (see **Chapter 2**) and has been the subject of much judicial opinion, as have its predecessor sections.

Where the statutory duties are contravened, the court may impose a range of civil penalty orders. Section 1317E lists a number of provisions under the Corporations Act which are designated as 'civil penalty provisions'. Most of the directors' duties provisions (ss 180–183, 588G) are included in this list. If a civil penalty provision is contravened, ASIC may apply for a declaration of contravention from the court under s 1317E. If a declaration is granted, ASIC may then seek:

- a pecuniary penalty order (basically a fine) under s 1317G;
- a civil penalty compensation order on behalf of the company under s 1317H; and/or
- an order disqualifying a person from managing a corporation under s 206C.

As directors' and officers' duties are owed to the company, the company may seek a civil penalty compensation order for any damage caused by the contravention under s 1317H. The definition of damage in this context includes any profit made by the director or officer in breaching their duties: s 1317H(2). The company is not required to obtain a declaration of contravention in order to obtain compensation as only ASIC can apply for a declaration. It is important to remember the increased penalties for breach of directors' duties under the new penalty regime introduced by the Treasury Laws Amendment (Strengthening Corporate and Financial Sector Penalties) Act 2019 (Cth).

Before attempting the questions below, check that you are familiar with the following issues or terms:

✓	Who may be a director of a public/proprietary company?
✓	When may a director of a public/proprietary company be removed?
✓	What is meant by 'fiduciary'?
✓	What are the fiduciary duties owed by directors?
✓	To whom are fiduciary duties owed?
✓	Who may sue for a breach of fiduciary duty and what remedies are available?
✓	Who may sue for a breach of statutory duty and what consequences flow?
✓	When are directors required to disclose that they have a conflict of interest?

✓ What is the content and purpose of the prohibition on financial benefits to related parties in Ch 2E?

✓ What is the ambit and content of the duty to prevent insolvent trading under s 588G?

Question 21

Lin is a director of Lucky Dragon Pty Ltd. There are four other directors. At a board meeting a resolution is passed removing Lin from her office of director.

In her stead the board appoints Lee as a director. The next AGM for the company is in eight months' time.

Advise Lin whether she can challenge the resolution and appointment. Would her position be any different if Lucky Dragon was a public company?

Time allowed: 15 minutes

Answer Plan

This question is concerned with the power to appoint and remove company directors. As this is a short answer question with limited time there is no need for headings.

- The source of the power to remove directors could be in the constitution, the replaceable rules or the Corporations Act.
- The power to remove a director and appoint a replacement will reside with either the board or the members in general meeting (the company), depending upon whether the company is public or proprietary.
- If the board has no power to remove then what is the status of the resolution?
- You need to determine how a director can be appointed; whether there needs to be an election or whether the board can appoint directors.
- If the board can appoint a director, are there any limitations to this power?
- If Lucky Dragon Pty Ltd was a public company would s 203D resolve the issue regarding Lin's removal?

Answer

6-2 Lucky Dragon Pty Ltd is a proprietary company. In respect of proprietary companies there is no certain authority or power under the Corporations Act which permits the removal of a director prior to the end of his or her term of office. However, s 203C, a replaceable rule, provides that:

A proprietary company:

(a) may by resolution remove a director from office; and

(b) may by resolution appoint another person as a director instead.

This power is expressed as being a power which is vested in the company; that is, the members in general meeting and not the board. There is only a requirement for an ordinary resolution; that is, a simple majority for the removal.

It is possible for a proprietary company to have an internal rule which empowers the board to remove a director, and many smaller proprietary companies have such a rule.

Lin would need to check the constitution, if any, of Lucky Dragon Pty Ltd to see whether there is a power of removal vested in the board. If the board does have that power, then there is little that she can do to challenge the resolution, assuming that the resolution was passed in good faith: *Australian Metropolitan Life Assurance Co Ltd v Ure* (1923) 33 CLR 199 (which considered challenges to the power of the board of directors to act based on an alleged lack of good faith). It is possible that the constitution excludes the operation of s 203C (a replaceable rule) and does not permit a director to be removed by the board. If the board does not have the power to remove, it would be acting without power and in breach of the statutory contract formed by the constitution: s 140. Normally, a breach of the constitution would permit the wronged party, here Lin, to bring an action against the company for a declaration that the resolution was void and an injunction preventing the company from acting upon it.

In respect of the appointment of Lee, again s 203C is relevant as it also refers to the power to appoint another person to replace the removed director. Section 201H is also relevant. This section, a replaceable rule, empowers other directors to appoint another director. In the absence of anything in Lucky Dragon Pty Ltd's constitution about the removal and appointment of directors, s 203C would only permit Lin's removal by the members in general meeting, but an appointment of a director could be either by the members (s 203C(b)) or by the other directors (s 201H(1)). Of course, if Lin's removal was not valid then any subsequent appointment, by whatever means, would be invalid as there would be no vacant director position.

If Lucky Dragon Pty Ltd was a public company the position would be more certain. Section 203D of the Corporations Act provides for a right to remove a director from office by the members in general meeting. The procedure for doing so is by an ordinary resolution of which there has been two months' notice of the intention by the members given to the company. The worth of this notice is somewhat questionable in the light of the qualification contained in s 203D where the company calls a meeting after receiving the notice and the meeting is scheduled to occur within the two-month period. Notably, under s 249H(3), 21 days' notice is required for a general meeting and this time cannot be abridged where there is a motion for removal of a director.

The notice of intention to move for removal must be given to the director concerned: s 203D(3). The director has the right to be heard on the resolution at the meeting and the director may also require the company to send written representations regarding the removal to every member of the company: s 203D(4), (5) and (6). This procedure, in particular that the power to remove is to be exercised by the members in general meeting, applies notwithstanding anything in the company's constitution and must be complied with: Scottish & Colonial Ltd v Australian Power & Gas Co Ltd [2007] NSWSC 1266. Further, s 203E effectively prevents removal of a director of a public company by the other directors by making any such action, or even a request that the director vacate office, void.

Lin could rely on ss 203D and 203E, therefore, to preserve her position as a director of a public company in the face of the actions of the board or at least delay her removal.

Examiner's Comments

6-3 It would be useful to speculate on the practicalities or realities of Lin's position. If the remaining board members are hostile to Lin then they are likely, even if she successfully challenges the resolution, to adopt tactics which will make it difficult for her to fulfil her role as a director. For example, they may filter the information provided to her before board meetings or give only short notice of the meetings. There are no requirements under the Corporations Act for notice or periods of notice of directors' meetings, nor for specified information to be given to directors. Rules regarding these matters are contained, if they exist, in the constitution: s 248C.

Further, while a purported removal of a director in circumstances where the board does not have the power to do so will be subject to challenge, the remedy of an injunction is an equitable remedy and, generally, equity will not force unwilling parties to act in what can be characterised as a personal relationship of cooperation in business decision-making: Atlas Steels (Aust) Pty Ltd v Atlas Steels Ltd (1948) 49 SR (NSW) 157.

Given that Lin would be required to retire and seek re-election at a future annual general meeting, she may find it difficult without the support of fellow directors to be re-elected as a director. Thus, any potential benefits from a challenge to the board's resolution may only be temporary.

You could also add that if there is no power in the constitution of Lucky Dragon Pty Ltd empowering the board to remove a director then, if the other board members command the requisite majority, they could alter the constitution to include such a power: s 136(2).

An area of some interest is the interplay between ss 203C and 201H in relation to the appointment of directors. For a company with the replaceable rules, the question of who has the power to appoint a director may cause some conflict depending upon the reading of these two sections. Section 203C refers to a power residing in members to appoint a director, while s 201H appears to give the power to appoint another director to the board. Under s 201H, the power to appoint appears to be temporary, in that the appointment either must be confirmed within two months in the case of a proprietary company and at the next AGM for a public company. The power is likely to exist to ensure that the board always has a full complement of members. A director may vacate office either because of resignation, disqualification, death or removal. If this does not conveniently occur around the time of the company's AGM then the company may find it an expensive exercise to fill the casual vacancy if it must convene a general meeting to elect another director.

 # Keep in Mind

- Do not confuse the different positions between public and proprietary companies on this issue. Section 203D only applies to public companies. The constitution or replaceable rules are the principal source of power in this regard for proprietary companies.
- Do not overlook the fact that it is the board making this resolution and not the company in general meeting. The power of a company in general meeting to remove a director prior to the expiry of his or her term of office is clear: ss 203C and 203D.
- There are divergent judicial views as to the effect of s 203D. In *Scottish & Colonial Ltd v Australian Power & Gas Co Ltd* [2007] NSWSC 1266, the court held that failing to follow the s 203D procedure (by failing to give two months' notice) rendered the removal of a director invalid because s 203D is mandatory. But in *State Street Australia Ltd (Trustee) v Retirement Villages Group Management Pty Ltd* [2016] FCA 675, the court held that while s 203D would apply where inconsistent with the provisions in a company's constitution, s 203D is not an exhaustive code for removing directors.

 # Question 22

Harry, Irene and Henry are the directors and shareholders of Tomb Raider Pty Ltd. Tomb Raider Pty Ltd is a swimming pool construction company.

The market for pools in Australia is very strong and highly competitive. Each of the directors deals with this by devising expensive advertising campaigns and attempting to undercut their competitors' prices.

Unfortunately, Harry, Irene and Henry are not good financial managers. In recognition of this they employ a financial accountant, Brad, to manage the financial side of the business. Brad is paid a good salary for this but has no say in the company's activities.

Brad advises Harry, Irene and Henry that they have to refrain from their price undercutting practices because their cash flow position is in peril. The directors tell Brad not to interfere in managerial decisions but just make sure there is money to pay the subcontractors. Brad finds this increasingly difficult and begins to undertake a program of only paying select creditors. The company has few options left to generate sufficient cash to fund continuing operations.

In frustration with the company's troubles, Brad resigns. The directors are then served with a director penalty notice from the Australian Taxation Office for unpaid corporate taxes and they respond by putting the company into voluntary liquidation.

The liquidator investigates the actions of Harry, Irene and Henry in the months leading up to the liquidation and seeks your advice as to whether they may be liable for insolvent trading.

Time allowed: 45 minutes

Answer Plan

This question is concerned with the directors' duty to avoid insolvent trading.

Section 588G governs the liability of directors for debts incurred whilst the company is insolvent and in considering its application to the present problem you would need to determine whether, broadly:

- Harry, Irene, Henry and Brad were directors at the relevant time;
- the debts were incurred during the time that any of them were directors; and
- at the time of incurring the debt there were reasonable grounds for suspecting that the company was insolvent.

Was the company insolvent?

- Apply the statutory test for solvency under s 95A.

Liability for insolvent trading

- Apply the elements of s 588G.
- Determine if any defence in s 588H or s 588GA (safe harbour provision) may be available.

Consequences of insolvent trading

- Discuss civil penalties and compensation provisions.
- Consider prospect, if any, of criminal penalties.

Answer

6-4 This question concerns the potential liability of Harry, Irene and Henry for insolvent trading. The company appears to have been experiencing financial difficulties for some time and eventually collapsed into liquidation after enforcement action by the Australian Taxation Office (ATO). There are several elements to the insolvent trading prohibition which will be considered below.

Was the company insolvent?

6-5 Solvency is defined in s 95A as the ability to pay debts as and when they become due and payable. In this situation it appears that the company has been unable to pay its debts for some time. This is supported by a range of facts from the question:

- Brad has notified the directors that the company's discounting program has put its financial position in peril.
- Brad has had to pay select creditors only because of insufficient cash to pay all debts which means some creditors have gone unpaid.
- The ATO has served a director penalty notice because the company has failed to pay its tax obligations.
- The company appears to have run out of financing options to fund ongoing trading.

Therefore, applying the standard of commercial reality, it appears the company was insolvent prior to the liquidator being appointed because it was unable to pay all of its debts that were due and payable: *Southern Cross Interiors Pty Ltd (in liq) v Deputy Commissioner of Taxation* (2001) 53 NSWLR 213; [2001] NSWSC 621. (Insolvency is discussed further in **Chapter 10**.)

Liability for insolvent trading

6-6 Liability for insolvent trading requires proof of a number of elements under s 588G:

- *Was the person a director of the company?*

The facts of the question indicate that Harry, Irene and Henry are directors of the company. It should be noted that Brad was employed as an accountant and was not a director. Unless it could be proven that Brad was a shadow or de facto director he will not be liable for insolvent trading. It would seem that Brad was acting in a professional capacity and would not be a director under the definition in s 9.

- *Was a debt incurred?*

There are no facts in the question that suggest the existence of any deemed debts as described under s 588G(1A). However, the facts do indicate that the company was incurring debts prior to the liquidator being appointed as it was stated that certain creditors were not being paid. Furthermore, the continued trading operations of the business would involve debts such as wages and tax liabilities being incurred. Therefore, it can be assumed that debts were being incurred prior to the appointment of the liquidator.

- *Were there reasonable grounds to suspect the company's insolvency?*

The facts show a number of indicators of insolvency including debts going unpaid, creditor management, director penalty notices and a lack of alternative financing sources: *ASIC v Plymin* [2003] VSC 123. This would lead a reasonable person to suspect that the company was unable to pay its debts as and when they became due and payable. In *Queensland Bacon Pty Ltd v Rees* (1966) 115 CLR 266, it was stated that 'a suspicion that something exists is more than a mere idle wondering whether it exists or not; it is a positive feeling of actual apprehension or mistrust, amounting to a slight opinion, but without sufficient evidence'. The existence of several indicators of insolvency would constitute reasonable grounds to suspect the company's insolvency.

- *Awareness of reasonable grounds to suspect the company's insolvency*

In order to be found liable for insolvent trading it must be established that the directors, Harry, Irene and Henry, were aware of the reasonable grounds to suspect insolvency or that a reasonable person would have been aware. This can be established from the facts of the question because Brad warned the directors that their cash flow position was in peril if they continued their practice of undercutting and presumably paying for advertising. If they were not aware then it would be clear that a reasonable director in a company in similar circumstances would have been aware. This is similar to what occurred in *Hall v Poolman* [2007] NSWSC 1330, where this was sufficient to establish reasonable grounds to suspect insolvency. It is unclear whether the directors were aware that Brad was paying only selected creditors. Reasonably diligent directors would have put in place systems to enable them to effectively monitor the company's financial performance (*Daniels v Anderson* (1995) 16 ACSR 607) and would have therefore been aware of the grounds to suspect insolvency.

- *Potential defences (s 588H)*

As the directors have not taken an active role in monitoring the company's financial performance it is unlikely that they could have had a *reasonable* expectation that the company was solvent: s 588H(2). Being ignorant of the company's financial affairs is not a defence: *Statewide Tobacco Services v Morley* (1990) 2 ACSR 405. Nor is being hopeful of corporate solvency adequate for purposes of this defence: *ASIC v Tourprint International Pty Ltd v Bott* [1991] NSWSC 581. The directors are also unlikely to be able to prove that they had good reason for not taking part in the management of the company simply because of their lack of financial skill: s 588H(4); *Deputy Commissioner of Taxation v Clark* (2003) 57 NSWLR 113. The directors did nothing to prevent the company incurring further debts so there will be no defence under s 588H(5). The directors would also be unable to establish a defence under s 588H(3) as Brad did not advise them that the company was solvent.

- *Safe harbour (s 588GA)*

There is no supporting evidence in the given facts to show that the directors took steps to develop a corporate rescue plan. The safe harbour provisions in s 588GA, therefore, will not apply and protect the directors from personal liability for insolvent trading. But even if the directors developed a corporate rescue plan that was reasonably likely to lead to a better outcome for the company, the directors will still be precluded from reliance on s 588GA due to the company's failure to pay taxes: s 588GA(4). See *Re Balmz Pty Ltd (in liq)* [2020] VSC 652.

Consequences of insolvent trading

6-7 If the liquidator can prove that the directors contravened the insolvent trading provision, he or she may claim compensation from the directors in respect of the debts that were incurred after the company became insolvent: s 588M(2). The amount of compensation is measured by losses suffered by the company's creditors as a result of the insolvent trading.

The directors may face insolvent trading actions even if the liquidator does not bring proceedings, as ASIC (s 588J) and creditors of the company may also take action (s 588M(3)). If ASIC brings proceedings against the directors, it will seek a declaration of contravention under s 1317E and may then also seek an order disqualifying the directors from managing corporations under s 206C: see, for example, *Elliott v ASIC* (2004) 10 VR 369. Should there be evidence of dishonesty or recklessness, ASIC can seek criminal penalties for insolvent trading which can include imprisonment for up to five years or a pecuniary penalty or both: s 588G(3). See, for example, *R v Young* [2021] QCA 131.

🔍 Examiner's Comments

6-8 It may be useful to briefly discuss the possibility of relief from liability under s 1317S, as occurred in *Hall v Poolman* (2007) 65 ACSR 123; [2007] NSWSC 1330. However, the failure of the directors to actively monitor the financial position of the company would render relief from liability highly unlikely. Compare the situation in *Re McLellan; The Stake Man Pty Ltd v Carroll* [2009] FCA 1415 (where the director was very active in monitoring the financial situation). For a useful illustration of the judicial approach to relief from liability under s 1317S, see *Re Balmz Pty Ltd (in liq)* [2020] VSC 652 where relief was declined — albeit that the liquidator did not contend that the spousal directors of a family company acted dishonestly. The court held the directors' conduct did not have regard to the interests of all the unsecured creditors of the company.

Keep in Mind

- Note that s 588G applies *only* to directors. In this sense, it is more specific than other statutory duties.
- Brad, as a financial accountant or expert giving advice on financial management, is not necessarily a shadow director.
- For a useful collection of legal authorities on the meaning of insolvency (under s 95A), see *Quin v Vlahos* [2021] VSCA 205 at [42]–[64].
- For useful indicators of insolvency, see *ASIC v Plymin* [2003] VSC 123. For an example of the practical application of insolvency indicators, see *Quin v Vlahos* [2021] VSCA 205 at [144]–[162].
- Passive (or sleeping) directors, or directors who fail to take reasonable steps to acquire information about the company's financial state which could be reasonably required of company directors, will not be able to prove a defence under s 588H(2): *Statewide Tobacco Services v Morley* (1990) 2 ACSR 405; *Tourprint International Pty Ltd v Bott* [1991] NSWSC 581.
- Access to the safe harbour is conditional on meeting employee entitlements, tax reporting obligations and directors fulfilling existing obligations to provide assistance in the event of administration or liquidation: s 588GA(4). For example, see *Re Balmz Pty Ltd (in liq)* [2020] VSC 652.

Question 23

Quentin is a non-executive director on the board of the Rotweil Merchant Bank Ltd. Cool Partners is a financial consulting firm which has had dealings with Rotweil. Mark is a partner of Cool Partners and is also a non-executive director of Rotweil.

Cool Partners has proposed a permanent consulting role with Rotweil which would generate huge fees for Cool. Mark is a vocal advocate for the proposal and lobbies his fellow directors to accept the deal. While the other directors know that Mark is a partner of Cool, they are not told that Mark will be paid an extra commission if the consulting deal is approved.

Quentin's role on the board of Rotweil has been fairly insignificant as he is not considered to be 'in the club' by the other directors. He is suspicious of Mark but believes that whatever he says will be ignored by the other directors and his vote will not change the decision. Quentin does not turn up for the board meeting at which the decision is to be made and, not surprisingly, the other directors vote in favour of approving the consultancy.

Advise both Quentin and Mark of any potential breach of directors' duties.

Time allowed: 60 minutes

Answer Plan

This question is concerned with the directors' duty of care and diligence and equitable duties (particularly the duty to avoid conflicts of interest). The steps to answering this question would be as follows:

- Briefly identify the duties attaching to the office of director.
- Distinguish between executive and non-executive directors.
- Discuss Quentin's potential breach of the duty of care and diligence.
- Discuss Mark's potential breach of his equitable duties.
- Identify what consequences may flow from breaching these duties.

Directors' and officers' duties

- Outline the range of directors' duties.
- Explain to whom the duties are owed and how they may be enforced.
- Identify how they apply to non-executive directors.

Quentin's potential breach of duty

- The duty of care, skill and diligence.
- The statutory duty of care and diligence.
- Potential defences.

Mark's potential breach of duty

- The duty to avoid conflicts of interest under equitable principles.
- The statutory duty to avoid conflicts: ss 181 and 182.
- Potential defences.

Consequences of breaching duties

- Remedies at general law.
- Statutory consequences.

Answer

6-9 This question requires an examination of the potential liability of Mark and Quentin for breach of directors' duties.

Directors' and officers' duties

6-10 Company directors occupy positions of power and authority over the affairs of the company. The vulnerable position that companies and most shareholders find themselves in justifies the imposition of legal and equitable duties to restrain the exercise of directorial power in order to ensure that directors act properly and with due care. Directors are subject to both general law and statutory duties. The general law duties centre on the common law duty of care, skill and diligence: *Daniels v Anderson* (1995) 16 ACSR 607. The equitable duties include the duties:

- to act in good faith for the benefit of the company as a whole;
- to keep discretions unfettered;

- to exercise powers only for proper corporate purposes; and
- to avoid conflicts of interest.

In addition, there are statutory duties imposed on directors and other officers by the Corporations Act. The principal source of these duties is ss 180–184. These duties overlap with the general law duties already set out.

Both the general law and statutory duties are owed to the company and not to individual shareholders (*Percival v Wright* [1902] 2 Ch D 421; for limited exceptions, see *Crawely v Short* [2009] NSWCA 410), nor are they owed to the company's creditors (*Spies v R* (2000) 201 CLR 603) or employees (*Parke v Daily News Ltd* [1962] Ch 927).

Both Quentin and Mark are stated in the question as being non-executive directors. The Corporations Act does not distinguish between executive and non-executive directors. The role and responsibility assumed by the defendant will be relevant in determining what their legal and equitable duties are: *Shafron v ASIC* [2012] HCA 18. An executive director is a director who performs other managerial duties for the company, usually for a salary and under the terms of a separate contract of service. Executive directors take part in the day-to-day decision-making of the company and usually have high levels of individual responsibility within the business. A non-executive director holds no other position within the company and merely attends board meetings to make decisions and provide general oversight of the company's management and strategic direction. Despite this distinction, all directors are subject to the same duties and the obligations imposed on non-executive directors are not of a lesser standard than those imposed on executive directors: *Daniels v Anderson* (1995) 16 ACSR 607. There is no information in the facts that suggests that Quentin or Mark have executive management responsibilities, but rather that they are serving on the board in an advisory capacity. As directors they have a fundamental duty to monitor the company's performance and to properly read and consider matters brought before the board for consideration: *ASIC v Healey* [2011] FCA 717.

Quentin's potential breach of duty

6-11 The *AWA* case recognised that all company directors have a minimum obligation to establish internal monitoring systems that allow them to remain informed about the company's ongoing financial performance. This will typically involve attending all board meetings when they are reasonably able to do so: *Vrisakis v ASIC* (1993) 11 ACSR 162. The essence of director negligence is failing to properly balance the foreseeable risk of harm against the potential benefits that could reasonably have been expected to accrue to the company: *Vrisakis* (per Ipp J). See also *Vines v ASIC* [2007] NSWCA 75; *Cassimatis v ASIC* [2020] FCAFC 52.

On the present facts, there may be a risk that the consulting contract will not be beneficial to the company which must be weighed against any potential benefit flowing from the contract. Quentin has decided not to participate in the meeting or discussion as he does not believe that his views will be considered. This is evidence of not properly weighing up the benefits and potential risks, and it is therefore not conduct that a reasonable person would engage in if they were a director of the company in similar circumstances: see, for example, *Gold Ribbon (Accountants) Pty Ltd (in liq) v Sheers* [2006] QCA 335.

If Quentin has knowledge about potential harm that may be caused by the transaction, he should seek to protect the company's interests: *Permanent Building Society (in liq) v Wheeler* (1994) 14 ACSR 109; *ASIC v Adler* (2002) 42 ACSR 80. It should, however, be noted that both of these cases concerned the positive obligation imposed on chief executive officers. It is arguable that if a reasonable person had actual knowledge of potential harm to the company on which they were serving as a director they would take steps to disclose that potential harm and argue against the transaction: *ASIC v Macdonald (No 11)* [2009] NSWSC 287 (where non-executive directors were held to be negligent for failing to oppose the release of a misleading press release).

It would appear that Quentin has failed to act with due care and diligence by failing to participate in the board discussion concerning the consulting contract. This would be a breach of both the general law obligation and the statutory obligation in s 180(1). However, as negligence is an unintentional tort it must still be proved that the failure to act with due care caused the company harm. Causation of harm is not, however, necessary for a breach of the statutory provision: *Permanent Building Society (in liq) v Wheeler* (1994) 14 ACSR 109. As in *PBS v Wheeler*, if all of the other directors had been determined to approve the transaction it is doubtful that Quentin's negligence could be said to have caused the harm suffered by the company as the result would have been the same regardless. This need not be proved if the action is brought under the statute: *ASIC v Flugge* [2016] VSC 799 at [1864]. Furthermore, if ASIC were bringing the action, it may not necessarily be seeking compensation for loss suffered by the company, but rather a banning order against Quentin.

It seems unlikely that Quentin would have any defence to an action for breach of the duty of care and diligence. Quentin could not use the business judgment rule defence in s 180(2) as he either failed to make a business judgment (s 180(3)) or because he was not properly informed: *Gold Ribbon (Accountants) Pty Ltd (in liq) v Sheers* [2006] QCA 335; see also *ASIC v Rich* [2009] NSWSC 1229. Quentin did not exercise an independent judgment about information provided by others and therefore cannot rely on the defence in s 189 either.

Mark's potential breach of duty

6-12   As a director of Rotweil Merchant Bank Ltd, Mark is bound by a fiduciary duty to avoid conflicts of interest between his personal interests and those of the company: *Aberdeen Railway Company v Blaikie Bros* (1854) 1 Macq 461. Clearly, by representing both the company and his consulting partnership Mark is acting under a conflict of interest by acting for both vendor and purchaser (as occurred in *Blaikie Bros*). It is also important to determine whether the company had ameliorated the strict equitable prohibition against conflicts by allowing certain conflicted transactions under the company's constitution as long as the conflicted director gave full disclosure. The question does not specify what is contained in Rotweil's constitution, so it is assumed that such a provision exists.

This raises the question as to whether Mark has given sufficient disclosure to enable the transaction to stand because of the relief granted by the constitution provision. This was the issue in *Imperial Mercantile Credit Association v Coleman* (1873) LR 6 HL 189, where it was held that disclosure by a director that he 'had an interest' in the transaction was insufficient to confer protection and the details of the conflict and any profit had to be disclosed. See also *Groenveld Australia Pty Ltd v Wouter Nolten (No 3)* [2010] VSC 533; *Hylepin Pty Ltd v Doshay Pty Ltd* [2020] FCA 1370.

In this case, it is difficult to determine what level of disclosure was given by Mark. The question states that the other directors know that Mark is a partner in Cool Partners but there is no evidence that they are aware that Mark is receiving an additional commission if the transaction goes ahead. It would seem therefore that Mark has not given sufficient disclosure to gain the protection of the constitutional provision and the transaction would be voidable at the option of the company.

Mark's conduct in seeking to gain a benefit for himself through the transaction would be likely to be in breach of s 182 by improperly using his position to gain an advantage for himself rather than Rotweil: see, for example, *Re HIH Insurance Ltd (in liq); ASIC v Adler* [2002] NSWSC 171 (where Adler used his position on the HIH board of directors to obtain a benefit for himself and his private family company). It could also be argued that by knowingly seeking to gain a private benefit for himself Mark has not acted in good faith in the best interests of the company, but rather in his own best interests: s 181(1)(a). Such conduct would also be likely to constitute failing to act for a proper purpose; that is, failing to act only in the best interests of the company: s 181(1)(b).

Lastly, Mark may also have contravened s 191 by failing to give proper notice of his 'material personal interest' in the transaction. However, as noted above, this is based on the assumption that Mark has only disclosed his interest in the Cool partnership and has not disclosed his secret commission. If he had given such notice to the board this provision would not be contravened. If we assume that Mark attended and voted at the board meeting that Quentin missed, he would also have contravened s 195 (as Rotweil is a public company) unless he obtained approval from the other directors under s 195(2), although this requires full disclosure. It is also possible that the transaction confers a financial benefit on a related party (Mark) which would require shareholder approval under Ch 2E (related party transactions), although the consulting contract might fall within a carve-out such as an arm's length transaction (s 210) and not need approval.

If Mark has not given proper disclosure of his interest in the transaction to Rotweil it is difficult to see how he could have any valid defence. A fiduciary who acts under a conflict of interest may have a defence if they have given full and frank disclosure to the company (preferably the shareholders): *Regal (Hastings) Ltd v Gulliver* [1967] 2 AC 134. It does not appear that Mark has done this and so he is unlikely to have any defence available.

Consequences of breaching duties

6-13 Mark's conduct in acting under a conflict of interest may allow the company to invalidate the transaction by rescission of contract, although this will only be possible if both parties can be returned to their prior state. As Mark has likely also breached his statutory duties, the company could seek compensation under s 1317H as both ss 181 and 182 are civil penalty provisions. Mark may also face action from ASIC which could apply for a declaration of contravention under s 1317E and pecuniary penalty orders under s 1317G, and/or banning orders under s 206C (as occurred in *Adler's* case).

Section 180(1) is also a civil penalty provision and Quentin could face similar consequences under the Corporations Act. As noted above, the primary remedy at general law for breach of the duty of care is damages.

🔍 Examiner's Comments

6-14 The discussion of conflicts and acting for a proper purpose in this question depends heavily on exactly how detailed Mark's disclosure to the company was. It is possible that Mark could have obtained the consent of the company to take his actions which would give rise to a question as to whether his conduct would have been in good faith and acting properly. While ratification by the company (particularly the shareholders) would render the company (probably) unable to take action, it would not prevent ASIC from suing for a breach of the statutory duties.

As for Quentin, it is important to discuss what his role and responsibilities within the company were. Although he was a non-executive director, he may have taken on greater individual responsibilities (such as serving on a sub-committee of the board of directors dealing with conflicted transactions) which could give rise to more onerous responsibilities: see, for example, *ASIC v Rich* [2003] NSWSC 85.

Keep in Mind

- Remember to stick closely to the specific question posed; for example, do not get caught up in describing any possible breaches of duty by the other directors.
- Do not confuse statutory duties with general law or equitable duties. While their content may be similar, the statutory duties are expressly defined in the Corporations Act. Further, the relevant person to commence any legal proceedings may be different and the consequences of any breach are also different under the particular source of law being enforced. For example, breach of the Corporations Act can attract criminal penalties and is enforced by the corporate regulator, ASIC.
- There will be no breach of the conflict rule or the profit rule of fiduciary obligations if the director establishes that he or she obtained the company's fully informed consent to the transaction. As Brennan CJ, Gaudron, McHugh and Gummow JJ made clear in *Maguire v Makaronis* [1997] HCA 23; (1997) 188 CLR 449 at 466:

> ... if the [fiduciary was] to escape the stigma of an adverse finding of breach of fiduciary duty, with consequent remedies, it was for [it] to show, by way of defence, informed consent by the respondents to the appellants' acting, in relation to the mortgage, with a divided loyalty. What is required for a fully informed consent is a question of fact in all the circumstances of each case and there is no precise formula which will determine in all cases if fully informed consent has been given.

For an explanation of fully informed consent in this context, see Samuels JA in *Woolworths Ltd v Kelly* (1991) 22 NSWLR 189 at 207–11; *Blackmagic Design Pty Ltd v Overliese* [2011] FCAFC 24; *Hasler v Singtel Optus Pty Ltd* [2014] NSWCA 266; *Rahme v Benjamin & Khoury Pty Ltd* [2019] NSWCA 211; *Atanaskovic Hartnell v Birketu Pty Ltd* [2021] NSWCA 201 at [46]–[50]; *Mualim v Dzelme* [2021] NSWCA 199 at [111]–[115].

Question 24

Wallett Ltd is a listed company. Coin Ltd holds 40 per cent of the issued shares in Wallett and Note Ltd has 35 per cent of the shares. The remaining 25 per cent is held by a diverse group of shareholders.

Wallett has tendered for the construction of a large timber mill and is likely to be the successful bidder. It will need an injection of funds to construct the mill. The directors are concerned that Coin, which has other timber milling interests, will launch a takeover of Wallett and they will lose their positions. They are also concerned that Coin will terminate the employment of many of Wallett's workers as Coin has a reputation of using foreign workers rather than local workers.

At a board meeting the directors resolve to allot a substantial number of shares to Note in consideration for a promise that Note will arrange finance for the construction of the mill. The allotment to Note varies the shareholding power of Coin such that, after the allotment, Coin will only command 10 per cent of voting power.

Advise the directors about the possibility of any legal challenge to their actions.

Time allowed: 40 minutes

Answer Plan

This is a problem type question about the power of directors to issue shares. You should consider the following issues:

- What is the nature and extent of the power to issue shares?
- Is there any legislative or common law limit to the exercise of this power?
- At common law, directors have a duty to only exercise their powers for a proper purpose.
- Is this share issue for a proper purpose?

Directors' and officers' duties

- Outline the range of directors' duties.

Acting for a proper purpose

- Operation of the proper purpose rule.
- Possible defences.

Consequences of contravention

- Statutory and general law.

Answer

6-15 This question gives rise to issues concerning the validity of the actions of Wallett Ltd's directors in issuing shares to Note Ltd, specifically whether the directors of Wallett Ltd have acted in breach of their legal obligations as company directors by misusing their powers.

Directors' and officers' duties

6-16 Company directors occupy positions of power and authority over the affairs of the company. The vulnerable position that companies and most shareholders find themselves in justifies the imposition of legal and equitable duties to restrain the exercise of directorial power in order to ensure that directors act properly and with due care. Directors are subject to both general law and statutory duties. The general law duties centre on the common law duty of care, skill and diligence while the equitable duties include the duty:

- to act in good faith for the benefit of the company as a whole;
- to keep discretions unfettered;
- to exercise powers only for proper corporate purposes; and
- to avoid conflicts of interest.

In addition, there are statutory duties imposed on directors and other officers by the Corporations Act. The principal source of these duties is ss 180–184. These duties overlap with the general law duties already set out.

Both the general law and statutory duties are owed to the company and not to individual shareholders (*Percival v Wright* [1902] 2 Ch D 421; for limited exceptions, see *Crawely v Short* [2009] NSWCA 410), nor are they owed to the company's creditors (*Spies v R* (2000) 201 CLR 603) or employees (*Parke v Daily News Ltd* [1962] Ch 927). The directors are bound to act in the best interests of the company and the identification of those interests lies ultimately with the directors and not with the courts: *Re Smith and Fawcett Ltd* [1942] Ch 304. The courts are not responsible for setting what the commercial objectives of the company should be or determining how those objects are best obtained. The focus is on whether the directors have sought to achieve those goals in good faith. This is known as the general law business judgment rule: see *Howard Smith Ltd v Ampol Petroleum Ltd* [1974] AC 821.

This question concerns the duty of company directors to use their powers for a proper purpose to benefit the company. Most companies place the management of their affairs in the hands of the board of directors and this is in fact provided as a default rule: s 198A (a replaceable rule).

If Wallett Ltd has this replaceable rule then it is clear that the power to issue shares (ss 124(1)(a), 254A) will be vested in the board. It is common, in the case of companies with a constitution, that there will be a similarly expressed power in favour of the directors. The Corporations Act does not require share issues to be decided or approved in the general meeting. Raising capital by the issue of shares is clearly a managerial power and it is specifically vested in the directors by ss 198A and 124. Thus, unless the constitution of Wallett Ltd restricts the use of this power then the board is generally free to exercise it in any way that they see fit, although it is a corporate power that is being exercised and it must therefore be used only in good faith and for a proper purpose.

The proper purpose rule

6-17   Although directors may exercise their managerial powers in any manner they see fit, the powers must be exercised for a proper purpose: *Mills v Mills* (1938) 60 CLR 150.

This leads to the question: What is the proper purpose of issuing the shares? There is no clear statement of law that defines the proper purpose of this power. Courts generally try to identify some objective purpose of the power and in this regard they may be guided by the terms of the constitution: *Whitehouse v Carlton Hotel Pty Ltd* (1987) 162 CLR 285. However, as a general rule, the objective purpose of a share issue is to raise capital for the company: *Howard Smith Ltd v Ampol Petroleum Ltd* [1974] AC 821. Having established the objective purpose of the power in the particular company then the court will inquire into the purpose which actually motivated the exercise of the power in this circumstance.

Thus, in *Ngurli v McCann* (1953) 90 CLR 425, it was held at [24] that:

> The power must be used bona fide for the purpose for which it was conferred, that is to say, to raise sufficient capital for the benefit of the company as a whole. It must not be used under the cloak of such a purpose for the real purpose of benefiting some shareholders or their friends at the expense of other shareholders or so that some shareholders or their friends will wrest control of the company from the other shareholders.

Similarly, in *Howard Smith Ltd v Ampol Petroleum Ltd* [1974] AC 821, the Privy Council held that directors will breach their duty to exercise their power for a proper purpose if they use the power to issue shares to create a new majority. This is so even if they honestly believe that the share issue is in the best interests of the company because there is a threat of takeover by the existing majority.

If the directors of Wallett Ltd are motivated by a desire to change the majority voting power then on the basis of *Ngurli v McCann* (above) and *Howard Smith Ltd v Ampol Petroleum Ltd* (above) the share issue is tainted by an improper purpose and the directors would be in breach of their duty.

However, in the case of Wallett Ltd, there appear to be two purposes for the issue of the shares. One purpose may be to defeat a potential takeover bid and the other is to raise capital. There have been a number of cases in which the question of mixed purposes for the share issue has been considered. The High Court in *Whitehouse v Carlton Hotel Pty Ltd* (above) settled the matter by stating (at [10]):

> As a matter of logic and principle, the preferable view would seem to be that, regardless of whether the impermissible purpose was the dominant one or but one of a number of significantly contributing causes, the allotment will be invalidated if the impermissible purpose was causative in the sense that, but for its presence, 'the power would not have been exercised': *Mills v Mills* (1938) 60 CLR 150.

In both *Pine Vale Investments Ltd v McDonnell and East Pty Ltd* (1983) 1 ACLC 1294 and *Darvall v North Sydney Brick & Tile Co Ltd* (1989) 16 NSWLR 260, courts examined situations where a company made a share issue for the dual purpose of raising finance and thwarting a takeover bid. In each case, the evidence from the directors and the company records was sufficient to establish that the obligation to raise finance was brought about by the desire of the directors to take advantage of a good commercial opportunity for the company and that the share issue was 'caused' by the need to raise the necessary finance.

By contrast, in *Howard Smith Ltd v Ampol Petroleum Ltd* (above), there was also a dual purpose. The evidence in that case was, however, such that the directors appeared to be largely motivated by the desire to thwart the takeover and the issue of the shares to the other shareholder to raise the finance was at a special price. Initially, Ampol had made a takeover bid and there was then a higher takeover bid by Howard Smith. The board wanted to ensure the success of the Howard Smith offer, so the allotment was made to Howard Smith at a price that was significantly lower than their offer price but marginally higher than the offer price by Ampol. The price was also far less than the asset backing per share. While it was clear that the company needed to raise capital, it was also established by the evidence that the directors had acted to ensure the success of Howard Smith's bid and any consideration of the need to raise finance was cursory as no other finance-raising techniques were considered by the board.

The non-cash consideration for the share issue to Note Ltd is going to be the major stumbling block for the directors of Wallett. While the answer cannot be certain — for there would need to be a thorough examination of the evidence of the directors' meetings — the consideration for the shares would tend to suggest that the primary cause of the issue was to change the voting power of the majority rather than to raise finance. It is likely that the directors have exercised their power for an improper purpose and the issue would be rescinded.

A failure to act for a proper purpose under equitable principles will also constitute a breach of s 181(1)(b).

Consequences of breaching the proper purpose rule

6-18 Acting for an improper purpose has tainted the share issue and the company may seek to have it set aside: *Whitehouse v Carlton Hotel Pty Ltd* (1987) 70 ALR 251. A contravention of s 181 may allow the company (or ASIC) to seek compensation under s 1317H as s 181 is a civil penalty provision. ASIC may apply for a declaration of contravention under s 1317E and pecuniary penalty orders under s 1317G and/or banning orders under s 206C.

Examiner's Comments

6-19 The Listing Rules of a stock exchange, such as the Australian Securities Exchange (ASX), may require that certain share issues be put to the company in general meeting. These Listing Rules are not a separate law which determines what a company may or may not do, but rather a set of rules, compliance with which is necessary for the company to be listed and its securities quoted on the ASX. The rules will be expressed such that the company's constitution will need to comply with the rules before the ASX grants listing. Non-compliance with the rules will mean that the ASX may suspend trading in the company's shares or de-list the company. The aim of the Listing Rules is to ensure high integrity and efficiency in the share market. Thus, it is likely that there will be restrictions upon directors preventing them from making allotments which will have the effect of altering voting control, without a general meeting.

Wallett Ltd may also face a complaint to the Takeovers Panel about the potential for the share issue to constitute 'frustrating action' which may allow the Panel to make a declaration of 'unacceptable circumstances' under s 657A, including orders under s 657D.

The answer could discuss the distinction between the subjective assessment of the duty of good faith and the objective assessment of the duty to act for a proper purpose: see the discussion in *Westpac Banking Corporation v Bell Group Ltd (in liq) (No 3)* [2012] WASCA 157.

There is also an interesting issue as to what extent the directors may act in the interests of employees. While *Parke v Daily News Ltd* [1962] Ch 927 confirmed that directors have no duty to employees, that case concerned a business that was closing where the directors made ex gratia payments from the sale of the business to the terminated employees. The decision in *Teck Corp Ltd v Millar* (1973) 33 DLR (3d) 288 (BCSC), which was approved by the Privy Council in *Howard Smith Ltd v Ampol Petroleum Ltd* [1974] AC 821, considered similar circumstances where directors were concerned about the effect of a hostile takeover bid on the company, the minority shareholders (that is, those who did not sell to the bidder) and the workers. The court seemed to acknowledge that directors have a wide compass to determine what the interests of the company may be and it is up to the party alleging breach of duty to bring evidence of bad faith or an improper purpose. Merely noting that the directors are concerned about employees would not be enough to establish this.

One final area for elaboration would be to address the question of who may bring an action for the breach of duty. Generally, only the company can bring proceedings for a breach of duty under the rule in *Foss v Harbottle* (1843) 2 Hare 461. However, in *Residues Treatment & Trading Co Ltd v Southern Resources Ltd (No 4)* (1988) 14 ACLR 569, it was held that shareholders have a personal right to ensure that the voting power of their shares is not reduced or diminished by an improper share issue. The existence of a statutory derivative action under Pt 2F.1A of the Corporations Act could be addressed here.

Care needs to be taken in relation to orders to set aside a share issue on the grounds that it was an improper exercise of power. Such transactions are merely voidable for they are an excess of power rather than an absence of power. In these cases, third parties who acquire rights as a result of the share issue may not be subject to an order to set it aside unless there is notice of the improper purpose: *Whitehouse v Carlton Hotel Pty Ltd* (above).

Keep in Mind

- Do not assume that the only proper purpose of a share issue is to raise finance. Share issues can be used for a variety of legitimate purposes, some of which may be expressed in the company's constitution. The fact that the share issue also defeats a takeover bid or some other control balance will not of itself defeat the share issue. Questions of proper purpose are a delicate balance of causative or motivating purposes which cannot always be readily divined without a very thorough examination of the evidence.
- For a collection of legal principles on the power to issue shares, see *Re Alon Pty Ltd* [2021] NSWSC 1021; *Re Pacific Springs Pty Ltd* [2020] NSWSC 1240 at [115]–[125]; affirmed on appeal in *Mualim v Dzelme* [2021] NSWCA 199.
- Do not assume that you need the company in general meeting to decide whether or not to issue shares. Ultimately, the power to issue shares will be set out in the constitution or replaceable rules and it is rare for this power to be anywhere other than within the managerial power of the board of directors. Subject to Listing Rule limits or total limits in the constitution on authorised capital, the power to issue shares is solely a matter for the board.

Question 25

Fassbinder is a director of Port Hotels Ltd. He is also a director and controlling shareholder of Buildenbust Pty Ltd, a construction company.

Fassbinder convinces the board of Port Hotels that the company could improve its position by renovating and expanding one of its major tourist resorts and, indeed, his proposal is reasonable given the tourism prospects in the area. The expansion program, however, would require council approval.

Fassbinder obtains plans and a written quote for the expansion work from Buildenbust for $2 million. He obtains quotes from other companies which far exceed the quote from Buildenbust, because the quote from Buildenbust is well below the cost of the project.

The directors of Port Hotels Ltd are convinced as a result of Fassbinder's representations that the application will be approved by the council and they sign the contract with Buildenbust. The terms of the contract with Buildenbust require an advance payment of $500,000. Buildenbust commences building prior to council approval and demands a progress payment of a further $500,000 which is duly paid.

The council does not grant approval because the site is environmentally sensitive. Buildenbust has an issued capital of $2 and no capacity to complete the project. The advance payments have been used to pay other debts of Buildenbust and the work done at the site was minor demolition. Port Hotels has now paid $1 million to Buildenbust, has partly demolished premises and no council approval for construction has been granted. Buildenbust is being wound up.

The directors of Port Hotels seek your advice about any action they may take against Fassbinder.

Time allowed: 40 minutes

 ## Answer Plan

Fassbinder has devised an elaborate fraud on a not-so-clever board to gain up to $2 million from Port Hotels Ltd to prop up his construction company, Buildenbust.

There are a number of breaches of fiduciary duty and statutory duties by Fassbinder that may be pursued by the directors of Port Hotels such as:

- breach of duty to avoid a conflict of interest; and
- breach of duty to act bona fide in the interests of the company as a whole.

Directors' and officers' duties

- Outline the range of directors' duties.

The no conflict rule

- Operation of the no conflict rule (general law and statute law).
- Possible defences.

Consequences of contravention

- Statutory and general law.

 ## Answer

6-20 This question is concerned with Fassbinder's plan to divest Port Hotels Ltd of $2 million in favour of his construction company. The key issue is whether this is a conflict of interest and a breach of directors' duties.

Directors' and officers' duties

6-21 Company directors occupy positions of power and authority over the affairs of the company. The vulnerable position that companies and most shareholders find themselves in justifies the imposition of legal and equitable duties to restrain the exercise of directorial power in order to ensure that directors act properly and with due care. Directors are subject to both general law and statutory duties. The general law duties centre on the common law duty of care, skill and diligence while the equitable duties include the duty:

- to act in good faith for the benefit of the company as a whole;
- to keep discretions unfettered;
- to exercise powers only for proper corporate purposes; and
- to avoid conflicts of interest.

In addition, there are statutory duties imposed on directors and other officers by the Corporations Act. The principal source of these duties is ss 180–184. These duties overlap with the general law duties already set out.

Both the general law and statutory duties are owed to the company and not to individual shareholders (*Percival v Wright* [1902] 2 Ch D 421; for limited exceptions, see *Crawely v Short* [2009] NSWCA 410), nor are they owed to the company's creditors (*Spies v R* (2000) 201 CLR 603) or employees (*Parke v Daily News Ltd* [1962] Ch 927).

The no conflict rule

6-22 Fassbinder's elaborate plan to divest Port Hotels Ltd of $2 million in favour of Fassbinder's construction company would seem to be a clear case of acting under a conflict of interest. As a director, Fassbinder is under a fiduciary duty to avoid a conflict of interest: *Aberdeen Railway Company v Blaikie Bros* (1854) 1 Macq 461. This can be strictly applied to cover even situations where there is no clear conflict in terms of the activities being undertaken by the director but where there is a 'real sensible possibility of conflict': *Phipps v Boardman* [1967] 2 AC 46.

In Fassbinder's case, the facts go much further than a possibility of conflict, for in his case he is serving only the interests of Buildenbust, instead of Port Hotels, when he convinces the board to act as they have. Indeed, the method used by Fassbinder has employed fraud, dishonesty and trickery to achieve his purpose of acting to better the financial position of Buildenbust. This would clearly establish that he has not acted in good faith in the best interests of the company: *ASIC v Adler* (2002) 41 ACSR 72 (seeking to deliberately avoid detection of misconduct). When a director acts knowingly under a conflict of interest then he or she also does not act in the interests of the company as a whole. In Fassbinder's case, he is certainly not acting in good faith. The duty can strictly be breached when a director has interests in another company other than the company of which he or she is a director: *Transvaal Lands Co v New Belgium (Transvaal) Land and Development Co* [1914] 2 Ch 488. The object of the duty is to ensure that the director gives his or her impartial deliberation to the affairs of the company rather than being affected by personal or other interests.

The fiduciary duty to avoid a conflict of interest is more often breached in situations where the director has an interest in a transaction with the company, either because he or she personally is involved or because another company associated with the director is involved.

A company is entitled to the unbiased and independent judgment of each of its directors. A director of a company who is also a director of another company may owe conflicting fiduciary duties. Being a fiduciary, the director of the first company must not exercise his or her powers for the benefit or gain of the second company without clearly disclosing the second company's interest to the first company and obtaining the first company's consent: *R v Byrnes* (1995) 17 ACSR 551.

At the very least, Fassbinder should have disclosed his interest in Buildenbust Pty Ltd to the directors of Port Hotels and probably should not have taken part in any deliberation or voting: *Jenkins v Enterprise Gold Mines NL* (1992) 6 ACSR 539. This is also a requirement of ss 191 and 195 of the Corporations Act. It has also been held that directors owe a positive duty to protect the company's interests by taking action to prevent the transaction from going ahead when the transaction is clearly of no benefit to the company, but rather will cause harm to the company: *Permanent Building Society (in liq) v McGee* (1993) 11 ACSR 260. Failing to protect the company's interests in such a situation may also give rise to a breach of the duty of care and diligence: see *ASIC v Sydney Investment House Equities Pty Ltd* (2008) 69 ACSR 1 (failing to protect the company from incurring loans to insolvent companies); *ASIC v Cassimatis (No 8)* [2016] FCA 1023; affirmed by majority on appeal in *Cassimatis v ASIC* [2020] FCAFC 52 (directors have a duty to take reasonable care to avoid any foreseeable risk of harm to their company — including through reputational damage or regulatory action — that would result from it breaking the law).

Consequences of breaching the no conflict rule

6-23 Breach of a fiduciary duty gives rise to a right in the company to pursue equitable relief against the director. Relevantly, the directors would seek to rescind the contract with Buildenbust Pty Ltd in order to avoid the possibility of further obligations and to recover, if possible, any amounts already paid. For the court to make an order for rescission, Port Hotels would need to show that Buildenbust knew of the breach of duty: *Transvaal Lands Co v New Belgium (Transvaal) Land and Development Co* (above). This ought not be difficult given Fassbinder's role in the company. Port Hotels must also show that *restitution in integrum* is possible. This may be difficult now that Buildenbust is being wound up.

As against Fassbinder, Port Hotels would be seeking an order to recover their losses. Where a breach of fiduciary duty causes loss then the court has power to award monetary compensation called equitable compensation: see *V-Flow Pty Ltd v Holyoake Industries (Vic) Pty Ltd* [2013] FCAFC 16; *Mudgee Dolomite & Lime Pty Ltd v Robert Francis*

Murdoch; *Re Mudgee Dolomite & Lime Pty Ltd* [2020] NSWSC 1510; *Schmidt v AHRKalimpa Pty Ltd* [2020] VSCA 193.

In addition to fiduciary duties which are owed to the company by directors, directors are also subject to statutory duties. The statutory duties mirror the fiduciary duties quite closely. Section 182 in particular would apply to Fassbinder, with the possibility that Fassbinder would also be liable for the criminal offence set out in s 184(2). ASIC is the relevant body to pursue a breach of statutory duty or a criminal offence: ss 1317J and 1315. The directors of Port Hotels do not have standing to pursue a breach of statutory duty. However, this does not mean that they are powerless in this regard. ASIC is a public body charged with the administration and prosecution of offences under the Corporations Act. There is nothing to stop the directors from reporting this matter to ASIC for investigation and possible prosecution.

Section 182 is a civil penalty provision: s 1317E. This renders a defendant liable to not only a pecuniary penalty (fine) but in serious cases to an order that the person not manage a corporation for a specified period of time: ss 1317G and 206C. It is possible, if ASIC did pursue the matter, that they would prosecute for a criminal offence as it is likely that they would be able to prove that Fassbinder acted knowingly and dishonestly and with intention to gain an advantage for Buildenbust: s 184(2). This would make Fassbinder liable to a fine and/or imprisonment of up to 15 years. Whether ASIC pursues either a civil penalty order or a criminal prosecution, there are proceedings incidentally available for the company to recover loss occasioned as a result of the activity: ss 1317H and 1317J(2).

Examiner's Comments

6-24 As well as the fiduciary and statutory duties there are some specific requirements under the Corporations Act designed to mitigate conflict of interest situations.

Section 195 prohibits directors of public companies from voting on or being present when a matter in which he or she has a material interest is being considered by the board. Section 191 requires disclosure of a material personal interest by a director. Notably, s 193 preserves the operation of the general law in respect of disclosure of interests and gives effect to any specific requirement under the company's constitution regarding personal interests of directors. It is common for companies to require disclosure under their constitution, and in equity there is a need to give full disclosure if any benefit is to be retained.

By contravening s 195, Fassbinder does not invalidate any contract which arises from the board resolutions (s 195(5)), although it would still be voidable as discussed in the answer. Contravention of this section is a strict liability offence where the director votes or participates in the deliberation and has not obtained any relief under s 195(2) and (3).

It is doubtful that the board of Port Hotels would have given Fassbinder permission to participate or vote if they had had adequate disclosure about the nature of his interest anyway. The penalty for breach of this section is dealt with under the general penalty section: s 1311.

The other problem for this 'deal' is that it probably breaches Ch 2E. Port Hotels is a public company and is prevented from giving a financial benefit to a related entity. Buildenbust would be a related entity because it is an entity over which a director has control: s 228(4). The contract would be a financial benefit according to s 229; in particular, s 229(3)(d): s 243G.

These prohibitions relate to financial benefits given after 1 February 1993. Thus, the date of the contract would be important. These benefits may only be given if they are within the exceptions in Pt 2E.1. Relevantly, the only exception for Port Hotels is that the benefit was given in respect of a transaction conducted on normal commercial terms: s 210. Alternatively, the transaction would need to be approved by a general meeting under the procedure set out in Pt 2E.1. The consequences of giving an unauthorised financial benefit are set out in s 209 and, unfortunately, the directors of Port Hotels may find that they, along with Fassbinder, would be in contravention of the prohibition and may face civil penalty proceedings. They may need to seek relief under s 1317S.

 # Keep in Mind

- Avoid falling into the trap of setting out all of the duties, both fiduciary and statutory, and then trying to apply them all to the facts. (In answering a problem question about directors' duties, many students will be tempted to do this.) The answer is filled with irrelevant material, when the activity involved is readily identifiable with a particular duty. In this question, it is clear there is a conflict, and in some conflict cases there will also be a breach of the duty to act honestly or for the best interests of the company. In this case, the breach of one also includes a breach of the other.
- Do not confuse fiduciary with statutory duties. While their content may be similar, the persons who can bring proceedings may be different and the consequences are also quite distinct.
- Not all personal interests come within the conflict rule. The interest must give rise to a conflict or a real or substantial possibility of conflict: *Hospital Products Ltd v United States Surgical Corporation* (1984) 156 CLR 41 at 103; *Coope v LCM Litigation Fund Pty Ltd* [2016] NSWCA 37 at [106].
- The test for the existence of a conflict or a real and substantial possibility of a conflict is objective. It is to be determined from the standpoint of the objective observer with knowledge of all relevant

facts and circumstances: *Boardman v Phipps* [1967] 2 AC 46 at 124; *Coope v LCM Litigation Fund Pty Ltd* [2016] NSWCA 37 at [109].

- A breach of fiduciary duty is excused 'by way of defence' if the fiduciary shows that the beneficiary has given informed consent to the breach. What is required to demonstrate fully informed consent is a question of fact in all the circumstances and there is no precise formula which will determine in all cases that fully informed consent has been given: *Maguire v Makaronis* (1997) 188 CLR 449 at 466; *Coope v LCM Litigation Fund Pty Ltd* [2016] NSWCA 37 at [110]; *Mualim v Dzelme* [2021] NSWCA 199 at [111]–[115].

Chapter 7

Share Capital Transactions

Key Issues

7-1 In this chapter we will look at the doctrine of maintenance of capital from the common law and how this principle has been dealt with under the Corporations Act. We will examine some common transactions that a company may undertake which will eliminate or reorganise the capital structure of a company as well as some of the regulations impacting on share control of companies.

Maintenance of capital simply means that a company must not return or reduce its issued capital to shareholders except when the company is being wound up. The principle arose in the case of *Trevor v Whitworth* (1887) 12 App Cas 409. The purpose of the rule was to protect the interests of creditors of the company who relied upon issued capital as a measure of a company's worth and its ability to pay. The manner in which the company's capital is to be used, together with creditor expectations, is explained below in the *Whitworth* case by Lord Watson at 423–4:

> Paid up capital may be diminished or lost in the course of the company's trading; that is, a result which no legislation can prevent; but persons who deal with and give credit to a limited company naturally rely on the fact that the company is trading with a certain amount of capital already paid, as well as the responsibility of its members for the capital remaining at call; and they are entitled to assume that no part of the capital which has been paid into the coffers of the company has been subsequently paid out, except in the legitimate course of its business.

Modern corporate regulation still strives to protect creditors, but the strict rule requiring maintenance of capital is no longer seen as the most appropriate means of achieving this aim. The Corporations Act protects creditors in specific ways such as the provisions of ss 588G–U which impose personal liability upon directors for insolvent trading (ss 588V–X impose liability upon a holding company in similar circumstances). The requirement that dividends can only be paid in certain circumstances (s 254T), and the priority of payments in a winding up which ensures that creditors are paid before members, are among the specific provisions designed to protect the interests of creditors.

A key means of protecting creditors as well as investors and existing shareholders is by regulating to ensure that there is adequate and accurate information about companies so that creditors and investors can make informed decisions before they give money or credit to a company. The Corporations Act is replete with regulations to ensure the availability of adequate and accurate information; some of those provisions specifically relate to reductions of capital and yet others relate to various transactions which affect corporate control such as takeovers. For disclosing entities, such as public companies that are listed on the ASX (or another licensed financial market), there are also continuous disclosure obligations under Ch 6CA.

Reductions of capital are now regulated in Ch 2J of the Corporations Act. Reductions of capital can be transactions which cancel shares, cancel the amount unpaid on shares or reduce capital to account for lost capital during the course of business. A reduction of capital can also be effected by a company buying back its own shares. Share buy-backs and reductions of capital are all permitted subject to the rules provided for these transactions in Ch 2J. The express purpose of these rules is contained in s 256A:

... The rules are designed to protect the interests of shareholders and creditors by:

(a) addressing the risk of these transactions leading to the company's insolvency;
(b) seeking to ensure fairness between the company's shareholders;
(c) requiring the company to disclose all material information.

Accordingly, companies may now more effectively manage the amount of issued capital and create a more flexible structure to engage in various enterprises either in conjunction with other companies or on their own. This flexibility ought not prejudice the initial aim of the maintenance of capital rule to protect creditors, and it will go further by providing a measure of protection to shareholders who will always be affected either by a loss of share entitlements or a loss of voting power in these changes to share capital.

Capital reductions and buy-backs, particularly selective buy-backs, can change voting control in a company. In addition to these methods there are other means by which voting control can be changed. Minority shareholders can be forced to sell their shares to the majority (as opposed to selling to the company) either under the constitution of the company, or by virtue of the provisions in Pt 5.1 for a reconstruction of the company or as a result of a compulsory acquisition when the majority achieve 90 per cent shareholding under Ch 6A. The structure and ultimate control of a company can be changed dramatically as a result of the court-approved procedure in Pt 5.1 for reconstructions and mergers. Companies can be streamlined by the merger of subsidiaries, or unprofitable subsidiaries may be separated and wound up. Finally, control of a company can be changed by a takeover under the provisions of Ch 6.

Compulsory acquisition of minority shareholdings was the subject of judicial opinion in *Gambotto v WCP Ltd* (1995) 127 CLR 432 where the court held that principles of fairness and disclosure were essential to the process. These principles of disclosure and fairness are a common theme throughout the transactions that can affect voting control in a company such as reductions of capital, buy-backs and takeovers.

Before attempting the questions below, check that you are familiar with the following:

✓ What is the rule arising from *Trevor v Whitworth* and what is its purpose?

✓ What is a 'reduction of capital'?

✓ What is a 'share buy-back'?

✓ What are the rules for a lawful reduction of capital?

✓ What are the permitted types of buy-backs?

✓ What is the significance of a selective reduction or buy-back and what different requirements are there for these transactions?

✓ When can the majority shareholder compulsorily acquire the shares of the minority?

✓ What is the effect of *Gambotto's* case in these share control transactions?

✓ What is a 'scheme of arrangement' and what purpose does it serve?

✓ What companies are affected by the takeover provisions of Ch 6?

✓ What are the basic rules governing takeovers and what are the principles behind them?

Question 26

Is the common law doctrine of maintenance of capital still a part of the law in Australia?

Time allowed: 20 minutes

Answer Plan

This is a short essay-style question, but it requires not just exposition of the law — rather, it requires exposition and comparison. Logically, the answer should:

• define the doctrine of maintenance of capital;

- identify instances of the doctrine in the Corporations Act; and
- interpret the provisions of the Corporations Act to determine whether they coexist with or replace the common law doctrine.

 ## Answer

7-2 The doctrine of maintenance of capital was recognised in the well-known case of *Trevor v Whitworth* (1887) 12 App Cas 409. Briefly, the case involved the repurchase of shares by the company. The shareholder was seeking to recover the balance of the purchase money from the company's liquidator (Trevor). The court refused to order the repayment, for to do so would prejudice the right of creditors to assume that the company's capital was always available to repay its debts, subject to capital lost in the ordinary course of business. *Trevor v Whitworth* was an example of what is now termed a self-acquisition. Broadly speaking, it is one means by which a company might seek to return capital to shareholders prior to a winding up. Historically, a company's capital was used as an indicator of the company's ability to repay its creditors. This was an important issue because the limited liability provided to a company's shareholders means that the likelihood that a creditor will be repaid depends upon the company's financial capacity to repay its debts. One measure of a company's financial capacity is its level of fully paid-up equity capital, typically made up of shares. The reasoning behind the ruling in *Trevor v Whitworth*, therefore, was to protect creditors by ensuring that companies maintain their capital, and that it can only legitimately be returned to shareholders once the company is wound up and after creditors have been paid.

In modern times, it is not unusual for companies to be registered with a very low capital — as little as $1. The amount of capital may therefore offer little comfort to a potential creditor. Creditors tend to rely on other information about a company's financial position in order to judge whether or not to give credit. Profit and loss statements, asset valuations and share price (for a listed company) are among the pieces of financial information that are considered more reliable indicators of a company's ability to pay its creditors than capital. In the absence of good financial information then creditors may either not give credit or would take some form of security over the assets of the company or a guarantee from the company's director(s).

The doctrine of maintenance of capital has not been removed under amendments made to the Corporations Act in 1998; it underpins Ch 2J of the Corporations Act albeit in a modified form: *Connective Services Pty Ltd v Slea Pty Ltd* [2019] HCA 33. The commercial reliance on capital as an indicator, however, has gradually been eroded. In addition, companies need to be more flexible in modern global markets and, in particular, they need to be able to change in size and be more malleable so they can either 'downsize' or merge with other companies in a joint enterprise. In most western European and United States markets, companies are no longer restricted by the doctrine of maintenance of capital.

Amendments to the Corporations Act in 1998 (Company Law Review Act 1988 (Cth)) permit changes to capital under a different and more streamlined regime. Changes to capital are now essentially internally driven and not subject to outside approval. The permitted changes to capital are regulated by the stated purpose for reductions under Pt 2J.1 which is set out in s 256A. This section states that the rules are designed to protect shareholders and creditors by addressing the risks of these kinds of transactions in so far as they might lead to insolvency and seeking to ensure fairness amongst shareholders, part of which is covered by the requirements for disclosure. By legislating this way, the Corporations Act is permissive in regard to reductions and self-acquisitions, but it still gives credence to the purpose of the maintenance of capital doctrine by attempting to ensure that these changes to capital do not materially prejudice creditors: ss 256B(1)(b) and 257A(a). The legislation aims to strike a balance between policy considerations while ensuring that creditors and members will not be unduly prejudiced: *Re CSR Ltd* [2010] FCAFC 34. It further maintains the doctrine by prohibiting in s 259A any other type of self-acquisition apart from the permitted buy-backs or other special circumstances in Pt 2J.2: s 256B(1).

As well as the rules about permitted reductions and buy-backs, the Corporations Act also provides more comfort for creditors in two ways:

- First, by linking buy-back agreements to the regime of personal liability for directors for insolvent trading under s 588G. A buy-back agreement is deemed to be a debt by virtue of s 588G(1A). This goes some way to ensure that the buy-back does not materially prejudice creditors in that it shifts the risk that a buy-back may lead to insolvency to directors who will no doubt have devised or decided to engage the company in a share buy-back: ss 257A and 256A.
- Second, contraventions of the reduction of capital and buy-back procedures are also dealt with by placing personal liability on those who devise or control these activities. The company is not held accountable; rather, individuals involved in the transaction are liable: ss 256F and 259F. For example, see *Knauf Plasterboard Pty Ltd v Plasterboard West Pty Ltd (in liq) (recs and mgrs apptd)* [2017] FCA 866.

In conclusion, the strict application of the doctrine of maintenance of capital as stated in *Trevor v Whitworth* no longer exists under the Corporations Act. What remains is a strong recognition of the purpose of the doctrine; that is, to protect creditors. The current statutory regime permits reductions of capital and buy-backs as a means of self-acquisition through a strict system of disclosure and shareholder approval, and always with a view to protect creditors. If the rules are not followed and the purpose not honoured, then there is the potential for personal liability for those who are involved in the activity. This is the policy trade-off made under the modern legislative approach which has to some degree relaxed the strict application of the maintenance of capital rule compared with the traditional approach.

Examiner's Comments

7-3 The answer identifies the principal purpose of maintenance of capital as being to protect creditors. It could be more fully explained that creditors need some kind of protection in respect of a company's ability to repay its debts simply because of the separate entity theory and the corporate veil. Creditors who deal with a company cannot look to anyone else other than the company for the repayment of their debts. The Corporations Act has to some extent provided keyholes through which the corporate veil may be lifted and in most instances the purpose for these provisions is for the protection of creditors.

Chapter 2J of the Corporations Act deals directly with changes to share capital, and its purpose of preventing material prejudice to creditors is expressly stated.

It is useful, however, to identify other parts of the Corporations Act which are designed to or which simultaneously protect creditors.

Examples include:

- rules regarding the payment of dividends: s 254T;
- the rule which requires redemptions of redeemable preference shares to be made either out of profits or a new issue of shares: s 254K;
- rules against a company giving financial assistance for the purchase of shares in itself: Pt 2J.3;
- rules designed to prevent insolvent trading: ss 588G–588Y;
- rules for public companies which control and effectively prohibit related party transactions: Pt 2E.1; and
- order of priority of payment in a winding up: Pt 5.6 Div 6 Subdiv D.

Keep in Mind

- The rule in *Trevor v Whitworth* was concerned with capital maintenance but the rationale for the statutory prohibition came to be understood as operating on a wider basis of protecting against abuse of the rights of the company's creditors and shareholders, particularly minority shareholders: *Connective Services Pty Ltd v Slea Pty Ltd* [2019] HCA 33 at [10].
- The key to this question is in identifying the purpose of maintenance of capital. By simply viewing the provisions of Ch 2J it is easy to mistakenly conclude that maintenance of capital is now abolished and in its place there is a corporate freedom to change capital at any time. Even the title of this chapter in the Corporations Act has been changed to the more liberal title of 'Transactions Affecting Share

Capital' rather than the former title for Div 4 of 'Maintenance of Capital'. While it is true that there is now no need to seek court approval for a reduction of capital, the procedure for a lawful reduction or buy-back is clearly designed to achieve the purpose of the common law doctrine of maintenance of capital.

- The penalties for failure to abide by the procedure can be harsh. Under *Trevor v Whitworth*, the end result was that the transaction was not enforced. Under the current statutory regime, the transaction may still be valid (ss 256F and 259F), but there will be grounds to obtain an injunction under s 1324 if the transaction is not complete.
- Individuals involved may suffer prosecution under the civil penalty provisions or under the criminal provisions as well as being liable to compensate the company under s 1317H.
- For a fuller discussion on the maintenance of capital rule, see the High Court judgments in *Beck v Weinstock* [2013] HCA 15 and *Connective Services Pty Ltd v Slea Pty Ltd* [2019] HCA 33.

Question 27

ABC Pty Ltd is a large media and technology company. Eighty-eight per cent of its shares are owned by XYZ Ltd and its associates. The remaining shares are owned by small investors in various-sized parcels. XYZ Ltd wishes to own 100 per cent of ABC Pty Ltd as it would gain considerable administrative and taxation savings from doing so. However, several small investors in the company are unwilling to sell out to XYZ Ltd.

Advise the directors of XYZ Ltd on the best way to achieve full ownership of ABC Pty Ltd.

Time allowed: 40 minutes

Answer Plan

There are several different ways to achieve this end. Each type entails a procedure and has certain pitfalls or risks. Each one needs separate treatment.

Share buy-back

- Discuss different methods of reducing ABC Pty Ltd's share capital to give XYZ Ltd full control.

Compulsory acquisition

- Outline the procedure for compulsory acquisition.

Constitutional alteration

- Discuss how ABC Pty Ltd's constitution may be altered to give XYZ Ltd the power to acquire the minority holdings.

Answer

7-4 This question is concerned with the ability of a majority shareholder to compulsorily acquire minority shareholder shares in order to achieve the benefits that come with full ownership of the company. There are basically several possible means of acquiring the remaining shares. XYZ Ltd could conduct a buy-back of the shares under Ch 2J, they could instigate a creeping takeover and then complete a compulsory acquisition, or they could enter into a members' scheme of arrangement. XYZ Ltd could also seek to have ABC's constitution changed to give it the power to compulsorily acquire the minority shares. Each of these options poses potential risks which are discussed below.

Share buy-backs

7-5 The Corporations Act permits companies to buy back their own shares even though to do so would appear to be contrary to the principle of maintenance of capital as expressed in *Trevor v Whitworth* (1887) 12 App Cas 409. Companies are permitted to buy back their own shares provided they strictly follow the procedure set out in Pt 2J.1 Div 2: s 257A. The procedure is designed to preserve the essence of the doctrine of maintenance of capital while allowing companies some measure of flexibility as to their capital structure. Any buy-back or self-acquisition that does not comply with the procedure would be unlawful.

Section 257A provides, inter alia, that a company has the power to buy back its own shares; however, the section does not preclude situations where a particular company may have a constitution which prevents buy-backs or imposes restrictions on the power to buy back shares. The question is silent on any constitutional restrictions — it is therefore assumed that there are none.

There are five permitted methods of buying back shares under s 257B. The only relevant type here is a selective buy-back, because this will allow specific shareholders to sell their holdings to the company. A selective buy-back is one that is made to specific shareholders only or to holders of a particular class of shares. The procedure for such a buy-back differs from other methods because of the potential for abuse and preferential treatment that does not exist in the equal access or on-market methods. For a selective buy-back there is a requirement for special shareholder approval under s 257D. The approval must come from a meeting which has all material information about the buy-back before it, and the resolution must be either a special resolution with no votes being cast by those shareholders who will be the object of the buy-back or it must be a unanimous vote by all ordinary shareholders.

Unfortunately, the section is not explicit as to which kind of resolution is appropriate in any particular circumstance. It merely provides two alternatives. The relevant vote required must be deduced from the purpose expressed in s 256A which includes the desire to ensure fairness as between shareholders. By reference to the purpose, it seems that if a particular class of shareholders would clearly benefit from the buy-back then it would be inappropriate to allow those shareholders to vote and thus skew the outcome to secure a benefit for themselves. The procedure under s 257D(1)(a) is more appropriate in such a case.

If the buy-back is directed at certain individual holders of ordinary shares, as required in this question, then it is more appropriate that there be unanimous agreement by the ordinary shareholders under s 257D(1)(b). For a company such as ABC, where there is an 88 per cent shareholder and then smaller shareholders, a special resolution of 75 per cent would be very simple to obtain and would not achieve fairness as between the shareholders. It is notable that the offer to buy back can be made before the approval is given, but the offer must be conditional upon the approval. This allows the company to make the offer to determine whether or not it will be accepted before holding the general meeting for approval.

A buy-back is really an offer to buy particular shares. The shareholder is not under any compulsion to sell. This poses a significant problem for XYZ as at least some of the minority shareholders seem to be hostile to the proposed acquisition by XYZ of 100 per cent ownership. Of course, XYZ may make the offer terms very attractive to the minority shareholders to encourage them to accept the buy-back offer.

If, however, XYZ can persuade shareholders with at least two per cent of the votes to accept the buy-back then it can be classed as a 90 per cent holder for the purposes of Ch 6A and may therefore undertake a compulsory acquisition of the remaining 10 per cent holdings.

Compulsory acquisition

7-6 If XYZ can obtain at least 90 per cent of the ordinary shares in ABC it has the right under s 664A to compulsorily acquire the remaining 10 per cent of the shares, regardless of whether the minority shareholders agree or not. As a 90 per cent holder, XYZ may notify the holders of the remaining 10 per cent that it wishes to purchase their shares: s 664C. The compulsory acquisition notice must be given to the minority shareholders within six months after XYZ becomes a 90 per cent holder of the shares: s 664AA. Given that XYZ needed to acquire at least a further two per cent of the shares in order to reach the 90 per cent threshold, it would need to disclose the terms of this purchase in its compulsory acquisition: s 664C.

Minority shareholders have the right to object to the proposed compulsory acquisition under s 664E; however, that objection may be overridden by XYZ if the objecting shareholders do not hold 10 per cent in value of the company's shares. Where 10 per cent of ABC's shareholders (in value) object to the proposed compulsory acquisition, XYZ may approach the court for approval of the acquisition: s 664F. The only ground upon which the court may refuse to approve the compulsory acquisition is that its terms do not offer fair value for the shares: s 664F(3).

Constitutional change

7-7 If XYZ cannot become a 90 per cent holder of shares in ABC by persuading at least two per cent of the shareholders to accept its offer to purchase shares then it may call a general meeting and resolve to alter ABC's constitution to confer on it a right to expropriate either the two per cent needed to become a 90 per cent holder in ABC or the whole 12 per cent remaining shares in ABC. However, there are several problems posed by this option.

First, any change to the constitution would require a special resolution: s 136(2). This would seem to be easily achievable as XYZ already controls 88 per cent of the shares in ABC (assuming that each share in ABC confers a single vote). However, such use of majority voting power may be susceptible to arguments under s 232 that XYZ is acting oppressively.

Second, it is likely that this action would be successfully challenged by any of the minority shareholders as the majority were expropriating property rights for the improper purpose of seeking complete control: see *Gambotto v WCP Ltd* (1995) 182 CLR 432. In that case, the High Court found that merely obtaining economic benefits through complete ownership was not, in and of itself, a valid reason for expropriating the minority shareholders' property rights (that is, the ownership of their shares).

Examiner's Comments

7-8 A simple way to improve this answer would be to analyse each method comparatively and draw out the inconsistency between policies in relation to each method. In relation to compulsory acquisition provisions under Ch 6A, the policy is to permit the overwhelming majority shareholder (90 per cent holder) to fully achieve the administrative and taxation benefits that accrue from full ownership. The policy in permitting selective buy-backs is to allow companies to have greater and more flexible control over their capital.

However, with the exception of McHugh J in the High Court in *Gambotto's* case, compulsory acquisition through a rule change is not considered a proper purpose when the motive is to achieve those same administrative benefits and control over capital that is clearly permitted in other instances under the Corporations Act. The inconsistency seems even starker when the ruling in *Gambotto's* case is confined to situations where the constitution is being changed to permit compulsory acquisition. A new company may be formed with a constitution that already has such a rule in it. The use of such a rule would not be subject to the same challenge because there is no relevant exercise of voting power by the majority to change the rule which could be the subject of a claim of fraud on the minority.

A further point of comparison can be drawn from the different tests of fairness which are applicable in relation to the different methods. A buy-back, being a type of reduction of capital, is required by s 256B(1)(a) to be 'fair and reasonable to the company's shareholders as a whole ...'.

A selective reduction of capital or selective buy-back is not considered unfair per se. Courts have applied the test of fairness by reference to all shareholders: *Nicron Resources Ltd v Catto* (1992) 8 ACSR 219; *Elkington v CostaExchange Ltd* [2011] VSC 501. 'Fair and reasonable' is to be read as a composite phrase: see the discussion in *Elkington v CostaExchange Ltd* [2011] VSC 501. In that case, the court held (at [60]) that '[o]ne of the aims of the selective capital reduction provisions is to ensure fairness between the company's shareholders'.

In permitting the majority to compulsorily acquire shares, the courts and the parliament have recognised that there can be strong financial and economic advantages for companies to be able to acquire minority shareholdings. It is also recognised that there can be circumstances where the minority can oppress the majority by demanding an excessive price for their shares; this is popularly known as 'greenmail'. Thus, there are good grounds to permit a procedure for a fair acquisition by the majority.

The test in *Gambotto's* case, however, is clearly a test of fairness to the individual shareholder, and the onus of establishing that the offer was fair is upon the company. *Gambotto*, however, was a case involving changes to the constitution for the purpose of conferring power on the majority shareholder to compulsorily acquire the shares of the minority. Different considerations apply where the power to acquire the shares is given by statute.

It is notable in relation to the changes to the Corporations Act in July 1998 that the provisions relating to capital reductions (in particular the statutory test set out in s 256B(1)(a) (above)) were expressly referred to in the Explanatory Memorandum to the Company Law Review Bill. In essence, the statutory test is said to focus on the effect rather than the purpose of the reduction and it was specifically inserted to avoid the application of *Gambotto's* case to these kinds of activities. Such statements may possibly indicate a desire on the part of parliaments to reduce the impact of the proper purpose test and the individual fairness test which was the high-water mark for members' rights under the *Gambotto* ruling.

Students could also improve this answer by working through the five different types of permissible buy-backs and explain why a selective buy-back is the only appropriate option.

Keep in Mind

- Do not fall into the rather common trap of thinking that a buy-back is a form of compulsory acquisition. A buy-back is an offer to buy.

If the offer to buy is accepted then there is an agreement or contract to transfer the shares at the offered price. This agreement would be enforceable like any contract, but there is no compulsion to enter the agreement.

- Do not fail to recognise that buy-backs will result in a cancellation of the acquired share capital, while a compulsory acquisition is the acquisition of issued shares of a particular shareholder by another, usually the majority, shareholder. Therefore, there is no consequent share cancellation or reduction of capital.
- Avoid discussing, in the context of available methods, each of the permissible means of buy-back or other capital reductions. Do not waste time by discussing all buy-back processes; confine your answer to those processes that are relevant to the facts in the question.

Question 28

Ron Low is a major shareholder and director of First Investments Pty Ltd; he is also a major shareholder and the managing director of Yesman Pty Ltd.

First Investments Pty Ltd engages in various investments such as lending, share acquisitions and other investments for the Low family. Yesman Pty Ltd manufactures toys and children's clothing.

Ron Low is also chairman of the board of Folleys Ltd, a large retailing chain, and he owns shares in Folleys Ltd.

First Investments wanted to borrow $10 million and put a proposal to Folleys that it borrow from Folleys at a very favourable interest rate for Folleys. Ron Low absented himself from the board at the time of the discussion over the proposal and did not vote. However, the Folleys board agreed to lend to First Investments because of the high interest rate and security over a portion of First's investment portfolio.

The money was advanced to First Investment who subsequently lent the money to Yesman, unsecured and at the same interest rate. Yesman then purchased shares in Folleys on the market over a period of approximately three weeks for $10 million.

Advise the board of Folleys as to whether the actions of Ron have contravened the Corporations Act in these transactions. Do not consider potential breaches of Ch 6 (takeovers).

Time allowed: 35 minutes

 Answer Plan

These transactions are often best understood by means of a diagram to show the flow of money or assets:

- The first part of the diagram would show Folleys Ltd with Ron Low as chairman and shareholder.

- Money is then lent upon security to First Invesments Pty Ltd with Ron Low as major shareholder and director.
- The same money is then lent to Yesman Pty Ltd with Ron Low as major shareholder and managing director.
- Yesman then uses the same money to acquire shares in Folleys Ltd.

Having prepared a rough diagram, each transaction should be first analysed with a view to identifying potential breaches of the Corporations Act. Then the overall effect of the transactions needs to be examined to identify any other breaches of the Corporations Act.

Material personal interests

- Explain how Ron Low's different interests may conflict and how these conflicts can and should be managed.

Financial assistance

- Discuss whether the financial assistance requirements in Pt 2J.3 have been complied with.
- Set out what the potential consequences may be of failing to comply with these provisions.

This question does appear to cover quite a range of issues; however, a significant limiting factor is that it is restricted to possible breaches of the Corporations Act and not any common law or fiduciary principles.

Answer

7-9 This question gives rise to a range of potential breaches of the Corporations Act, including conflicts of interest and share capital transactions. The facts may also give rise to issues under general law; however, I have not been asked to comment on these and will therefore restrict my discussion to potential breaches of the Corporations Act.

Material personal interests

7-10 The Corporations Act requires that all company directors who have a 'material personal interest' in the subject matter of a decision being considered by the company's board give notice of that interest to the other directors, unless an exception applies: s 191(1). An interest will be material if it has the capacity to influence the director's vote on a particular matter before the board: *McGellin v Mount King Mining NL* (1998) 144 FLR 288. Directors of public companies are subjected to a further requirement that they not participate in board discussions concerning such matters: s 195.

The first transaction is a loan between Folleys Ltd and First Investments Pty Ltd. The loan was considered by the board of Folleys and apparently approved. Ron Low absented himself from the board vote on the transaction which may mean that he disclosed his interest in the subject matter in compliance with s 191. Alternatively, Ron may have given standing notice to the board members of Folleys (under s 192) in which case he would not need to give further notice to the board under s 191. Furthermore, Ron did not participate in the vote, thereby complying with s 195, although it has been recognised that directors with particular positions of responsibility within the company may have a further positive obligation to protect the company's interest rather than simply absent themselves from the discussion: see *Permanent Building Society (in liq) v Wheeler* (1994) 14 ACSR 109. In that case, the CEO could not absolve himself simply by being absent from the board meeting where he had knowledge of the risk to the company and thereby needed to take positive steps to protect the company. It may be arguable that Ron's status as chairman of Folleys gives rise to this added obligation. A failure to take reasonable steps to protect the company could give rise to a claim for the breach of the duty of care: s 180(1). However, the terms of this loan to Folleys seem to have been beneficial as the loan was made at a favourable interest rate for Folleys. Security for repayment was offered and obviously acceptable. In all respects, the loan appears to be on commercial terms and, as such, the transaction would not breach the Corporations Act.

The problem with the transaction is really a problem which affects Ron in his position as director of Folleys and his interest and control of First Investments. The transaction may be a financial benefit to a related party under Pt 2E.1. First Investments would be classified as a related party of Folleys Ltd by virtue of s 228. The granting of a loan would be a financial benefit within the meaning of s 229: see further *ASIC v Adler* [2002] NSWSC 171. However, this loan may well come within the general exceptions under s 210 in that it is probably a financial benefit on arm's length terms. The limited information as to the terms of the loan tends to suggest that it is a loan on good commercial terms, although these terms would be closely examined. If it was not a loan at arm's length then the transaction will not be permitted under the Corporations Act unless there is approval by the company in general meeting under Pt 2E.1 Div 3.

The second transaction is between proprietary companies and so the provisions of Pt 2E.1 do not apply to non crowd-sourced funded proprietary companies. That the loan is made unsecured suggests that, despite the commercial interest rate, it is probably not a transaction at arm's length but this may only be relevant in determining whether Ron has breached any duty to the company. Again, there is a conflict of interest for Ron in this transaction. Section 191 is relevant here. This section requires directors to disclose material interests that they have in any resolutions before the board. Given the nature of Ron's shareholdings and control, it is likely that there is adequate evidence of disclosure in this transaction.

Financial assistance

7-11 The Corporations Act does not prohibit corporations giving financial assistance to others to facilitate the purchase of their own shares, provided that certain requirements are complied with. For present purposes, these requirements are either that:

- the financial assistance does not materially prejudice the interests of the company or its shareholders or prejudice the ability of the company to pay its creditors: s 260A(1)(a); or
- the transaction was approved by the members of the company: s 260B.

In this case, it is clear that Folleys Ltd has apparently unwittingly provided the funds for acquiring shares in itself. The facts of the question do not disclose any approval by the general meeting, and it would appear that but for Ron Low the board was probably unaware of the ultimate use of the funds in the purchase. Therefore, s 260B cannot be relied upon.

Section 260A(1)(a) may, however, provide support as there is nothing in the question to suggest that the loan would materially prejudice the creditors of Folleys, particularly because the loan is given with security (although the secured property is an investment portfolio which may fluctuate in value). The question of material prejudice to the company and its shareholders is a more difficult question. It is possible that the acquisition of the shares may affect the balance of control for shareholders. This, arguably, would constitute a material prejudice to the interests of the company and its shareholders. However, problems with the control of the company may result in an application to the Takeovers Panel which is outside the scope of the question.

Section 260D preserves the validity of the transactions that constitute the financial assistance, but imposes liability upon the persons who contravene the provisions. It would appear that Ron may be in breach of s 260A in addition to a breach of his statutory duty under s 181 to act in good faith in the best interests of each of the companies that he is a director of. Both of these provisions are civil penalty provisions.

Examiner's Comments

7-12 This answer could be improved by students commenting on the attitude that ASIC takes to exemptions and modifications as expressed in ASIC Regulatory Guide 51. A full consideration of the possible breach by Ron of his duties owed to each company would improve the answer. It is important to point out that directors owe an independent duty to each company they are director of: *Walker v Wimborne* (1976) 137 CLR 1. Therefore, Ron cannot prejudice the interests of Folleys in order to benefit First Investments without breaching his duties to Folleys.

Keep in Mind

- Do not get caught up in determining whether or not Ron has breached any fiduciary duties to the company. Undoubtedly, he has, but the question only seeks to identify breaches of the Corporations Act and the answer is best confined to this limit. While this question may seem complex and involve a number of transactions, it only requires an opinion about whether or not there has been a breach of the Corporations Act.
- The concept of financial assistance is undefined in the Corporations Act and has no technical meaning. However, the financial assistance need not involve a money payment by the company to the person acquiring the shares. Any action by the company can be financial assistance if it eases the financial burden that would be involved in the process of acquisition or if it improves the person's 'net balance of financial advantage' in relation to the acquisition: *Connective Services Pty Ltd v Slea Pty Ltd* [2019] HCA 33.
- The courts focus on the commercial realities of the transaction when deciding if financial assistance has been given: *Connective Services Pty Ltd v Slea Pty Ltd* [2019] HCA 33.
- The question of material prejudice to the interests of the company or its shareholders or creditors is fact sensitive. This means that it requires an assessment of and comparison between the position before the giving of the financial assistance and the position after it to see whether the company or its shareholders or its ability to pay creditors is in a worse position: *Connective Services Pty Ltd v Slea Pty Ltd* [2019] HCA 33 at [26].

 Question 29

GJ Boles Ltd is a holding company. It has four subsidiaries. Two of the subsidiaries are wholly owned and subsidiaries 3 and 4 are partly owned. The capital structure of subsidiaries 3 and 4 is that GJ Boles owns 80 per cent of the ordinary shares and the remaining ordinary shares are owned by other shareholders. There are also 1000 preference shares issued which carry a seven per cent dividend rate and 1000 redeemable preference shares with an eight per cent dividend rate. Subsidiaries 1 and 2 have consistently returned a profit. On the other hand, subsidiaries 3 and 4 have not been performing well for some years and the dividend on the preference shares is cumulative. There have been no distributable profits for ordinary dividends and each subsidiary has been unable to pay preference dividends for the last two years. The directors of both subsidiaries 3 and 4 are concerned about the future solvency of the company. The business of the four subsidiaries together forms an integrated enterprise in which each subsidiary is dependent on the activity of the other for its own prosperity.

Advise the directors of GJ Boles Ltd of their legal options with respect to the group's capital structure in response to the above concerns.

Time allowed: 30 minutes

Answer Plan

The problem posed in this question is one which prompts a consideration of a reconstruction and merger of the subsidiaries using the process of a scheme of arrangement under Pt 5.1. Schemes of arrangement are designed to bring about an agreement between the company and its creditors and/or members to effect a corporate structure to suit the company's financial position. Matters to be examined include the following:

- What is the best outcome for GJ Boles in terms of corporate structure?
- Can this be accommodated in a scheme of arrangement?
- What is the necessary procedure to produce such a scheme?

As this is a relatively short descriptive question no headings will be used.

Answer

7-13 The main problem for GJ Boles Ltd is the potential insolvency of subsidiaries 3 and 4, and in relation to these companies there are other shareholders to consider as well as creditors. Subsidiaries 1 and 2 pose less of a problem because they are wholly owned and there is no apparent risk of insolvency. However, given that the businesses are integrated, a loss of subsidiaries 3 and 4 may well impact later on the other subsidiaries. The cause of the financial problems for subsidiaries 3 and 4 is not known, nor is it relevant for this question. However, it would seem that the group of subsidiaries as a whole is probably profitable and they certainly need each other. It would seem therefore that some combination or amalgam of the subsidiaries would solve the difficulties, protect creditors and probably satisfy the preference shareholders.

There is no immediate threat of a liquidation from creditors; however, the holders of redeemable preference shares would be in a position to petition for a winding up of the company. It is suggested that a convenient means of satisfying the redeemable preference shareholders and the creditors of subsidiaries 3 and 4 would be to transfer the assets and liabilities of these two subsidiaries to either subsidiary 1 or 2, or to incorporate some new company to subsume the balance sheets of all four subsidiaries. There may be a range of merger possibilities in between these two alternatives but they would all require the same processes and produce a similar outcome.

A scheme of arrangement under Pt 5.1 could readily accommodate such a corporate restructure. The terms of s 411 are attracted when a Pt 5.1 body (a company or Australian registered corporation: s 9) proposes a compromise or arrangement between itself and its creditors or its members. Courts have interpreted these terms widely to cover a variety of proposals for reconstructions and mergers without the need to establish an underlying dispute (*Re Guardian Assurance Co* [1917] 1 Ch 431) and without the threat of insolvency (*Re Crusader Ltd* (1995) 17 ACSR 336).

The court's powers under s 413 seem ideally suited to these kinds of arrangements as they include the power to transfer the undertaking of a company to another; to allot shares, debentures and other interests in the company; to order the deregistration of a company, without winding up; and to deal with any persons, members or creditors who dissent from the compromise or arrangement.

Indeed, if GJ Boles had difficulty in achieving agreement with subsidiaries 3 and 4 then it is possible to achieve a takeover of these subsidiaries, subject to s 411(17), by way of a scheme of arrangement and the compulsory acquisition of dissentient members' shares under s 414, especially in circumstances where there is a need to take over more than one class of shares: *Re ACM Gold Ltd* (1992) 7 ACSR 231.

Schemes of arrangement are instigated through court proceedings. Thus, the proponent for the scheme will approach the court under s 411 and, provided that the scheme is an arrangement or compromise, then the court will order meetings of creditors and members. In relation to subsidiaries 1 and 2, who would also need to be involved in the scheme, the application can be made in respect of more than one company (*Re Safety Fix Pty Ltd* [1962] VR 467) and the meeting in respect of those companies can be a meeting of one person; namely, GJ Boles (*Re Hastings Deering Pty Ltd* (1985) 9 ACLR 755).

At the meetings of creditors and/or members there must be approval of the scheme by a prescribed majority under s 411(4). GJ Boles, in holding 80 per cent of the ordinary shares, should have no difficulty in achieving the required majority, although it should be noted that court approval to implement the proposal is still required even after the required majority vote approves the transaction. Furthermore, the majority required is 75 per cent of the votes but these votes must be held by at least 51 per cent of the members of the company. Clearly, GJ Boles will not be able to force through the proposal.

It is also important to note that using a scheme of arrangement to effect a merger or amalgamation in this case would also require separation of differing interests of each group into separate classes. Section 411(1) refers to classes of members and classes of creditors, for in each case members and creditors may have different interests. Thus, in this situation the holders of redeemable preference shares would need special consideration, and the 20 per cent ordinary shareholders of subsidiaries 3 and 4 may well have different interests from GJ Boles as majority and sole shareholder of the other subsidiaries. As for creditors, there may be no need to hold a meeting of creditors because it would be unlikely that the interests of creditors would be compromised; rather, they may be enhanced by the arrangement: *Re AGL Sydney Ltd* (1994) 13 ACSR 597.

Integral to the process is the provision of information to the members and/or creditors. Pursuant to s 412, the proponent of the scheme must provide an explanatory statement which is approved by the court and sent to members or creditors along with notice of the meeting. Information material to the decision whether to vote in favour or not is the key to the type of information required, along with disclosure of the interests of or benefits to any directors from the scheme.

The explanatory statement and the proposed scheme are to be lodged with ASIC for approval and, of course, ASIC's lack of approval can spell the demise of the scheme: s 411(17). Listed companies are also required to notify the ASX under the relevant Listing Rules and to make arrangements in situations where new shares may be issued to replace existing shares.

If the relevant creditors' or members' meetings approve the scheme then the matter is referred back to the court for judicial approval. The resultant scheme of arrangement is made by an order of the court and it arises not as a mere acknowledgment of the approval of members or creditors but because of a separate judicial process: *Re Garner's Motors Ltd* [1937] Ch 594. The court must be satisfied that the scheme complies with the Corporations Act, has been approved on the basis of adequate information and that it is reasonable: *Re Stockbridge Ltd* (1993) 9 ACSR 637; *Re Chevron (Sydney) Ltd* [1963] VR 249. The court considers the interests of the members bound by a scheme and those of broader stakeholders: *Centro Properties Ltd v PriceWaterhouseCoopers* [2011] NSWSC 1465.

Along with the order to approve the scheme the court also will appoint a scheme manager to administer the arrangement: s 415. Certain persons who are not able to show independence from the company are not permitted to administer the scheme: s 411(7).

Examiner's Comments

7-14 Compare the scheme of arrangement process and its purpose with voluntary administrations under Pt 5.3A. Compared to the history of schemes, voluntary administrations are relatively new methods of achieving compromises with creditors. They are in respect of a suspect insolvency of a single company and, while useful as a salvage operation of such companies, their outcomes are limited. A scheme of arrangement is broader in that it focuses upon members as well as creditors and can affect many companies in a corporate conglomerate.

The question is fairly broad as it does not give specifics of the actual terms of a scheme of arrangement and there can be many variations upon a theme. Often the terms of the scheme are matters for accountants and business or finance experts rather than lawyers. However, it may be useful to illustrate the answer with examples of schemes of arrangement which utilised the court's powers to transfer the undertaking of one company to another or that issued shares in a new company in substitution for those in the original company. Another example may be where the redeemable preference shares were substituted with debentures in the new or transferee company.

📢 Keep in Mind

- Do not assume that because of the bad performance of subsidiaries 3 and 4 they will become insolvent and are therefore candidates for administration or liquidation. It is common for a company to split its undertaking into different companies as a means of insulating the fortunes of one part of the business from the other by relying on the shield of limited liability.
- Unlike a voluntary administration, the agreement of the members or creditors does not mean that the scheme of arrangement can go ahead. Court approval is more than just a rubber stamp of the members' or creditors' decision. These decisions can come about as a result of inadequate information or because of inadequate identification of the interests of each member or group of members and/or creditors.
- The general principles applicable to the court's role in making an order for the convening of a scheme meeting and subsequently to the approval of a scheme are well settled. There are three stages to an application under s 411. These stages are identified in *Re CSR Ltd* [2010] FCAFC 34; (2010) 183 FCR 358 at [7] per Keane CJ and Robson J; *Re Boart Longyear Ltd* [2017] NSWSC 567; affirmed on appeal in *First Pacific Advisors LLC v Boart Longyear Ltd* [2017] NSWCA 116.

Chapter 8

Members' Rights and Remedies

Key Issues

8-1 Membership of a company brings with it a range of rights and remedies which arise from the:

- contract of membership (particularly the terms of the share issue);
- company's constitution and/or replaceable rules; and
- Corporations Act.

This chapter is concerned primarily with rights and remedies that arise out of the Corporations Act.

The Corporations Act provides company members with a number of personal rights, including the right to:

- vote on proposed changes to the company's constitution: s 136;
- have protection from changes to the company's constitution, unless they consent in writing, that require the members to take up additional shares, contribute additional capital or limit the transfer of existing shares: s 140(2);
- inspect registers maintained by the company without charge: s 173;
- request a court order to inspect the company's books: s 247A;
- receive notice of upcoming company meetings: s 249J; and
- attend and vote at company meetings, either in person or by proxy: see Pt 2G.2. Members may be asked to vote on a range of issues including:
  - appointing or removing company directors: ss 201G, 203C, 203D;
  - approval of related party transactions: s 208;
  - proposed changes to capital structure: s 256C, Pt 2J.1 Div 2 s 260B;
  - a proposed solvent winding up of the company: s 491.

Aside from general and specific rights given to company members, the Corporations Act also provides a range of important remedies for members. When dealing with members' remedies it is important to distinguish remedies that only apply to breaches that affect the members' rights as a member (such as enforcing the company's constitution under s 140) and remedies that apply to members even where the contravention might not relate specifically to membership (such as the oppression remedy and the statutory injunction).

The rights of members to sue have been developed to overcome the potential for individuals to lose or have their rights compromised at the hands of directors or the majority shareholders. In large listed companies where the shareholder is primarily motivated by earnings, members' rights are not such acute issues. The dissatisfied shareholder will sell the shares and invest in another company and this may adversely affect the company's share price (if a large number of shares are sold). In this way, the role of the market is to temper the potential for misconduct in the company.

Shareholders in proprietary companies, however, do not enjoy the same ease of transfer of their shares in the event of dissatisfaction or oppression by the majority. Many proprietary companies impose restrictions on transferring shares in their constitutions or give directors the absolute discretion as to whether they will register share transfers: s 1042G. The sale of the shares may be difficult because the value of the shares is not ascertainable without access to the financial records of the company. A means of resolving this problem is to provide members with rights of access to these records: s 247A. This right is also a valuable means of procuring evidence which may point to misconduct of officers of the company which, in turn, may constitute grounds for further action and orders regarding the company.

Members' remedies are often concerned with the conduct of company directors which is understandable given that it is the board of directors that is generally responsible for managing the company's business: s 198A (directors' duties were discussed in **Chapter 6**). However, members' remedies can also be used to address situations involving the misuse/abuse of power in certain situations where the Corporations Act provides members with personal remedies.

Directors owe their duties to the company and not to individual members: *Percival v Wright* [1902] 2 Ch 421. However, particular circumstances may create independent duties between particular directors and particular members: *Coleman v Myers* [1977] 2 NZLR 225 (applied by the New South Wales Court of Appeal in *Brunninghausen v Glavanics* (1999) 46 NSWLR 538); *Crawley v Short* [2009] NSWCA 410. The cases in which it has been held that a director is in a fiduciary relationship with a shareholder relate to companies with few shareholders, very few directors and where their relationships are not impersonal but close. It is more likely that a fiduciary relationship will be found between directors or between directors and shareholders in closely held companies because it is more likely that the members will place trust and confidence in each other in such companies. However, it is the mutual cooperation, trust and confidence that is the factor giving rise to the fiduciary relationship not merely the fact of the company being closely held: *Wright v Lemon (No 2)* [2021] WASC 159 at [693]–[698].

Breaches of directors' duties can generally only be pursued by the company, unless the Corporations Act gives a member the power to pursue the action in the company's name: see Pt 2F.1A. The problem of prosecuting breach of directors' duties is exacerbated when the director(s) or officer(s) themselves have sufficient control over the board to prevent an action being pursued. To overcome this difficulty of the company being able to exercise its rights, there are three matters to consider. First, the company in general meeting has power to excuse, forgive or ratify a director's breach of duty: *Regal (Hastings) Ltd v Gulliver* [1967] 2 AC 134. This may not, however, prevent ASIC from taking action for a contravention of the Corporations Act. Second, there is potential for the general meeting to condone the breach by the director(s) when those persons control the voting power at the general meeting. Third, the Corporations Act now provides a statutory derivative action in Pt 2F.1A that permits a member to bring an action on behalf of the company.

The member must seek court approval to bring proceedings in the company's name: s 237. A statutory derivative action may still be pursued where the members of the company have ratified the director's conduct in a general meeting: s 239. For a useful review of the legal principles on the operation of statutory derivative action under s 237, see *Blakeney v Blakeney* [2016] WASCA 76; *Huang v Wang* [2016] NSWCA 164; *Mount Gilead Pty Ltd & Hobhouse v L Macarthur-Onslow* [2021] NSWSC 948.

As well as the majority being in a position to condone a director's breach of duty (as stated above), the majority also is in the position of acting in other ways which may prejudice the rights of individual members. Commonly, these issues arise when the majority exercises its voting power to change the constitution. Normally, a company's constitution can be altered by a 75 per cent vote: s 136(2). Thus, it is possible for a majority to change or eliminate rights attaching to shares. Altering rights attaching to a class of shares is regulated by Pt 2F.2, and it provides a mechanism to ensure greater procedural and substantive fairness on these matters. Other changes to the constitution, however, may cause great injustice to minority shareholders.

The majority are not in any fiduciary relationship to the company or to other shareholders, and so as a general rule they can exercise their vote in any way they please: *Peters' American Delicacy Co Ltd v Heath* (1939) 61 CLR 457. There is an equitable limitation on the power of the majority which is based on principles developed and classed as abuses of power. The limitation is that the majority may not act in such a way as to effect a fraud on the minority. Fraud on the minority has been authoritatively explained by the High Court in *Gambotto v WCP Ltd* (1995) 182 CLR 432. This limit will affect the majority in any circumstance where there is power to vote in general meeting (although the *Gambotto* case concerned the alteration of the constitution to empower the expropriation of shares). Where there is fraud on the minority, the minority can bring action on its own behalf and not as a derivative action on behalf of the company.

Finally, the Corporations Act provides a range of statutory remedies for members. Chapter 2F contains the broad oppression remedy: s 232. This may apply either where the conduct is contrary to the interests of the members as a whole (s 232(d)) or where the conduct is oppressive to, unfairly prejudicial to, or unfairly discriminatory against a member or members whether in that capacity or in any other capacity (s 232(e)). The term 'oppressive' was explained by the court in *John J Starr (Real Estate) Pty Ltd v Robert R Andrew (A'asia) Pty Ltd* (1991) 6 ACSR 63 as including 'something done against a person's will and in his despite' and 'the acts of oppression must result from some overbearing act or attitude on the part of the oppressor'. In the important decision in *Wayde v NSW Rugby League Ltd* (1985) 180 CLR 459, Brennan J defined unfairness by discussing whether the decision would have been undertaken by reasonable directors having regard to the benefits and detriments caused by the decision. The scope of the oppression remedy in s 232 extends to mere breaches of duty or contraventions of the Corporations Act: *Thomas v HW Thomas Ltd* (1984) 2 ACLC 610. The central focus in s 232(e) is 'commercial unfairness': *Morgan v 45 Flers Avenue Pty Ltd* (1986) 5 ACLC 222. The High Court confirmed in *Campbell v Backoffice Investments Pty Ltd* [2009] HCA 25 that s 232 should be interpreted broadly. Where s 232 is contravened, the court has broad powers to make orders under s 233 including an order that the minority member be bought out by the majority. Only members, former members, share transferees and those authorised by ASIC can apply for an order for breach of s 233: s 234. The principles underpinning the oppression remedy were discussed in *Tomanovic v Global Mortgage Equity Corp Pty Ltd* [2011] NSWCA 104.

The applicable principles under the oppression remedy in ss 232–233 were summarised by Stevenson J in *Munstermann v Rayward* [2017] NSWSC 133 at [22] as follows (citations omitted):

(1) The test of oppression is an objective one of unfairness ...

(2) The court must look to determine whether on the balance of probabilities the objective commercial bystander would be satisfied that the affairs of the company were being conducted unfairly ...

(3) A director may act oppressively in the sense relevant to the operation of s 232 and yet not breach any fiduciary or other duty owed as a director ...

(4) Conduct of a company's affairs may be oppressive even though the conduct is otherwise lawful ...

(5) Conduct that has the effect of paralysing a company in the operation of its business is properly characterised as conduct contrary to the interests of the members as a whole ...

(6) A shareholder of 50 per cent of the shares in a company can seek relief for oppressive conduct because they do not have control in the form of power to prevent the oppression, particularly where individual strong arm tactics are used ...

(7) The court must formulate an opinion about oppression or unfair prejudice as at the date of the institution of proceedings and the issue of relief under s 233 must be determined at the date of the hearing ...

(8) The discretion under s 233 is wide as to the appropriate remedy ...

(9) The nature of the remedy chosen by the court under s 233 will be dependent upon the conclusions drawn by the court as to the type of oppression with which the court is dealing and the court will choose the remedy which is least intrusive ...

(10) The aim of any order under s 233 must be to put an end to the oppression ...

(11) The court should only look to wind up an otherwise solvent company as a 'last resort' ...

(12) As a remedy for oppression, an oppressor can be ordered to sell their shares to the oppressed party ...

(13) If an order is to be made for the purchase of shares under s 233 the task of the court is to fix a price that represents a fair value in all the circumstances.

More generally, members also have a right to seek an injunction against the company or its officers in the event of or in anticipation of a breach of the Corporations Act: s 1324. This statutory remedy can be quite broad and possibly even give rise to an award of damages instead of an injunction: s 1324(10). However, the Queensland Court of Appeal held that this provision could not be used as a side wind to bypass the enforcement mechanisms in Pt 9.4B: *McCracken v Phoenix Constructions (Qld) Pty Ltd* [2012] QCA 129.

Last, but not least, is the member's right to petition the court that a company be wound up under s 461. Section 461 provides a number of grounds which attract the discretion of the court. They include grounds such as the directors acting in their own interests, oppressive conduct and that it is just and equitable for the company to be wound up. Once any of these grounds for relief are established, the court has a discretion to order a winding up, although it will generally only do so in serious circumstances. For a summary of the legal principles underpinning the 'just and equitable' ground for a winding up order under s 461(k), see *Re TM Fresh Pty Ltd* [2019] VSC 383; *Re Pure Nature Sydney Pty Ltd* [2018] NSWSC 914.

Re Docklands Chiropractic Clinic Pty Ltd [2020] VSC 364 at [22] provides a summary of the matters relevant to the question of whether a just and equitable winding up order should be made. These include (citations omitted):

(a) a failure of the main object of the company's formation;

(b) a deadlock in the management of the company;

(c) a breakdown in the relationship between the shareholders;

(d) a lack of confidence in the conduct and management of the affairs of the company;

(e) where there has been fraud, misconduct or oppression in relation to the affairs of the company;

(f) serious concerns about the company's compliance with its statutory obligations, including the filing of tax returns; and

(g) a risk to the public interest that warrants protection.

Before attempting the questions below, check that you are familiar with the following issues or terms:

✓	What circumstances need to be established before a member can bring a statutory derivative action?
✓	In what circumstances may the vote of the majority affect minority shareholders?
✓	Are there any limits to the power of the majority to vote in the way it/they please?
✓	What is meant by 'fraud on the minority'?
✓	What is the rule established by *Gambotto v WCP Ltd*?
✓	What is the difference between a member's personal right and corporate rights?
✓	How are personal rights protected at common law or under the statute?
✓	What statutory rights exist for members?

Question 30

Hardware Pty Ltd was incorporated in 2010. In its constitution, each of the five subscribers agreed to take up 100 shares at the issue price of $200 per share. Each of these initial members also became executive directors of the company. The company's start-up capital was sufficient for it to commence its business of conducting a computer retail shop. In 2020, four of the company's members, who are also directors, were of the view that they should expand to take up a franchise agreement and open two more stores. The fifth member and director, Jessica, did not want to expand because she thought the risks were too high and she was not able to contribute any more capital. At a board meeting it was decided to issue 2000 $100 preference shares with a 10 per cent cumulative dividend. Jessica voted against this proposal and did not purchase any of the newly issued preference shares as she did not have sufficient funds and also because she was opposed to the expansion. Six months later, a members' meeting was called along with notice of the following motions:

- That the constitution be amended to specify that no dividends will be paid to members holding ordinary shares for a period of 10 years to allow the company to finance its expansion. This restriction does not apply to holders of preference shares.

- That the constitution be amended to require each director to acquire 400 preference shares.

> • That the constitution be amended to allow holders of preference shares to acquire ordinary shares of existing members at the issue price within one month of the date of the meeting by making a written offer.
> Jessica seeks your advice.
>
> **Time allowed: 1 hour**

Answer Plan

There are two features to this problem: (1) the issue of the shares and the proposed constitutional amendments; and (2) the fact that they need to be dealt with separately.

The power to issue shares

- Explain that the company may issue shares (s 124) and such a power is usually vested in the board of directors: s 198A.

Constitutional amendment

- Determine whether the proposed amendments to the constitution are valid.
- Advise on any action that may be taken to prevent or overturn the alteration.

Minority rights and remedies

- Discuss s 232.
- Outline general law equitable limitations on the exercise of majority power.

Answer

8-2 This question concerns Jessica's rights and remedies in a situation where the majority shareholders seem intent on squeezing her out of the company. This question raises legal issues concerning the scope of the directors' power to issue shares, the alteration of the company's constitution and the compulsory acquisition of minority holdings.

The power to issue shares

8-3 Hardware Pty Ltd, while a company, seems to have five members and five directors thus making it, in terms of management, probably little different from a partnership which may be relevant if Jessica wishes to seek a winding up order (discussed below). However, there is a board of directors and it would be reasonable to assume that this company probably had replaceable rules which allocated the power to manage the business of the company to the board of directors: s 198A. The power to issue shares is a specific example of a managerial power as it is one of the means of raising capital for the company to continue its enterprise.

The company has the power under s 124 to issue shares. Section 254A recognises that this power includes the power to issue preference shares. Even if the company's constitution fails to provide for the ability of directors to issue share capital, the broad managerial discretion under s 198A would allow the directors to issue shares on behalf of the company. The fact that the company's five members are also directors would indicate that decisions of the board would be identical to decisions of the company in general meeting, even if the power to issue shares was reserved to the members in general meeting.

The board, as an organ of the company, would have the power to issue preference shares (s 254A) on any terms that it sees fit: s 254B.

The share issue is of a different class of shares, being preference shares. The share issue then would need to comply with s 254A(2). The question refers to some of the terms of issue; the directors, however, would need to address other terms as required by subparas (a), (b), (d) and (e) in order to ensure that the issue was valid. The company would also need to lodge a notice with ASIC that it had resolved to divide the share capital into classes of shares, although this need only be done within 14 days of the resolution: s 246F.

The decision to issue shares, being a discretion of the board of directors, is subject to fiduciary duties: fiduciary duties are examined in **Chapter 6**. Briefly, the principal challenge to the exercise of the discretion to issue shares is that the issue is not for a proper purpose.

In determining whether or not a power has been exercised for a proper purpose, courts first determine the objective purpose of the power and then determine the purpose which actually motivated the use of the power: *Howard Smith Ltd v Ampol Petroleum Ltd* [1974] AC 821. It is rare for a company's constitution to state the purpose for which the power to issue shares may be used, but it would be a clear indication of what the power could be used for: *Whitehouse v Carlton Hotel Pty Ltd* (1987) 162 CLR 285.

Many of the cases which examine the purpose of the power to issue shares are concerned with share issues used for purposes other than raising capital. Thus, the courts have been engaged in reasoning by which the range of purposes of share issues can be enlarged to cover purposes such as altering voting control. The *Howard Smith* case certainly seemed to be based on the acceptance that capital raising was a valid purpose, but that it was not the only purpose.

For Hardware Pty Ltd, it would appear that the main motivating purpose (and it would be a matter of evidence) was to raise capital for the expansion. The proposals to amend the constitution may reveal a subsequent ulterior purpose, but the share issue decision preceded these motions. Even if it was the case that the other directors had an ulterior motive in making the share issue, if the ulterior motive was not the substantial motive (applying a 'but for' test) then the issue was made for a proper purpose according to the rule laid down in *Whitehouse v Carlton Hotel Pty Ltd* (1987) 162 CLR 285. As the High Court said in *Ngurli Ltd v McCann* (1953) 90 CLR 425 at 440:

> ... [the director] could take advantage of the power to benefit himself if such a benefit was incidental to a bona fide exercise of the power but he could not use the power ostensibly to benefit the company but really to benefit himself at the expense of [minority shareholders].

On the question of whether the shares can be issued, it would appear that the board has the power to issue these shares. Provided that the issue is done in accordance with s 254A(2), the issue is valid. Jessica would bear the onus of establishing a breach of fiduciary duty in relation to the issue: *Metropolitan Life Assurance Co Ltd v Ure* (1923) 33 CLR 199. It would appear that the issue was not voidable, as the substantial purpose would probably be to raise capital and hence a valid exercise of power.

Constitutional amendment

8-4 As far as the proposed amendments to the constitution are concerned, the answer could be quite different.

Section 136(2) provides that a company's constitution can be amended by a special resolution, unless there is a further requirement of compliance in the constitution: s 136(3). Thus, in the absence of any further requirement, the proposed amendments could be passed by a 75 per cent vote. Jessica, with her shareholding, will be facing an 80 per cent vote. It may be possible, though, for Jessica to at least delay the meeting if she can establish that the procedure for calling a members' meeting has not been validly followed. It is assumed that the other members will attend, so it is likely that the meeting will have a sufficient quorum: s 249T. Jessica should examine the nature of notice provided by the company in calling the meeting: see Pt 2G.2 Div 3. There is nothing in the facts to suggest that the proposed meeting has been improperly called. Jessica may, however, challenge the substance of the amendments. Each amendment needs to be examined separately as they each affect different rights.

The first amendment prevents dividends for the next 10 years to allow the company to finance its expansion. It must be questioned as to why this amendment is even needed. The power to declare dividends is a managerial function and therefore does not depend on member consent (unless such consent is required by the constitution itself). It may be possible to argue that the payment of dividends to preference shareholders and not to ordinary shareholders is not 'fair and reasonable to the company's shareholders as a whole' (s 254T(1)(b)) and therefore the dividend payments would breach the Corporations Act.

It may be that this change can be characterised as an attempt to alter existing rights attached to the company's ordinary shares. The variation of class rights is governed by s 246B and requires 75 per cent approval of the proposed variation (in the absence of a specific procedure set out in the constitution). The act of issuing a new class of shares in itself is an act which can be taken to vary class rights: s 246C(5). For Hardware Pty Ltd, the members of the class of ordinary shares are the same as members of the whole company and there will be no difficulty in achieving the required 75 per cent majority.

Jessica's rights, however, are not limited to voting. Section 246D would permit her to lodge an objection to the court against the variation. The court will set aside the variation if it is of the view that the applicant (Jessica) is unfairly prejudiced.

The deferral of dividends for 10 years, and even then the subordination of her dividend payment rights to those of the preference shareholders would certainly be a matter prejudicial to Jessica, although it could be argued that she had the opportunity to participate but refused based on a disagreement about management policy.

In relation to the first amendment, therefore, the company must hold a meeting of all ordinary shareholders and a general meeting and achieve a 75 per cent vote at each meeting for the amendment to be effective. There is nothing to prevent these meetings being held concurrently. Jessica would have an opportunity to lodge an objection to the amendment within one month. The objection is made to the court on grounds that the amendment is unfairly prejudicial to her.

The second amendment, if passed by the requisite 75 per cent (s 136(2)), would mean that Jessica would be required to take up more shares in the company. This would seem to trigger the protection of s 140(2); however, Jessica is being asked to take up the shares in her capacity as a director and not as a member so s 140 is not engaged. It is permissible to require directors to maintain certain shareholdings as a qualification for membership of the board of directors.

The third amendment is of much more concern. This amendment would operate to permit the other members, who, it is assumed, will acquire the preference shares, to compel Jessica to sell her shares at the same value as their issue price. The amendments all form a scheme to freeze out Jessica (or other persons who are not wanting to expand the company) by actively flushing out her intentions in amendment two, reducing the value and saleability of her shares by amending the dividend entitlement and then providing a means of divesting her of her shares at least cost to the other members. This is obviously an expropriation of the minority's property rights. A share is considered an item of personal property (s 1070A) and there are rare instances within our legal system which enable expropriation of property by a non-government body. The Corporations Act, however, does not explicitly prevent any amendment which effectively appropriates property rights. The statutory restrictions imposed on variations or amendments are essentially driven by the broad principle of majority rule. The majority shareholders, unlike directors, owe no fiduciary duties to the company or to shareholders and as a general rule they may vote to promote their own interests: *Peters' American Delicacy Co Ltd v Heath* (1939) 61 CLR 457. Literally applied, a majority shareholder can vote in any way he or she pleases notwithstanding that to do so would be detrimental to the company or to other shareholders. Equity, however, does impose a limit on the voting power of the majority. The limit is known as 'fraud on the minority'. Thus, the majority cannot vote in such a way as to abuse their position of power, for to do so would be a fraud on the minority.

Dixon J in *Peters' American Delicacy Co Ltd v Heath* (1939) 61 CLR 457 at 511 stated that an abuse of voting power occurs when the power is used for some ulterior purpose such as:

> ... a means of securing some personal or particular gain, whether pecuniary or otherwise, which does not fairly arise out of the subjects dealt with by the power and is outside and even inconsistent with the contemplated objects of the power.

As a definition of fraud on the minority it is difficult to apply this ruling without a full-scale examination of the purpose of voting to amend a company's constitution. The High Court of Australia had cause to examine an instance of a majority vote where the minority alleged abuse of the voting power in similar circumstances to this problem. In *Gambotto v WCP Ltd* (1995) 182 CLR 432, the court considered a proposal to amend the constitution of a company where the amendment effectively expropriated shares of the minority at a price dictated by the majority. The court laid down a test to determine the validity of such amendments and thereby gave more precise content to the doctrine of fraud on the minority. The test has two stages. First, the amendment must be for a proper purpose. Second, it must be fair in the circumstances, and expropriation of minority property rights in order to further the commercial interests of the company will not be for a proper purpose. Furthermore, the High Court overruled earlier case law in relation to who bears the onus of proof in such cases. It was stated that the onus was on the company to prove that the amendment was for a proper purpose and that it was not oppressive. These principles only apply to amendments of the constitution that seek to take away property rights, as is the case here with Jessica's shares.

While there is now a test for fraud on the minority in relation to amendments of this nature, there is still a need to examine more closely what the test dictates before advising Jessica. In *Gambotto's* case, it was accepted broadly that there can be situations where expropriating shares or share rights was justifiable; that is, property rights are not sacrosanct. It was permissible to expropriate for a proper purpose. What, then, is a proper purpose? This was illustrated by example. In *Gambotto's* case, the purpose of the expropriation was to achieve 100 per cent ownership by the majority. WCP Ltd would become a wholly owned subsidiary of the majority which would then deliver certain administrative and taxation benefits to the majority and WCP Ltd. The High Court found that this purpose, while having some benefit to the company as a whole, was substantially nothing more than aggrandising the majority. Such a purpose was not a proper purpose. The court said in *Gambotto's* case (at 440):

> ... an expropriation may be justified where it is reasonably apprehended that the continued shareholding of the minority is detrimental to the company, its undertaking or the conduct of its affairs — resulting in detriment to the interests of the existing shareholders generally — and expropriation is a reasonable means of eliminating or mitigating that detriment.

Examples of a detriment which might warrant expropriation of shares were where the minority shareholder was a competitor of the company (*Sidebottom v Kershaw, Leese and Co Ltd* [1920] 1 Ch 154), or where statutory regulation required certain characteristics of shareholders (for example, citizenship) for the company to continue its undertaking.

The second part of the test requires that the amendment be fair in all the circumstances. The court noted that this includes both substantive and procedural fairness. Procedural fairness would be satisfied by full disclosure of the information material to the amendment proposal and an independent valuation of the shares. Substantive fairness was essentially concerned with the price of the shares, which may not be simply the market value of the shares but ought also include adequate recompense for the loss of the rights attaching to the shares.

For Jessica, the amendment appears open to challenge by applying *Gambotto's* case. There is nothing to suggest that Jessica's shareholding in the company is harming the business, which means that expropriating her shares would not be for a proper purpose. Furthermore, the price nominated, being the issue price, could not on any analysis constitute substantive fairness when the issue price is likely to be lower than the enterprise value of the shares when the company appears to be expanding its asset values by opening two new stores. Procedural fairness is also lacking as there is no attempt to provide an independent expert valuation.

It would appear that Jessica would have good grounds to challenge the third proposed amendment of the constitution on the grounds that it constitutes a fraud on the minority. Alternatively, Jessica could argue that the proposed amendments contravene the minority oppression provision in s 232.

Minority rights and remedies

8-5 This argument uses a similar analysis to *Gambotto's* case and would be based on commercially unfair behaviour in seeking to aggrandise the position of the majority at the expense of the minority. Applying the test used by Brennan J in *Wayde v NSW Rugby League Ltd* (1985) 180 CLR 459, it could be argued that reasonable directors would not seek to expropriate minority shares merely for the purpose of squeezing out the minority members. Jessica could also argue that the combination of the proposed amendments together also had the effect of operating unfairly as they sought to squeeze her out of the company. By removing the dividend entitlement (at least for the next 10 years) Jessica is effectively being prevented from any exposure to the economic benefits of running the business. The second amendment will presumably also lead to Jessica becoming ineligible to serve on the board of directors as she will be unable to purchase the preference shares.

As a member of the company, Jessica may apply for an order that her shares be purchased by the company for a fair value under s 233. Alternatively, Jessica may seek a winding up order on the basis that the relationship between the members and directors has broken down entirely: s 461(1)(k). However, the courts are usually reluctant to wind up solvent companies without proof of fraud or other contraventions of the law. It is more likely that Jessica will be unaffected by the second amendment and may be able to avoid the third amendment either on the basis of *Gambotto's* case or s 232.

Examiner's Comments

8-6 In relation to the share issue, it was concluded that it may constitute a proper purpose because the dominant purpose was to raise capital. If the directors make the share issue in the knowledge that certain members, being the minority, cannot take up the shares then this may be a relevant factor in determining whether the share issue was for a proper purpose: *Wallington v Kokotovich Constructions Pty Ltd* (1993) 11 ACSR 759 (on appeal, *Kokotovich Constructions Pty Ltd v Wallington* (1995) 17 ACSR 478).

In relation to the first proposed constitutional amendment, reference was made to an objection under s 246D. The basis for judicial interference in such cases is that the proposal to vary class rights is 'unfairly prejudicial' to the applicant. There is little or no judicial interpretation of this phrase in this section. The phrase is employed in s 232 and it may be useful to refer to cases under this section (or its predecessors, the former ss 246AA and 260) for guidance on what would constitute unfair prejudice.

The irony of the fate of amendments such as in *Gambotto's* case and in this problem is that companies may have a constitution upon registration which contains provisions for the expropriation of shares or which otherwise can prejudice minority interests: *Phillips v Manufacturers' Securities Ltd* (1917) 116 LT 290. Presumably, the exercise of the power of expropriation would then only be limited by the oppression remedy under s 232. The equitable limitation of fraud on the minority is a limitation on voting power of the majority, and this is why it is activated in situations of amending the constitution which must be done through a vote of the members.

Keep in Mind

- Do not confuse the role of the board of directors and the members in general meeting. It is the board which primarily makes the managerial decision to issue new shares and board decisions are subject to fiduciary obligations. It is the members in general meeting who vote to amend the constitution and there is no fiduciary obligation here. Even though the exercise of the powers in each instance can be invalidated under a 'proper purpose' test, the source of the limitation or obligation is different.

Question 31

> Daniel is the managing director and sole shareholder of Ezislice Pty Ltd, a major player in the commercial cheese distribution market. In order to obtain ideas about improving his business Daniel takes a four per cent strategic shareholding in his competitors, including Dairyslice Ltd. Daniel's four per cent shareholding gives him the ability to obtain a position as non-executive director of Dairyslice. This enables Daniel to gain information about their strategic forward planning, including their plans to streamline commercial distribution. This gives Ezislice a significant commercial advantage.
>
> Dairyslice is concerned about one of its directors and shareholders actively competing against the company. In order to prevent Daniel from obtaining sensitive commercial information, the other directors propose significant amendments to the Dairyslice constitution. The main change imposed by the amendments requires all shares issued or transferred to directors in the last six months to be acquired by the company for 'fair compensation'. Only Daniel has received shares in the last six months.
>
> Daniel is outraged at the proposed changes; however, the vote at the general meeting of the members obtains 96 per cent approval for both resolutions. (Daniel was the only shareholder to vote against the resolutions.)
>
> Daniel now comes to you and seeks advice concerning his rights under this situation.
>
> **Time allowed: 40 minutes**

Answer Plan

This question is concerned with members' remedies, particularly in relation to constitutional amendments and *Gambotto's* case (although this question may provide a different perspective to the previous question). This question is concerned with this narrow issue, with the result that a system of headings is probably unnecessary.

Answer

8-7 Daniel was a director and member of Dairyslice Ltd until he was removed from his position as a company director and his shares were expropriated by the company's majority shareholders. The loss of his position as a director and the expropriation of his shares took place as a result of an alteration to the company's constitution. The key issues in this question concern whether Daniel has any remedies against the company and/or its members in respect of the constitutional amendment and whether any defences are available in respect of Daniel's challenge to the constitutional amendment.

The power of the majority of members to amend the constitution must be exercised for a proper purpose: *Peters' American Delicacy Co Ltd v Heath* (1939) 61 CLR 457. Where the power to amend the constitution is misused by the majority of members it may be possible to challenge the amendment on the basis of 'fraud on the minority': *Gambotto v WCP Ltd* (1995) 182 CLR 432. Daniel may also seek to challenge the constitutional amendments using the oppression remedy under the Corporations Act: s 232. Both the *Gambotto's* case principle (particularly the second limb of the majority opinion) and oppression are concerned with the underlying fairness of the transaction. We may therefore discuss them together.

The Corporations Act provides Daniel with certain rights as a former member of the company. Section 232 provides that the court may make an order under s 233 if:

(a) the conduct of a company's affairs;

(b) an actual or proposed act or omission by or on behalf of a company; or

(c) a resolution, or a proposed resolution, of members or a class of members of a company;

  is either:

(d) contrary to the interests of the members as a whole; or

(e) oppressive to, unfairly prejudicial to, or unfairly discriminatory against, a member or members whether in that capacity or in any other capacity.

In order to apply to the court under s 232, Daniel must come within the class of persons referred to under s 234. Section 234(c) allows Daniel, as a former member, to seek the court's assistance. Daniel must, however, establish to the court that the constitutional amendment satisfies either paragraph (a) or (b) above.

In considering whether the constitutional amendment is oppressive, unfairly prejudicial or unfairly discriminatory, the court will examine whether 'objectively in the eyes of a commercial bystander, there has been unfairness, namely conduct that is so unfair that reasonable [business people] who considered the matter would not have thought the decision fair': *Morgan v 45 Flers Ave Pty Ltd* (1986) 5 ACLC 222 at 233 (see *Wayde v NSW Rugby League Ltd* (1985) 180 CLR 459). The problem that Daniel faces is that his conduct, in taking advantage of his position as a director of Dairyslice to obtain a commercial benefit for a competing business, would itself be seen as unfair. Therefore, it is difficult to see how the amendments to remove him and prevent the abuse from continuing would be seen by a commercial bystander as unfair.

Similar considerations arise in relation to the High Court's decision in *Gambotto's* case. This case found that a constitutional amendment which expropriated shares must be for a proper purpose and must be fair in all the circumstances. In that case, the majority of the company were obtaining a significant benefit by expropriating the minority's interests which the High Court found impermissible. In the present case, the minority are expropriating Daniel's shares because they wish to prevent him from obtaining a competitive advantage by having access to confidential information as a director of the company (by reason of his four per cent shareholding). Therefore, it will be difficult for Daniel to prove that the constitutional amendment expropriating his rights is oppressive, unfair or prejudicial as it appears that the members have a good reason for the amendment.

The High Court in *Gambotto's* case stated that there could be circumstances where the expropriation of minority shares could be justified. The High Court relied on the decision in *Sidebottom v Kershaw, Leese and Co Ltd* [1920] 1 Ch 154. This may provide a defence to the company against Daniel's action either under the fraud on the minority or under s 232 oppression.

The fact that Daniel is operating a competing business that is obtaining a competitive advantage through Daniel's shareholding is highly relevant and brings this situation within the scope of the High Court's exception in *Gambotto's* case outlined above.

A further requirement for the defence is that all relevant information must have been disclosed prior to the constitutional amendment being voted on (procedural fairness). The question does not specify what information was given before the vote took place. However, as a director Daniel would have voted on the proposal to call the members' meeting so it is reasonable to assume that he had access to all of the relevant information prior to the meeting.

In order to take advantage of the defence to oppressive conduct, the company must have also offered Daniel a fair price for his shares: *Gambotto's* case. The question specifically states that the resolutions offer Daniel a fair price for his shares.

In conclusion, Daniel may seek relief through the courts against the constitutional amendment by arguing that the amendment was a fraud on the minority or that it was a breach of the oppression remedy: s 232. However, the fact that this conduct was undertaken in order to prevent him from competing with the company, adequate information was given concerning the amendments, and fair value was paid for his shares may mean that the conduct will not be invalidated following *Gambotto's* case.

One further issue raised by the question concerns directors' duties. By using information obtained as a company director of Dairyslice to benefit his personal company, Ezislice, Daniel may be breaching his statutory and general law duties owed to Dairyslice. Daniel owes a duty to Dairyslice not to misuse his position as a director or to misuse the information he obtains in that position: ss 181–184. The misuse of his position as a director to directly compete with Dairyslice may also be in breach of Daniel's fiduciary duties. It may well be detrimental to Daniel's interests to complain about this situation as he may end up being sued for breach of directors' duties.

Examiner's Comments

8-8   One area where this answer could be improved is to provide a brief discussion of the procedures necessary for amending the corporate constitution. Section 136(2) provides that the company may amend its constitution by a special resolution which is defined as a resolution that has been subject to special notice under s 249L and must be approved by 75 per cent of the members eligible to vote. This may open up an avenue of challenge for Daniel if the statutory requirements for voting on the constitutional amendments were not met. If this were the case, Daniel could apply for an injunction under s 1324 to prevent his shares being expropriated by the company.

Daniel may also attempt to launch a statutory derivative action against his former board members for breach of directors' duties (in trying to remove him) under s 236. The difficulty faced by Daniel in this situation, however, is that in order to bring a statutory derivative action, Daniel must have the approval of the court which is unlikely to occur as Daniel will have difficulty convincing the court that his request is in good faith or in the best interests of the company: s 237(2). This is because Daniel wishes to retain his shares and his board position to obtain an unfair competitive advantage against Dairyslice.

Keep in Mind

- It is important that students distinguish between Daniel's capacity as a member and director, and as a member and former member.
- The majority of the High Court in *Gambotto v WCP Ltd* (1995) 183 CLR 432 at 446 (Mason CJ, Brennan, Deane and Dawson JJ) said:

  … an alteration to the company's articles permitting the expropriation of shares will not be valid simply because it was made for a proper purpose; it must also be fair in the circumstances. Fairness in this context has both procedural and substantive elements. The first element, that the process used to expropriate must be fair, requires the majority shareholders to disclose all relevant information leading up to the alteration ... The second element ... is largely concerned with the price offered for the shares. Thus, an expropriation at less than market value is prima facie unfair ... and it would be unusual for a court to be satisfied that a price substantially above market value was not a fair value ... Whether the price offered is fair depends on a variety of factors including assets, market value, dividends, and the nature of the corporation and its likely future.

Question 32

LandCo Pty Ltd is a land development company. It was formed originally with five members, including Rahul. Over the years further shares have been issued to the families of each original member. No one family has a majority. There are three directors. The constitution provides for the retirement of directors after two years and appointment of new directors or reappointment at the annual general meeting. Any member may stand for election as a director.

Rahul wishes to be a director and he nominates for election at the next general meeting. Rahul is a popular member of the company, but he has very little business acumen. The three incumbent directors issue additional shares to their families prior to the general meeting. The effect of the issue is to alter the voting power and make it impossible for Rahul to be elected.

Advise Rahul about any rights that he may have.

Time allowed: 40 minutes

 # Answer Plan

Rahul is effectively prevented from becoming a director of the company and at the same time his voting power has been reduced. There are a number of possible sources of relief:

- the personal action for breach of the constitution (if there is a breach);
- the statutory derivative action for breach of fiduciary duty to exercise powers for a proper purpose; or
- the statutory oppression remedy: s 232.

Enforcing the constitution

- Discuss the power of members to enforce the provisions of the constitution.

Statutory derivative action (SDA)

- Outline Rahul's ability to bring an SDA.

The oppression remedy

- Discuss whether Rahul may obtain relief under the minority remedy: s 232.

Answer

8-9 Individuals who invest in companies as shareholders in many cases seem to have to subordinate their personal wishes in favour of the notion of majority rule. Even their monetary contribution becomes subsumed into the property of the company with only a right to a residual claim in a winding up in return. There are, however, some important areas where individual or personal rights are secured and protected. The constitution of a company is the principal source of personal membership rights. The constitution or replaceable rules must set out the basic rights attaching to shares. There are other rights preserved in the Corporations Act, such as rights to attend meetings and to be given notice: s 249J.

The constitution or replaceable rules of a company have the same effect as a contract: s 140.

The parties to the contract are the company, each member and the directors and company secretary. Under this contract, each person agrees to observe and adhere to the constitution and rules so far as they apply to that person: s 140.

Under contract law, breach of the terms of the contract would entitle the wronged party to sue. The same applies to this statutory contract; however, the right to sue is limited to suing to enforce rules which affect members in their capacity as a member. Thus, if the constitution provides that a particular member cannot be engaged to give particular advice for a fee to the company, this is not a normal membership right and cannot be enforced as a right of membership: *Eley v Positive Government Security Life Assurance Co* (1876) 1 Ex D 88. The company could change its constitution by majority (s 136) and remove the individual right, making it necessary for the individual to identify some separate contract conferring the right: *Bailey v New South Wales Medical Defence Union Ltd* (1995) 132 ALR 1.

LandCo's constitution provides that any member may stand for election as a director. Such a rule is clearly one which confers a right upon a person in their capacity as member. Rahul, as a member, could therefore enforce this part of the contract.

An advantage of suing for a personal right is that it is not possible for the company in general meeting to excuse or ratify a breach of a personal right: *Pender v Lushington* (1877) 6 Ch D 70. By contrast, a corporate right which has been infringed may well be ratified or forgiven in this fashion.

The problem for Rahul is, however, that his right under the constitution is that he is entitled to stand for election. The directors have not prevented him from standing — rather, they have effectively prevented him from gaining sufficient votes by altering the voting power. The board of directors has the discretion, as part of their managerial discretion, to issue shares: s 198A. Unless there is some express rule in the constitution which prevents an issue of shares so as to alter the voting control or power of members then Rahul must look to the general law of equity to find some limit on the power to issue shares.

Certainly, there is the limit on the power to issue shares arising from the fiduciary duty upon directors to use their power for a proper purpose. This duty, however, is owed to the company and Rahul would be faced with the standard difficulties of taking action on behalf of the company. The statutory derivative action option will be discussed later.

However, in *Residues Treatment & Trading Co Ltd v Southern Resources Ltd (No 4)* (1988) 14 ACLR 569, the court identified authorities which supported a personal right to not have voting power reduced by the improper purposes of directors. King CJ said:

> A member's voting rights and the rights of participation which they provide in the decision making of the company are a fundamental attribute of membership and are rights which the member should be able to protect by legal action against improper diminution. The rule in *Foss v Harbottle* has no application where individual membership rights as opposed to corporate rights are involved.

It would seem, therefore, that Rahul could bring a personal action in respect of the share issue which then altered the voting power. This may not yet get him elected but the vote would not be compromised. Of course, Rahul would need to be able to establish that the share issue was made for an improper purpose and he would need to have regard to the cases which deal with improper purposes in respect of share issues. *Howard Smith Ltd v Ampol Petroleum* [1974] AC 821 and *Harlowe's Nominees Pty Ltd v Woodside (Lakes Entrance) Oil Co NL* (1968) 121 CLR 483 both held that a share issue designed primarily to create a new majority was an improper purpose. Similarly, the scheme in *Kokotovich Constructions Pty Ltd v Wallington* (1995) 17 ACSR 478 under which a new share issue rendered a shareholder's share parcel virtually valueless was also held to be an improper purpose. On the other hand, in *Australian Metropolitan Life Assurance Co Ltd v Ure* (1923) 33 CLR 199, the directors' refusal to register a transfer of shares was held to be a proper use of power because it was exercised with a view to preventing a particular person from becoming a director. It seems, from that case, that a company can prevent persons becoming directors when those persons may damage the company's reputation and business. Rahul would need to be careful to avoid a finding that his lack of business acumen became the turning point for him on this issue!

Arguably, business acumen is a matter that is more properly addressed by the process of permitting directors standing for election to provide statements of their suitability for the position.

Statutory derivative action (SDA)

8-10 If the wrong complained of is a wrong to the company, namely breach of directors' duty to exercise powers for a proper purpose, then

Rahul will have no standing to sue unless he can establish the grounds for an SDA which allow him to take proceedings against the directors on behalf of the company under s 236. In order to launch an action in the name of the company, Rahul must obtain court approval under s 237 which requires that:

(a) it is probable that the company will not itself bring the proceedings, or properly take responsibility for them, or for the steps in them; and

(b) [Rahul] is acting in good faith; and

(c) it is in the best interests of the company that [Rahul] be granted leave; and

(d) there is a serious question to be tried; and

(e) either:

  (i) at least 14 days before making the application, the applicant gave written notice to the company of the intention to apply for leave and of the reasons for applying; or

  (ii) it is appropriate to grant leave even though subparagraph (i) is not satisfied.

It may be difficult for Rahul to obtain approval to bring an SDA against the directors because he may have trouble establishing that he is bringing the case in good faith. In *Swansson v RA Pratt Properties Pty Ltd* (2002) 42 ACSR 313, Palmer J explained that good faith will not be proved where the applicant is seeking to bring the derivative suit for a collateral purpose as it would amount to an abuse of process. In this case, Rahul is clearly disappointed at his inability to obtain appointment to the board and would be using the SDA to pressure the directors and their families to drop their opposition which would not be acting in good faith. In *Chahwan v Euphoric Pty Ltd t/as Clay & Michel* (2008) 65 ACSR 661, Tobias JA summarised the good faith test from *Swansson* in the following way at [74]:

> ... as a current or former shareholder or director of the company, [the applicant] would suffer a real and substantive injury if a derivative action were not permitted provided that that injury was dependant [sic] upon or connected with the applicant's status as such shareholder or director.

This would be difficult for Rahul to establish, given his detriment is concerned with a desire to secure appointment as a director, although it may be possible to argue that such an appointment is an incident of membership under the company's constitution.

Once Rahul obtains court approval to launch a statutory derivative action he may carry out his case against the company. However, the problem faced by Rahul is that any amount of damages recovered on behalf of the company is to go to the company rather than Rahul. Rahul may, however, apply to the court for a costs order in his favour: s 242.

Minority oppression

8-11 Under s 232, a member of a company can bring action against a company on grounds of oppressive or unfairly prejudicial conduct. If the directors make a share issue with the main purpose of reducing a shareholder's voting control, especially when such a move damages some pre-existing mutual trust and cooperation in management, then such action can be unfairly prejudicial or discriminatory within the meaning of s 232: *Re Dalkeith Investments Pty Ltd* (1984) 9 ACLR 247. A disproportionate share issue not only reduces Rahul's proprietary interest in the company but it also prejudices his right to be involved in the management of the company. Even where the constitution has no express right for members to participate in management (other than voting rights and rights to stand for election as directors) there may be an implied right. An implied right is more likely in smaller companies formed on the basis of mutual trust and confidence than it is in large public companies with widely held shares. Thus, if Rahul is able to establish such a basis for the incorporation of LandCo Pty Ltd it is likely that he will have a legitimate expectation to participate in management. The share issue effectively excludes him and this would amount to oppression or unfairly prejudicial conduct: *Quinlan v Essex Hinge Co Ltd* [1996] 2 BCLC 417 (discussed with approval in *Smolarek v Liwszyc* (2006) 32 WAR 101; see also *Ebrahimi v Westbourne Galleries Ltd* [1973] AC 360; and obiter comments in *Campbell v Backoffice Investments Pty Ltd* [2009] HCA 25).

Under s 233, the court has a wide range of powers to redress the oppressive conduct. Apart from specific orders listed in paras (a)–(j), the court may make any order that it sees fit. Thus, it may invalidate the share issue or it may require the directors to make a proportional share issue to Rahul to redress the balance.

Conclusion

8-12 In summary, it would seem that Rahul could pursue a personal action based upon the general equitable right to have membership rights protected. There appears to be no direct infringement of his rights under the constitution to stand for election; however, his right is eroded by the reduction in his voting control as a result of the share issue. The authority in *Residues Treatment & Trading Co Ltd v Southern Resources Ltd* (above) supports him in categorising this as a personal right for which he has standing to sue. His alternative is to initiate proceedings under s 232 for oppressive conduct and seek orders to redress the balance of voting control prior to the election.

Examiner's Comments

8-13 One area worth developing is the restricted range of orders available for breach of the statutory contract. A member is not generally permitted to obtain damages that are reflective of the company's loss caused by the breach of duty: *Prudential Assurance Co Ltd v Newman Industries Ltd (No 2)* [1984] Ch 204 (see more recently *Central Coast Council v Norcross Pictorial Calendars Pty Ltd* [2021] NSWCA 75).

While the Corporations Act does not expressly limit the range of orders, the policy behind this arises because allowing members to sue for damages under the statutory contract may effectively defeat the claims of creditors against the company and s 563A defers all such claims until after creditors' claims are settled in a winding up. The appropriate remedies are therefore declarations and injunctions.

Keep in Mind

- It is important to recognise that the constitutional right is merely to be permitted to stand for election. Contract law relies upon strict interpretation of contractual terms and while the scheme of the directors in this case may prevent Rahul's election it does not prevent his standing for election. There cannot be a constitutional rule which provides that all members shall be elected, as this would deprive a member of a right to vote. There may be a constitutional rule which provides that each member shall have a 'turn' at being a director, although this would be something peculiar to a small 'quasi-partnership' company.

Question 33

> Jack and Jill decide to start up a retail nursery business. On advice from their accountant, they incorporate a proprietary company called Up-the-Hill Pty Ltd. The nursery is very successful and Jill expands the business to commence serving refreshments in the nursery shop. Jack always resisted the idea of serving refreshments because it was not part of the business plan and it diverted resources away from the nursery. Jill argued that it enhanced the business by drawing more customers, and that potentially the income from the refreshments would outstrip the nursery revenue.
>
> Gradually, their differences in opinion have become more acute until the relationship is now quite acrimonious. Decisions about the management of the business are difficult to achieve.
>
> As the adviser to Up-the-Hill Pty Ltd, what would you suggest they do?
>
> **Time allowed: 20 minutes**

Answer Plan

The options for a small company with only two members are limited. After a consideration of the difficulties in continuing the business in its current form, there is a need to consider how to end the business relationship. Generally, the options are:

- to buy out the other member;
- voluntary winding up; or
- compulsory winding up under s 461(1)(k).

As this is a short answer question there is no need for headings.

Answer

8-14 It is assumed that Jack and Jill are the only two members and directors of Up-the-Hill Pty Ltd. In one sense, the relationship in the business is probably not very different from a partnership. The breakdown in a partnership which is heavily reliant upon mutual trust and confidence usually means that the partnership must be ended in some way. Up-the-Hill Pty Ltd, however, is a separate legal entity and is independent, to a degree, from its members. The assets of the business belong to this entity and not the members. The conduct of the business of the entity as well as winding up its business is governed by the Corporations Act.

The management of the business is generally carried on by the board of directors (s 198A) who are, in this case, Jack and Jill. The board of directors makes decisions on the basis of a simple majority. If the two directors are having difficulties with each other then it is likely that there will be few occasions when there can be a board decision. The business of the company, therefore, is likely to deteriorate in these circumstances with a consequent loss of assets. If the relationship is acrimonious, then each member will seek to blame the other for the loss and possibly engage in costly litigation over the matter. To avoid such a development, and if Jack and Jill cannot patch up their differences, then it is time to end the relationship before any losses occur.

One means of ending the relationship is for one member to offer to buy all the shares of the other member. Up-the-Hill Pty Ltd would still continue, but it would be a single member/director company. The only issue in a buy-out would be valuing the shares. As directors, Jack and Jill each have access to the company's financial records (s 198F) to enable a fair valuation. A practical obstacle would be whether either of the members could afford to buy out the other, or if they both want to buy out the other. If a buy-out is not practical then they need to look at the other options of finalising the business and dividing the assets. The other options of either voluntary or compulsory winding up involve the end of the company and ultimately its deregistration.

Members can resolve to wind up a company themselves. This is called a voluntary winding up: s 491. The company must be solvent (s 494) and a liquidator is appointed by the members: s 495. Given that a voluntary winding up requires decisions or resolutions by members and directors over a number of matters, it is possible that a voluntary winding up could not be achieved because of the problems between the parties. A voluntary winding up has the benefit of the members being able to choose a liquidator themselves and the liquidator, as an independent third party, will take control of the business to divide the assets.

If a voluntary winding up is not achievable then the other option for a member is to apply to the court for an order that the company be wound up under s 461. The specific grounds in paras (1)(a)–(j) have no application to the current problem. Paragraph (1)(k) is broadly stated and is commonly called the 'just and equitable' ground. This ground has been used to order a winding up in a number of circumstances where the business of the company cannot be conducted because of changes since incorporation. An appropriate example of its application was in *Ebrahimi v Westbourne Galleries Ltd* [1973] AC 360. This case was similar in that it involved a company which was in size and management very similar to a partnership. One 'partner' tried to take over management of the company by attempting to remove the other 'partner' from the position of director. The court held that even though such a move may be permitted under the relevant legislation (there were three members to carry the vote) the majority shareholders had to act in accordance with the understanding between the members when the company was incorporated. If the company was formed on the basis of the same mutual trust and confidence required in a partnership then the members had to continue to act in this way. If they ignored or lost this understanding then it was just and equitable to wind up the company: see generally *Re 1A Eden Pty Ltd* [2021] NSWSC. In small companies there can often be a breakdown in mutual trust and confidence, but it will not in every case lead to an order for winding up. The statutory remedy for oppression under s 232 may be more appropriate in some cases, especially when there are more than two members and the capacity to oppress the minority. The courts are also reluctant to wind up solvent companies where to do so may adversely impact other stakeholders such as employees. In such cases, it may be preferable to bring an oppression action and ask for one of the members to be bought out. In *Carpenter v Carpenter Grazing Co Pty Ltd* (1986) 4 ACLC 18, the management structure was not as in a partnership, but rather a hierarchy of a governing director and his family who had equity but no voting power. There was a loss of trust and confidence, but the court did not order a winding up; rather, it made other orders in relation to share allotments to remedy the difficulty. Thus, for companies in the category of 'quasi-partnerships', winding up is an available remedy where the mutual trust and confidence underpinning the relationship is gone.

In summary, Jack and Jill must either decide to try harder to make the business work, and compromise, or they must finish the business relationship. One of them can buy out the other after an agreement as to the value of the shares, or they will need to resort to a winding up process. There is a process available to wind up the company regardless of whether or not they agree to wind up.

Examiner's Comments

8-15 The problems experienced by Up-the-Hill Pty Ltd are not unlike problems that can be experienced by partnerships. The current law tends to encourage businesses that would normally be partnerships to adopt the corporate form because of the benefit of limited liability. By way of comment, the current ease with which companies may incorporate, with automatic replaceable rules, means that problems in the future which arise from disagreement between 'quasi-partners' are not covered by the replaceable rules or a constitution. Deadlock between directors or members could be resolved if there was a provision in the constitution for casting votes or independent arbitration. Joint venture companies with equal 'partners' will generally take care to ensure that the constitution has provision to deal with deadlocks by providing for an orderly process of resolution or conclusion.

Another means of planning for these risks is to have a separate shareholders' agreement which may limit the way in which votes are cast to avoid positions of deadlock.

 Keep in Mind

- Just because there are only two members who now disagree, do not treat it like a partnership. Unlike partnerships, there is in existence a separate legal entity: the company. This company cannot just be abandoned; rather, its end must be formally dealt with as a means of protecting creditors.
- Whilst disagreements will frequently occur in the course of operating a company, much more is needed before the court will wind up a company by reason of such disagreements: *Re 1A Eden Pty Ltd* [2021] NSWSC 82 at [93].
- For a useful collection of legal principles on winding up on the just and equitable ground, see *Re 1A Eden Pty Ltd* [2021] NSWSC 82 at [90]–[100]; *Re Docklands Chiropractic Clinic Pty Ltd* [2020] VSC 364.
- Whilst winding up should be a last resort, there is no absolute rule that the court will not wind up a solvent company: *Mudgee Dolomite & Lime Pty Ltd v Murdoch* [2020] NSWSC 1510 at [293].

Question 34

Buildco Pty Ltd is a large construction company. The managing director, Tom Hammer, is paid a substantial salary package. Part of the package includes the ability to require the company to pay for reasonable decorating costs for his home which he then uses to entertain corporate clients. Mr Hammer embarks on an extensive program of costly renovations and additions to his home which are all paid for by the company. The expenses are revealed in the financial records reported to the board.

Some board members demand that Hammer repay the expenses to the company. Hammer, however, commands majority support on the board and the board resolves ultimately to allow the issue to be forgotten.

One of the disagreeing board members, Maya, finds the resolution to be unacceptable and wants to know what can be done to overcome it.

Time allowed: 40 minutes

Answer Plan

This question is reasonably complex and requires analysis of the wrong alleged and the procedure to prosecute the wrong:

- Has Hammer breached any fiduciary or statutory duty? The facts in this question do not provide much detail concerning the potential breach which may suggest that the question is more concerned with the enforcement of the potential breach than with the legal principles of proving a breach has occurred. This should be taken into account when determining how much time to devote to each issue.
- If there has been a breach, who has standing to prosecute the breach?
- If the company has standing, who decides to sue in the case of a breach of duty?
- Can the board of directors excuse the breach of duty?
- If not, can the company in general meeting excuse the breach?
- If both organs of the company purport to excuse the breach, are there grounds for a derivative action?
- Are there any statutory causes of action available to the director?

Breach of directors' duties

- Discuss Hammer's potential breach of fiduciary duties.

Enforcement of directors' duties

- Can the breach be excused?
- Explain the scope of ratification and discuss how it may apply here.

The statutory derivative action (SDA)

- Discuss the elements of the SDA.

Answer

8-16 This question concerns the issue of how potential breaches of directors' duties may be enforced.

Breach of directors' duties

8-17 Hammer, as a director, owes both fiduciary and statutory duties to the company. In essence, the wrong that would be alleged is that he has misappropriated company resources by using more of the company's funds for his own benefit than he was entitled to. In any claim of this nature there will always be an argument about the interpretation of what exactly Hammer was entitled to claim under his contract of service to the company. The answer to this question cannot be resolved without additional material. Clearly, however, if he is entitled to claim these expenses then there is no breach of duty and the decision to not sue could not be challenged.

It will be assumed, therefore, that there are reasonable grounds to argue that the amount obtained by Hammer exceeded his entitlements under his contract. If this is so then Hammer may be said to have acted improperly by misusing his position to gain an advantage for himself in breach of s 182. Hammer would also be found to have acted in breach of his fiduciary duty to the company by acting in his own interest and not that of the company, which involves a clear conflict of interest. The statutory and general law duties operate concurrently: s 185. In the event that Hammer is found to have breached his directors' duties he could consider asking the court to relieve him of liability under either s 1317S (for statutory duties, which are civil penalties) or s 1318 (in respect of the general law fiduciary duties). These sections permit a court to relieve or forgive a person from any liability for breach of duty, amongst other things. Hammer would have to show that he acted honestly and that in the circumstances he ought to be excused. His argument would, no doubt, be based on what he honestly believed he was entitled to under the terms of his service contract. It would also be relevant whether he gave full disclosure to the company about his dealings.

Enforcement of directors' duties

8-18 Fiduciary duties are owed to the company and so it would be the company who is entitled to sue: *Foss v Harbottle* (1843) 2 Hare 461. Statutory duties under ss 180–183 are civil penalty provisions (s 1317E) and may be enforced by either ASIC or by the company (at least in order to seek compensation under s 1317H). It has been held that ratification does not prevent a breach of the statutory duties from occurring, although it may alter the nature of the conduct so as to prevent it from being improper: *Angas Law Services Pty Ltd (in liq) v Carabelas* (2005) 226 CLR 507. In relation to the statutory breach, therefore, the decision by the board does not prevent ASIC bringing proceedings.

As for the company's decision whether or not to take action, the company may ratify what would otherwise be a breach of fiduciary duty: *Regal (Hastings) Ltd v Gulliver* [1967] 2 AC 134. Such a ratification may act as a waiver of the company's rights or an estoppel against the company taking action. Normally, the decision to instigate legal action is a managerial decision which is within the province of the board, if, as is normal, the board has power to manage the business of the company: s 198A. This managerial power and its classification are not always so clear-cut. Certainly, if the board decides to commence legal action, then the members in general meeting cannot stop it: *John Shaw & Sons (Salford) Ltd v Shaw* [1935] 2 KB 113. However, if the board decides not to bring legal proceedings then the position becomes less clear. This is so for two reasons. First, the duty is fiduciary in nature and, under general principles of fiduciary relations, only the principal can forgive or excuse a breach of duty. In this case, the principal would be the company. Thus, if all members agreed to excuse the breach then there is nothing more to be done. In some cases, excuse by a majority would be sufficient: *Regal (Hastings) Ltd v Gulliver* (above). Whether unanimous or majority assent is needed does not matter — the point is that the board itself cannot excuse the breach of fiduciary duty.

The second reason for questioning the power of the board to not instigate proceedings in this case is the very existence of the right under the Corporations Act for members to bring a derivative action: s 236.

It would seem, therefore, that the board's power to institute proceedings is positive, but its power to decide to not bring proceedings is limited in cases which certainly involve a breach of fiduciary duty.

If it is accepted that only the company, being members in general meeting, has the authority to excuse a breach of duty then it is conceivable, subject to any rules in the constitution, that a majority at the general meeting could excuse a breach of fiduciary duty. Thus, if Maya were to convince the board to refer the matter to a general meeting then the outcome may be the same if Maya does not command a majority vote. The answer to this problem may be found in the company's constitution. If the constitution provides either expressly or impliedly that a majority may excuse or ratify actions in breach of fiduciary duties then that is all that is required: *Regal (Hastings) Ltd v Gulliver* (above).

However, the power of the general meeting to excuse the breach is subject to the same equitable limitation that affects the majority voting power in other respects; namely, that it cannot amount to a fraud on the minority. Further, where the act which is purported to be excused involves a misappropriation of company resources and the majority in general meeting are controlled by the directors who seek to perpetuate the breach of duty, there is no power to excuse: *Miller v Miller* (1995) 16 ACSR 73. There is further authority for this in *Ngurli Ltd v McCann* (1953) 90 CLR 425 where the court said (at 438–9):

> Voting powers conferred on the shareholders and powers conferred on the directors by the articles of association must be used bona fide for the benefit of the company as a whole ... Nor can the majority of shareholders exercise their voting power in general meeting so as to commit a fraud on the minority. They must not exercise their vote so as to appropriate to themselves or some of themselves property, advantages or rights which belong to the company.

This limitation is consistent with the requirements for a derivative action.

The statutory derivative action (SDA)

8-19 A derivative action will not be permitted unless Maya acquires court approval to bring a derivative action under s 237(2). The court will only grant approval to bring a derivative action where it is in the best interests of the company and Maya is acting in good faith. The facts of the question do not provide that Maya has any ulterior motive apart from recovering the allegedly misappropriated money: compare

Swansson v RA Pratt Properties Pty Ltd (2002) 42 ACSR 313. Subject to the interpretation of Hammer's contract of service and his entitlements, it would appear that Hammer has appropriated more company resources than he was entitled to. Misappropriation is a serious matter and the company ought to have the benefit of its right to sue and recover its assets. Maya would also need to establish that there is a serious question to be tried which should involve, at least, the following matters:

- the character of the company — that is, the nature of the company's operations;
- the business of the company, so that the effects of the proposed litigation on the conduct of the business may be appreciated;
- whether there are other means of obtaining the same redress so that the company does not have to be brought into litigation against its will; and
- the ability of the defendant to meet at least a substantial part of any judgment in favour of the company so that the court may ascertain whether the action would be of practical benefit to the company.

(See *Ragless v IPA Holdings Pty Ltd (in liq)* (2008) 65 ACSR 700; [2008] SASC 90.)

Lastly, Maya would need to demonstrate that the company would be unlikely to bring the case against Hammer which should be easily established given the board's approval of the transaction.

In summary, if the use of company funds by Hammer is in excess of his entitlements and the majority is or is likely to excuse the misappropriation then Maya would be able to bring a derivative action on behalf of the minority and the company. The action would be for breach of fiduciary duty. Of course, any money payable in respect of the breach of duty would be payable to the company and not Maya, although she seems concerned about the company's welfare rather than her own so this may not be an important consideration. Maya could ask the court to order the company to pay her costs in bringing the SDA: s 242.

As earlier mentioned, the conduct may also constitute a breach of the statutory duties under ss 180–184. The prosecution of these breaches is a matter for ASIC and is independent of whether or not Maya pursues a derivative action. Maya could consider informing ASIC of the matter and hope that it devotes some resources to pursuing Hammer over the breach.

Examiner's Comments

8-20 An interesting area to develop in this answer would be the power of the company in general meeting to excuse a director for breach of statutory duty. There is authority to suggest that if a general meeting purports to excuse a breach of duty by a director or officer then the process of disclosure and approval may be relevant to whether or not the director has acted honestly: *Miller v Miller* (1995) 16 ACSR 73. Thus, if the duty breached is one which is focused upon honesty then ASIC would be hard-pressed to mount a prosecution in the face of disclosure and approval. The director or officer may also have thereby established grounds for the exercise of the court's discretion under ss 1317S and 1318. It could be noted that in this case there does not appear to be a unity of interest between the director in breach and the directors giving ratification: see *ASIC v Maxwell* (2006) 59 ACSR 373; [2006] NSWSC 1052; *Angas Law Services Pty Ltd (in liq) v Carabelas* (2005) 226 CLR 507.

In the case of a breach of s 184, based on misappropriation, it is difficult to see that approval in general meeting would be sufficient to prevent prosecution when the provision is clearly designed as a channel for public reprobation of these activities.

Keep in Mind

- Do not presume that because the board has the power to instigate legal proceedings, approval by the board is sufficient to stop or prevent legal proceedings. The power to control a company's right to sue is complex, and it is the main area where the company in general meeting has a reserve power and where the principle of fraud on the minority effects a limit on the majority voting power.
- Each of the five requirements of s 237(2) must be satisfied before the court is obliged to grant leave. The onus of proving each of the criteria falls on the plaintiff. For summary of the legal principles on the operation of the statutory derivative action, see *Re Zoe Corporation Pty Ltd* [2020] NSWSC 1431; *Blakeney v Blakeney* [2016] WASCA 76.

Chapter 9

Debt and Equity Fundraising

9-1 This chapter is concerned with the mix adopted by companies between debt and equity capital. In **Chapter 7** we discussed the concept of capital, particularly share capital and the rules relating to reductions in share capital. In this chapter we consider the various means by which a company obtains funds to carry out its ordinary business or to undertake new or expanded enterprise options. In each corporate finance problem, the legal requirements are often not determinative of which method of finance is chosen. The method will be determined by the company's gearing ratio (level of debt to equity), existing creditor and shareholder expectations, prevailing and expected interest rates, taxation benefits and the market for various types of investment.

Notwithstanding these very strong factors, it is important to understand that each finance option creates a different legal relationship with its own duties and rights.

'Debt capital' is that capital which is acquired through various types of lending contracts or instruments; for example, through single or syndicated loan facilities, debentures or unsecured notes. The capital contributor is a creditor and, apart from the creditor's rights during various types of external administration of the company (such as priority in a winding up), all these rights and obligations are determined by the terms of the contract between the company and the creditor. Principally, these terms can be categorised as rights to interest, repayment of capital and possibly security (depending on the particular instrument). While the making of ordinary loans is generally not regulated by the Corporations Act, debentures and unsecured notes can fall within the requirements of Ch 2L (debentures) and Ch 6D (public fundraising). Furthermore, the security granted by debtor companies is likely to come within the requirements of the Personal Property Securities Act 2009 (Cth) (PPSA). Corporate secured transactions were previously regulated by Ch 2K (charges) of the Corporations Act which was repealed in 2012 after a national system for dealing with security over personal property was introduced.

'Equity capital' is usually made up of shares except in companies limited by guarantee. The rights of shareholders are determined partly by the Corporations Act, partly by the statutory contract which is the company's constitution (s 140), and partly by the terms of the share issue. The rights of shareholders can be categorised into control rights (voting, right to stand for election as a director), dividend rights, information rights about corporate affairs and a right to repayment after creditors in a winding up.

Apart from these intrinsic differences between debt and equity capital, there are some other extrinsic differences, such as tax liability on income (interest/dividends), and deductibility of costs associated with each type. Each type of capital is a form of intangible property in the hands of the creditor or shareholder, with different rules at common law and under the Corporations Act for their transfer. Debt can be transferred as any chose in action can be transferred. Shares cannot be transferred without the assent of the corporation, which is signified by the registration of the transfer. Both types of capital, however, are termed 'securities' of a corporation (s 92) (note: debt may be classified as a debenture under s 9), and are subject to similar transfer documents at the relevant securities exchange: Pt 7.11.

While debt and equity capital display quite distinct rights and obligations, the terms of issue of shares and the terms of the contract in respect of the debt are highly negotiable. Examples of equity capital, such as redeemable preference shares, can quite closely mirror the rights and obligations of standard debt relationships. Debt capital can be issued on terms that it is convertible to equity at some future time. This flexibility in each type of capital means that a corporation's capital requirements can be structured to take advantage of prevailing interest rates and expected market changes to minimise the cost of the capital.

The choice of the type of capital, however, will be followed by various regulations under the Corporations Act. In respect of public issues of securities (either shares or debentures), there are strict and extensive requirements for the lodgment of a disclosure document (for example, a prospectus): Ch 6D. The Ch 6D requirements are closely monitored by ASIC in pursuance of that organisation's role in promoting an efficient capital market through investor protection. The primary function underlying Ch 6D is to address the imbalance of information between issuers of securities and potential investors: *ASIC v Axis International Management Pty Ltd (No 5)* [2011] FCA 60. The Ch 6D provisions are then supplemented by a range of civil liability provisions and offences to ensure due diligence and best practice in disclosure of information to potential investors.

Part 6D.3A (introduced piecemeal in 2017–18) provides the legal framework for equity-based crowd-sourced funding (CSF) by eligible companies and contains the reporting, audit and governance requirements applicable to unlisted public companies and proprietary companies making CSF offers.

Debentures, as a form of debt capital (see s 9), are also heavily regulated by the Corporations Act. As well as the prospectus requirements, a debenture issue is also governed by a regime whereby debentures must be secured and they must be subject to the imposition of a trustee and prescribed trust deed for the protection of debenture holders: Ch 2L. In recognising the inability of debenture holders to have any say in the management of the corporation and its fortunes, there are provisions to provide information to the trustee for debenture holders and to promise in the trust deed to use best endeavours in managing the corporation: Pt 2L.2.

Debt capital, like other borrowings, will often come with the need for the debtor company to provide security for its repayment. Companies can offer the same range of securities that individuals can (such as mortgages, liens and pledges) and further forms of security such as floating charges (as it was then called prior to security law reform in 2012). Prior to 2012, most (but not all) of these forms of secured transactions were regulated by Ch 2K of the Corporations Act as they were treated as company charges. That Chapter of the Act provided rules for the registration of charges, and detailed priority rules for competitions between registered and unregistered charges. On 31 January 2012 that system was replaced by the new Personal Property Securities Register (PPSR) (see <www.ppsr.gov.au>) and the regime brought in by the PPSA.

The PPSA moves away from the prior approach under Ch 2K of the Corporations Act because it is focused on the substance, rather than the form, of a transaction. This can be seen from the central concept of a security interest. Section 12(1) of the PPSA defines a security interest as 'an interest in personal property provided for by a transaction that, in substance, secures payment or performance of an obligation (without regard to the form of the transaction or the identity of the person who has title to the property)'. This means that the PPSA applies to the transaction regardless of whether it is categorised as a charge or a mortgage. The concept of a security interest also includes certain arrangements that are deemed to be security interests: s 12(3). If the PPSA applies to the transaction (note that some arrangements are excluded from the PPSA under s 8) then the range of priority rules under the PPSA applies. There is also a range of enforcement rules, but these do not apply to companies in receivership (s 116) or to deemed security interests. The priority rules focus on the concept of perfection, with a perfected security interest defeating an unperfected security interest (s 55(3)) much as a registered charge would previously beat an unregistered charge. Perfection is based on a number of steps (see PPSA ss 19–21), with perfected status not being achieved until all steps are satisfied at the same time. For most arrangements the secured party will need to register their interest on the PPSR (called registering a financing statement): see PPSA Pt 5.3. There are various rules that must be satisfied in order to effect a valid registration: see PPSA s 153 and Pt 5.4. The failure to perfect a security interest may lead to the secured party losing that security interest if the company enters formal insolvency (see PPSA ss 267–268; Corporations Act s 588FL) or losing a priority contest to another secured party (PPSA s 55). Certain types of security arrangements are given super priority under the PPSA: see, for example, ss 57 (perfection by control), 62 (purchase money security interests). In most compulsory corporate law subjects only a basic understanding of the PPSA is required.

Before attempting the questions below, be sure that you understand the following:

✓ What are the key characteristics of equity capital?

✓ What are the key characteristics of debt capital?

✓ All forms of capital have terms or conditions which are negotiable, leading to certain forms of capital displaying characteristics of both debt and equity — redeemable preference shares.

✓ What is the source of a company's power to issue shares and how is it regulated by the Corporations Act?

✓ All companies may raise capital — it is simply that proprietary companies (other than crowd-sourced funded proprietary companies) may not raise capital in such a way that they would require a prospectus.

✓ There are categories of capital raising or offers of securities which do not require a prospectus.

✓ There is a range of disclosure documents apart from a prospectus.

✓ If the capital raising requires a prospectus then there are extensive provisions in Ch 6D covering the content and quality of the information to be included.

✓ The Corporations Act provides for civil and criminal liability in respect of false and misleading material in disclosure documents and financial services in general.

✓ Defective disclosure may also give rise to common law liability for misleading or false statements for both the company, its directors and possibly advisers.

✓ Companies can give the same types of securities as natural persons as well as securities previously known as floating charges.

✓ The PPSA provides a system of registration of personal property securities and there may be adverse consequences for a secured party if they fail to perfect their security interest.

Question 35

Blinkie Blankets Pty Ltd manufactures bedding. The directors wish to upgrade the weaving processes at their plant so as to increase production. William Blinkie, the company accounts clerk, suggests to the board that they could finance the upgrade by issuing redeemable preference shares. The board is concerned that issuing such securities will impose an ongoing interest obligation.

Advise the board of directors.

Time allowed: 25 minutes

Answer Plan

Corporate finance questions can be very broadly based. Financing an acquisition can be achieved in many different ways and all with their own advantages or disadvantages. The difficulty is in confining the answer. This question is fairly focused on a particular finance method and a good answer will retain that focus primarily but also indicate that there may be other methods.

The answer ought to comply with the following pattern:

- What are redeemable preference shares?
- In answering the first question, there ought to be a reference to the difference between debt and equity and that these shares are a hybrid form of capital.
- Does this company, as a proprietary company, have power to issue such shares?
- How does a company issue such shares and what are the costs of doing so?
- What are the advantages and disadvantages of this type of finance?

Answer

9-2 I have been asked to advise the board of directors of Blinkie Blankets as to the suitability of raising further finance through the issue of redeemable preference shares.

Redeemable preference shares are a class of preference shares which are redeemable; that is, they may be bought back by the company that issues them. As a general rule, a company may not buy back its own shares as to do so would offend the rule in *Trevor v Whitworth* (1887) 12 App Cas 409 which requires a company to maintain its capital. Despite this rule, however, companies are permitted to issue redeemable preference shares but only if their constitutions permit them to do so and only on the terms upon which they are issued.

Section 254A(1)(b) provides that a company's power to issue shares includes the power to issue redeemable preference shares. This power is regardless of the existence of a power in the company's constitution. Section 254A(3) provides the range of circumstances in which redeemable shares may be liable to be redeemed. Certainly, they can only be redeemed on the same terms upon which they were issued unless the redemption is part of a reduction of capital or share buy-back under Ch 2J. Because these shares are an exception to the maintenance of capital doctrine it is not possible to convert shares into redeemable preference shares if they were not issued on such terms: s 254G(3).

There are restrictions upon the means by which a company can redeem these shares. So as not to prejudice creditors (and the doctrine of maintenance of capital) these shares may only be redeemed if they are fully paid up and then only out of profits or the proceeds of a new issue of shares made for the purpose of the redemption: s 254K. Shares are cancelled after they are redeemed: s 254J(1). See further *Heesh v Baker* [2008] NSWSC 711. A redeemable preference share has characteristics of both equity and debt capital. It is a share and as such it carries voting rights, although these may be restricted. It is entitled to a dividend, but as a preference share it will be at a predetermined rate in a similar fashion to interest being payable on a debt. If the preferential dividend is cumulative then it will be payable whether there is a profit or not as the amount of dividend simply accumulates until there is a profit from which it can be paid.

The main difference between debt and equity is the obligation to repay. A shareholder is only repaid by the company in a winding up, whereas a creditor is repaid at the end of the term of the loan. If, as is possible, the redemption date is at a fixed future time then the difference between a redeemable preference share and a debt is nominal only. Because redeemable preference shares can have a range of terms and rights attaching to them it is often said that they are a hybrid form of capital with elements of both debt and equity depending on the terms of issue.

Blinkie is a proprietary company. Redeemable preference shares can be issued by any company as there is no restriction of this class of shares to any particular form of company. Blinkie's restriction is contained only in the method of issuing or offering the shares. As a proprietary company it is not permitted to engage in any activity that would require the lodgment of a prospectus or other disclosure document, unless it is a crowd-sourced funded offer (which is not readily apparent in this case): s 113(3).

This restriction may not be a difficulty for Blinkie as it will probably be able to issue the shares without a disclosure document. The requirement to lodge a disclosure document is set out in ss 706 and 707. However, the requirement to lodge a disclosure document is predicated by exclusions set out in s 708. Blinkie needs to examine how much capital it needs for its upgrade program. If it is a relatively small amount then it may invite subscription either from large investors at a minimum of $500,000 or it may make a private offer to less than 20 investors for no more than $2 million in total: s 708. In each of these circumstances, there is no requirement for a disclosure document.

It is certainly a benefit in reduced costs to not require a disclosure document, although potential investors under these exceptions will undoubtedly require a large amount of information to be prepared and presented before deciding to acquire redeemable preference shares.

Before concluding whether or not to issue shares of this nature, Blinkie needs to examine other forms of finance to compare the costs and benefits. I am assuming that the capital requirements are not vast and they may be able to be acquired through a small private offer as outlined above. The obvious alternative for this scale of capital requirement is to borrow the money either from the same individual investors or from a financial institution. The lender becomes a creditor with no vote at all in the affairs of the company, but the certainty of interest payments and repayment of principal are the major concerns. To ensure repayment, the creditor will no doubt require security over some or all of the company's assets. Depending on the type of security required, Blinkie may be subject to some restrictions in its right to use or dispose of certain assets subject to the security.

For Blinkie, the obvious benefit of a redeemable preference share issue would be that there is no requirement for the grant of any security. The shareholder bears the risk as do the other shareholders in the company. The investor will want to make up for this perceived loss of security by requiring a higher return (dividend) on the investment, certainty of redemption date and a measure of voting control in the way the company is managed. At the very least, the investor will want information or access to information about the company's affairs so that it can reduce its risk if the company is not performing as expected.

In conclusion, the real question for Blinkie is whether redeemable preference shares are attractive enough for investors, or whether a standard borrowing arrangement with security is going to be more attractive. These are not legal questions but finance or investment decisions. Certainly, it is possible to raise the finance through a small or private issue of redeemable preference shares; however, there are other available methods of financing these ventures. Costs and marketability will largely determine the choice; however, there is a need to consider the basic question of whether the company wishes to further broaden its equity base and potential voting interests or to retain control and simply deal on a contractual basis with lenders. Redeemable preference shares can sometimes be viewed as a compromise in this choice between debt and equity capital because of the limited voting rights and the relative certainty of redemption.

 ## Examiner's Comments

9-3 In relation to the definition of a redeemable preference share, there could be some further development of what is meant by the term. Sections 9 and 254A(3) define these shares as a preference share in a body corporate that is liable to be redeemed. The share must be a preference share first, as well as having the option of or a set redemption date: *Heesh v Baker* [2008] NSWSC 711. If the only preference is an option for redemption then this is not a traditional preference share and therefore it could not be a redeemable preference share. A 'traditional' preference share, while not defined in the Corporations Act, gives a preferential right over ordinary shares to a dividend: *Re Brighton & Dyke Rly* (1890) 44 Ch D 28. It is worth noting that preference shares are designated as such by the terms of their issue and the terms of the company's constitution, not simply by their differing rights to other shares issued by the company: *Beck v Weinstock* (2013) 251 CLR 425. Certainly, s 254A(2) contemplates that preference shares will have certain rights over dividends and priority of repayment amongst other things, as these matters must be set out in the company's constitution or in a special resolution. By their separate and additional treatment in s 254A(3) in respect of the terms of redemption it is confirmed that an option to redeem only is not something which will cause the share to be categorised as a redeemable preference share.

It would also be of value to address the doctrine of maintenance of capital in the context of these types of shares. Clearly, if a company issued a minimum of ordinary shares and then a large number of redeemable preference shares that were redeemable at the company's option then this would defeat the doctrine of maintenance of capital. Listed companies are restricted by the ASX Listing Rules to only issuing certain amounts of redeemable preference shares expressed as a percentage of total capital. All companies are restricted to redeeming these shares only out of profits or from the proceeds of a new issue of shares for the redemption: s 254K. This provision thus preserves capital for the protection of creditors.

Of course, problems arise if the shares carry a set redemption date or a shareholder's option to redeem and there are no profits available to redeem. The judicial view was that in such a case the company clearly could not meet its contractual obligations under the terms of issue and that it could face being wound up, if it was not insolvent, upon the just and equitable ground in s 461: *TNT Australia Pty Ltd v Normandy Resources NL* (1989) 1 ACSR 1. However, since July 1998 the company may now avail itself of the buy-back procedure under Pt 2J.1 which would permit a buy-back even on terms different from the original issue, so long as there is no material prejudice to creditors and shareholders.

The buy-back, of course, can be funded out of capital. Blinkie Pty Ltd therefore would need to ensure that at the redemption date it has sufficient profits to redeem. Perhaps a redemption date at the company's option would assist in this regard, although this may not be attractive to investors.

Keep in Mind

- A common error in this type of question is to assume that all share issues are public issues and that they therefore require a prospectus. Proprietary companies are not prohibited from making a share issue; the prohibition is to not engage in issues or offers which require a disclosure document under Ch 6D (such as a prospectus), unless it is a crowd-sourced funded offer: s 113(3). Generally, subject to this exception in s 113(3), only public offers require a disclosure document.
- If Blinkie Pty Ltd approached a bank or a merchant bank, the bank may arrange for the capital to be 'advanced' to Blinkie in return for the issue of a parcel of redeemable preference shares or a debenture or some other form of security. The terms of issue of the redeemable preference shares, or other security, would reflect the terms of the loan. Be careful about mixing up equity and debt issues, both of which can be classified as 'securities' under s 92.

Question 36

> 'Companies must find the right mix of debt and equity to suit their corporate goals.'
>
> Critically evaluate this statement with reference to the commercial practicalities of debt and equity financing.
>
> **Time allowed: 25 minutes**

Answer Plan

Rather than posing a problem, this question requires an essay type of answer. The essay should start with an *introduction* in which the scope of the discussion is outlined.

The body of the essay should:

- define debt and equity finance;
- provide an outline of the different types of equity and debt financing;
- discuss the requirements of the Corporations Act for equity and debt financing; and
- weigh up the advantages and disadvantages associated with equity and debt finance.

Having discussed each of these matters, students should then address the central issue of the question — why companies should have an appropriate mix of equity and debt finance.

The conclusion should sum up all of the arguments raised in the essay into one coherent thread.

 ## Answer

9-4 There are many stages in a company's life when additional finance is necessary or beneficial to the business. When a company wishes to expand its operations, it is usually necessary for some form of finance to be sought outside of the company's profit reserves. Corporate finance is also necessary when companies face periods of low cash flow and may need additional financial support simply to keep the business going. Regardless of when additional finance is needed by a corporation, the decision between equity and/or debt finance techniques will be an important choice for the company and will have significant ramifications upon the future of the company.

Debt finance may be defined as the process by which companies can obtain loans from creditors. Equity finance can be defined as investments made in the company that expand the ownership base of the company. The major difference between debt and equity finance techniques is that debt finance does not generally confer an ownership right on the creditor, while equity finance creates a proprietary interest in the company for the investor. Members of a company are defined under s 231 and are most often persons who have purchased shares in the company and have had their share transfers registered by the company so that their name is recorded in the company's Register of Members. Members of a company have a range of rights and powers as against the company: see, for example, ss 232 (oppression remedy) and 249F (member's right to call meetings).

The first relevant consideration for any company that is attempting to raise additional capital is the extent to which the company wishes to dilute its present ownership structure. If a company is willing to take on additional members then equity finance may be suitable. If, however, a company does not wish to dilute the share capital which may reduce the stock price for a listed company (because each share represents a lower percentage in ownership of the company as a result of the new equity fundraising) then debt finance may be the most appropriate option.

Ownership is an important issue in relation to equity finance as membership of a company brings with it a range of rights and privileges that are not available to creditors. For example, a company that chooses to raise equity finance by issuing preference shares (s 254A(1)(b)) is creating a right in certain investors to a preferential dividend over a potentially long period of time (which could eventually account for more than the original investment): s 254A(2). By contrast, a simple bank loan would not create any rights in the bank creditor to receive dividends. An interesting point, however, is that ordinary investors are not normally entitled to receive a dividend unless the company declares one: ss 254U and 254V. Creditors, however, are almost without exception entitled to interest on their loan. Debt is a fixed claim on the company while equity is a variable claim (depending on the company's profits, constitution and the decisions of the board of directors).

An issue that is closely related to ownership is that of control. One advantage that significant creditors have in lending money to companies is that they are able to structure the loan agreement by attaching conditions that can give themselves a great deal of power over the debtor company's ability to trade. For example, a significant creditor will usually grant themselves the power in the loan instrument to appoint a receiver over the company's property to preserve the security for the loan. Members of the company, however, do not generally have the power to exercise control of the management of the company, which is left to the board of directors: s 198A. Members are generally restricted to voting for or against directors at the company's annual general meeting: ss 203C and 203D.

Debt finance may also have a negative impact on a company's share price as it will increase a company's gearing ratio (the proportion of the company's total capital that is sourced through debt finance). A company that is highly geared compared with similar businesses may not attract as high a share price as a lower geared company, particularly in times such as the financial crisis of 2007–09 when credit rationing made it difficult for companies to refinance large loan facilities. A company that has a low gearing ratio may, however, become a takeover target as corporate raiders seek to leverage off the extra gearing of the company's assets (a so-called 'lazy balance-sheet'). Therefore, the company must find an appropriate level of gearing that will not overburden the company with debt, but will maximise the finance leverage that can be gained against the company's asset base.

Taxation is always an important issue in determining the level of debt or equity financing. Generally speaking, interest costs on debt financing may be tax deductible, while dividend payments on equity finance are not tax deductible. This may present a significant benefit, particularly where the company is part of a group and the tax losses/deductions may be shared between the group companies.

Disclosure and liabilities flowing from defective disclosure is also an important consideration in deciding on a company's debt/equity mix. Where a company chooses to raise equity finance it will ordinarily be subjecting itself to a range of detailed and sometimes expensive disclosure requirements under Ch 6D of the Corporations Act that must be satisfied before the new issue may proceed. Applying for debt finance may, however, also require extensive disclosure in that creditors may require their own inspection of the company's financial position before lending money to the company. The PPSA also provides that the details of certain types of debt finance techniques must be perfected (usually by registration and compliance with the PPSA); for example, company charges. The difference, however, lies in the liability that may arise from the different type of finance. Equity finance techniques are required to comply with extensive requirements under Chs 6D and 7 of the Corporations Act. Where the equity issue is made using defective disclosure documents, investors have a general right to compensation under s 729 and persons involved in the contravention of s 728 (which prohibits misleading and deceptive statements and material omissions from disclosure documents) may be subject to civil and criminal penalties. Debt finance, on the other hand, does not have as onerous requirements and does not generally provide broad rights to compensation for creditors, although debenture holders do have compensation rights: s 283F. Debentures issued to the public under Ch 6D will also have disclosure and compensation rights.

In conclusion, it is clear that the statement reflects the commercial reality of modern corporate finance. Each company will have different future goals, and finding the right mix of debt and equity finance will be an important element in achieving those goals. As has been shown above, the choice of debt or equity finance will have a significant impact on the management, ownership and financial viability of the company. There is no magic formula for the optimal mix of debt and equity. Rather, each company must decide how to maximise the benefits and minimise the disadvantages associated with various debt and equity finance techniques and, more importantly, how these features match up with the future direction of the company.

Examiner's Comments

9-5 This answer could be improved by being more detailed on the disclosure requirements of equity and debt finance raisings. The response would also benefit by being more detailed about the range of equity and debt finance options. Several paragraphs explaining the advantages and disadvantages of company charges (now security interests) and debentures (debt) and different classes of shares and options (equity) would make the answer more comprehensive.

One important area that was not covered by the answer is the rules imposed by the ASX (the Listing Rules). These rules regulate how listed companies structure their businesses and they provide disclosure requirements that exist in addition to those contained in the Corporations Act.

 Keep in Mind

- This question is an essay that requires the student to do more than simply list relevant considerations in deciding between equity and debt finance. Ensure that the answer addresses the question by critically evaluating the need for an appropriate mix of both types of finance techniques.

Question 37

Aztec Mining Pty Ltd is a small gold mining company operating in Western Australia. It is looking to expand its exploration operations but needs more funds to do this. Company management is looking for ways to raise the necessary funds for the expansion, estimated to be approximately $10 million. Each of the directors of Aztec already has shares in the company as do most of the employees. Aztec management have also had discussions with the president of the Golden Nuggets Chamber of Commerce about developing some form of community investment in the company.

One of the major investors in the company is the wealthy Perth businesswoman Rina Lionheart. Management have previously approached Mrs Lionheart to see if she would be willing to make a larger investment in the company, but she has been hesitant. She now seems willing to make a larger investment but wants to obtain the protection of being a creditor, rather than taking on more equity (at least at this stage). Aztec has an existing secured loan facility with Eastbank which has registered an all present and after acquired security interest on the PPSR. The loan with Eastbank is fully drawn down and the bank has refused a request for an overdraft facility. Mrs Lionheart is keen to obtain the maximum priority for her debt investment.

Advise Aztec as to how it may structure a capital raising to raise $10 million.

Time allowed: 45 minutes

Answer Plan

This question concerns the fundraising options available to Aztec Mining Pty Ltd. The answer will need to start with a recognition that Aztec is a proprietary company and is therefore more limited in its options compared with a public company. The answer will need to discuss the range of debt and equity fundraising options.

Fundraising options

- What options does Aztec have?
- What relevant considerations will shape the decision?
- Consider debt and equity capital raising.

Will Ch 6D require a disclosure document?

- Will the fundraising involve the issuing of securities?
- Will Aztec need to issue a disclosure document?
- What consequences may arise for Aztec and its officers if it fails to comply with Ch 6D?

The priority of Rina's debt

- Does Rina Lionheart have a perfected PPSA security interest?
- What consequences may arise if Rina does not have a perfected PPSA security interest?

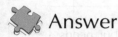 Answer

Fundraising options

9-6 Aztec Mining Pty Ltd appears to have a wide range of both debt and equity fundraising options. On the debt side, Aztec already has a debt facility with Eastbank which may restrict what further debt (at least secured debt) Aztec can enter into. Aztec may be able to raise further funds by negotiating a refinancing with Eastbank, but the bank's rejection of the overdraft facility would suggest this is unlikely.

Aztec may also consider issuing debentures, but these are categorised as securities and Aztec may need to comply with Ch 6D (discussed below). Debentures issued by Aztec may include convertible rights so that the debentures convert into shares at a future time, either at the option of the creditor or of the company. Aztec's constitution should be examined to ensure that such an arrangement is permitted (or at least not restricted or prohibited). This may appeal to existing shareholders who may be able to obtain a greater level of priority through debt while still getting access to future equity increases through the convertible rights. Debentures issued by Aztec may be either secured (covered by a PPSA security interest) or unsecured (in which case they are referred to as unsecured notes).

On the equity side, Aztec may issue ordinary shares (usually with one vote per share and a right to share in dividend distributions), preference shares (which have some measure of extra rights compared with ordinary shares) or options to acquire shares in the company at a future time.

The decision as to whether to issue debt and/or equity, and in what proportions, will be made according to a range of factors, including the following:

- The company's existing debt profile — can it support further debt? Will the bank allow further debt to be issued?
- The effect of an equity or convertible capital raising on the existing shareholders — how will they react to having their control positions diluted?
- The tax effects of any capital raising.

It is important to note that Aztec is a Pty Ltd company and as such it is prohibited from engaging in conduct that would require the release of a formal disclosure document under Ch 6D of the Corporations Act: s 113(3). It should be noted that this prohibition does not apply where an issue of shares that would require a disclosure document is made to existing shareholders or to employees. Thus, it is possible that Aztec could raise some or all of its $10 million target by offering shares to employees or existing shareholders. However, the capacity of existing shareholders must be considered. Proprietary companies are not permitted to have more than 50 non-employee shareholders: s 113(1). This means that the pool of potential shareholders who may take up the offer of shares is limited. We are also not told of the numbers of employees. Nonetheless an offer may be made. The exception in s 113(3) also only applies to shares. Existing shareholders (including the directors and employees) may not wish to take on more equity in the business, but may wish to diversify their investments. The need to prepare a disclosure document under Ch 6D (such as a prospectus) is also a disincentive to make an issue under s 113(3) as it would involve considerable time and money to complete, although an exemption may be available under s 708(13), (14).

Compliance with Ch 6D

9-7 Chapter 6D of the Corporations Act will have a significant impact on Aztec's fundraising activities. It is important to determine if Aztec's fundraising would involve the issue or sale of 'securities'. This term is defined in s 92(d) as having the meaning in s 700. Section 700 then refers to s 761A which includes the singular term security, defined as:

(a) a share in a body; or
(b) a debenture of a body; or
(c) a legal or equitable right or interest in a security covered by paragraph (a) or (b); or
(d) an option to acquire, by way of issue, a security covered by paragraph (a), (b) or (c) [paragraphs (e) and (f) are excluded by s 700].

Options to issue securities are also covered by Ch 6D: s 702.

Thus, if Aztec issues shares or debentures it will be issuing securities to which Ch 6D applies. A debenture is a chose in action that includes an undertaking to repay money lent to the company: s 9. If Aztec issues debt instruments to raise some or all of its $10 million target it will need to comply with Ch 6D because it will be issuing securities.

If Ch 6D applies then Aztec must issue a disclosure document for the securities unless exempted by Ch 6D; mainly ss 708 and 708A: ss 704 and 706. In this situation it seems that Aztec may use the small-scale exception under s 708(1)–(7). This would allow Aztec to raise up to $2 million, by making offers to no more than 20 investors within a 12-month period. It must be verified that Aztec has not raised any further capital by issuing securities in the prior 12 months: s 708(3). These securities may be offered to existing shareholders, including employees. Alternatively, these securities may be offered to members of the local community, although the offers must be personal offers (that is, no more than 20 offers may be made), but a broad audience may be canvassed before making the offers. It should be noted that s 734 will restrict advertising of these offers so Aztec should work with the local chamber of commerce to identify who may be suitable to participate in the offer.

In addition to this small-scale capital raising, Aztec may make offers to sophisticated investors under s 708(8). This may be targeted at Rina who may be able to buy at least $500,000 worth of securities and would seem to satisfy the assets and income tests (which would need to be verified by a qualified accountant). Any money raised by issuing securities to Rina would not be counted in the small-scale capital raising: s 708(5). Rina may also be a professional investor if she has or controls at least $10 million in assets: s 708(11).

Aztec may also be able to arrange for a financial services licensee to make the offers, perhaps to the members of the local chamber of commerce: s 708(10). However, this puts the risk onto the financial adviser, and they may be unwilling to undertake this for a private company.

Lastly, Aztec may issue securities to existing holders under s 708(13) (for shares) and s 708(14) (for debentures). It should be noted that the facts do not disclose any existing debenture holders so s 708(14) may not be available.

The failure to comply with Ch 6D is an offence under s 727. Aztec's directors and officers could also be in breach of their directors' duties if they allow the company to contravene Ch 6D: see *ASIC v Maxwell* (2006) 59 ACSR 373; *ASIC v Sino Australia Oil and Gas Ltd (in liq)* [2016] FCA 934; civil penalty decision in [2016] FCA 1488.

If Aztec issues debentures it may need to comply with Ch 2L. This usually applies only to public issues of debentures under a disclosure document, but s 283AA provides that an issue under s 708(14) must also comply with Ch 2L. This will require a debenture trustee to be appointed and the establishment of a debenture trust deed: s 283AA. However, as noted above, there do not appear to be any existing debenture holders so as long as Aztec issues the debentures under one of the other exceptions under s 708 it will not need to comply with Ch 2L.

The priority of Rina's debt

9-8 If Rina makes a secured loan to Aztec she should run a search of the PPSR which will reveal Eastbank's security interest. Eastbank will take priority over a simple secured loan by Rina under the priority rules in s 55 of the PPSA. This will occur regardless of whether Rina perfects her security interest or not. Rina should still perfect her security interest to ensure that she does not lose out to another secured party. Rina may negotiate with Eastbank to either buy out its debt or enter into a subordination agreement to elevate the priority of her debt: PPSA s 61.

Rina may enter into asset-based finance such as a finance lease to Aztec which could be classified as a PMSI and take priority over Eastbank, but only over the goods leased to Aztec: PPSA s 62.

Another option would be to issue Rina with convertible debentures which have equity upside, or to issue redeemable preference shares which have fixed payment rights as well as the right to redeem them (either at the company's option or at Rina's option): s 254A. Of course, shares are securities under s 92 and an issue to Rina will need to comply with Ch 6D (discussed above).

Examiner's Comments

9-9 This question covers a broad range of both debt and equity issues. There are a number of areas that need consideration:

- Consider the full range of potential fundraising options; don't just consider equity capital raisings.
- Consider what may be more or less appealing to investors and to the company. Discuss different features of particular forms of capital raisings.
- There is no need to go through the detailed provisions in Ch 2L; be guided by how much your course considered this issue.
- There is no need to go through too much detail on the PPSA unless your course covers this in detail. A basic knowledge of the consequences of failing to perfect and the main priority rules is usually sufficient.
- It could be useful to discuss potential liability outside of Ch 6D given a disclosure document is unlikely to be used: s 1041H.

Keep in Mind

- Do not get bogged down in giving general descriptions of how the law works (for example, going through each step in issuing a disclosure document). Not every part of Ch 6D will be relevant.
- Be sure to go over the definitions of key terms (for example, securities and debentures) carefully.

Question 38

> Poseidon NL wishes to raise $10 million for its proposed gold mine in North Queensland. There is a likely equity partner in the form of an offer of $3 million from another mining company, Prospector NL. The remainder of the funding, however, will have to be raised by issuing more shares.
>
> Advise Poseidon NL of the requirements of the Corporations Act in relation to this fundraising exercise.
>
> **Time allowed: 35 minutes**

Answer Plan

There are two fundraising issues in this problem. There is the $3 million contribution from Prospector NL and the public float for $7 million.

In each of these fundraising activities there is a need to look at the requirements of the Corporations Act.

The Prospector arrangement

- Consider the nature of the investment. Will it be a partnership/joint venture or basic share purchase arrangement?

The public float

- Consider whether a disclosure document under Ch 6D is needed: see ss 708 and 708A.
- If a disclosure document is needed, outline the main requirements of such a document.

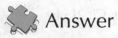

Answer

The Prospector arrangement

9-10 The offer of significant funds from Prospector NL may be made in a number of ways. It is common in the mining and exploration industry for individuals or corporations to form a joint venture for a specific project or undertaking. A joint venture is similar in many respects to a partnership, although there are some basic differences between them. A joint venture is formed through a contract, as is a partnership, and it may or may not be conducted through the medium of a manager which may be a separate corporation specifically formed for the venture. It was stated in the High Court in *United Dominions Corporations Ltd v Brian Pty Ltd* (1985) 59 ALJR 676 at 679 that a joint venture is not a technical term with a defined legal meaning:

> As a matter of ordinary language, it connotes an association of persons for the purposes of a particular trading, commercial, mining or other financial undertaking or endeavour with a view to mutual profit, with each participant usually (but not necessarily) contributing money, property or skill. Such a joint venture ... will often be a partnership. The term is, however, apposite to refer to a joint undertaking or activity carried out through a medium other than a partnership such as a company, a trust, an agency or joint ownership. The borderline between what can be properly described as a 'joint venture' and what should more properly be seen as no more than a simple contractual relationship may on occasion be blurred.

While there may be points of difference between partnerships and joint ventures, the point of commonality is that they are contractual arrangements between participants. The joint venture itself is not governed by the Corporations Act unless the participants incorporate a company for the purpose of managing the joint venture. In this case, the Corporations Act governs its incorporation and it would probably require a constitution setting out the terms of the joint venture. Joint ventures commonly also have separate shareholder agreements which further define the rights as between shareholders. It is also possible for the relationship between the companies to be characterised as a partnership, in which case the provisions of the partnership in the state where the business is operating would have effect.

If the contribution by Prospector is to be by way of an issue of shares then, apart from questions concerning any breach of duty by directors and changes in control of the company, Poseidon NL needs to examine whether or not such an issue of shares requires a prospectus.

Sections 706 and 707 require that all offers and invitations to subscribe for securities of a corporation must, unless exempted (primarily under s 708), be accompanied by a disclosure document.

Chapter 6D of the Corporations Act sets out a regulatory scheme for fundraising by the issue of securities and embodies the philosophy of investor protection through disclosure. The scheme recognises that not all investors need the degree of disclosure mandated by a prospectus. Therefore, it provides for a range of shorter disclosure documents (short form prospectus; profile statement) which may be issued after a full prospectus has been lodged with ASIC (investors are still entitled to request a copy of the full prospectus) or an offer information statement which may be used instead of a prospectus but requires ASIC approval.

The main class of exceptions to this disclosure regime is set out in s 708 and covers a great range of issues, offers and invitations. The common thread or attribute of these categories is, however, that the potential investor is sophisticated enough or well advised enough to be able to make decisions and demand information individually from the offering corporation. In particular, s 708(8) refers to offers, invitations or subscriptions where the minimum subscription for each investor is $500,000. It is assumed that investors of this calibre do not need the protection of a prospectus. Prospector would clearly come within this category and so there would be no need to lodge or register a disclosure for the $3 million share issue.

Poseidon and Prospector simply need to determine through negotiation the terms of the share issue. It is also possible that the share issue could come within the rights issue exception in s 708AA, although there is nothing in the facts of the question to suggest that this would apply.

The public issue

9-11   Unless the $7 million share issue can fit within one of the exceptions contained in s 708 or s 708A, then a disclosure document must be issued: s 706. The question does not specify what type of investors may take up the public issue. The exceptions relating to sophisticated investors (s 708(8) and (11)), issues through licensed financial services licensees (s 708(10)) and offers to existing securities holders (s 708(13)) or those persons associated with the company (such as directors: see s 708(12)) may apply, but the question does not provide sufficient information to make a positive determination. Therefore, it is assumed that these exceptions do not apply and the issue requires a disclosure document.

The most comprehensive form of disclosure document is a prospectus which must be lodged with ASIC. The difficulty associated with issuing a prospectus to the public is that they tend to be lengthy and complicated documents which are not always easily understandable by all types of investors. Therefore, Poseidon may wish to issue a short-form prospectus while lodging a full prospectus with ASIC that can be obtained by any interested investors.

The issuing of a profile statement or offer information statement would require the approval of ASIC: s 709(3). Offer information statements may only be used where the securities issue is valued at less than $10 million: s 709(4). However, there may be concern that lodging a shorter document may not provide sufficient information to attract investors, or may include less than full information which could lead to shareholder litigation if the company's future does not provide solid results. Therefore, I assume that Poseidon will issue a prospectus.

The fundraising requirements of the Corporations Act are based upon the desire to protect investors by forcing disclosure of material information which may affect the value of the securities offered and by imposing liability upon those involved in the preparation and publication of that information. Those who are involved in the preparation of disclosure documents are required to test the accuracy of the information with due diligence, or be liable for losses to investors as a result of that information: ss 728 and 729.

The content of a prospectus is governed by both general (s 710) and specific (s 711) requirements as to form and content. Section 713 applies to listed corporations which are already subject to the continuous disclosure provisions of the Corporations Act. This section relieves them of some of the disclosure requirements on the basis that this information has already been disclosed to the relevant securities exchange.

In addition to the form and content provisions, s 721 requires that the application form for subscriptions must be attached to the prospectus, this being one way to ensure that each subscriber at least will have available the information required by Ch 6D.

Section 710(1) imports a standard for the information which is commonly known as the reasonable investor standard. It is information which must be of sufficient quantity and quality for a reasonable investor to be able to make an informed decision about whether to invest in that corporation.

Given the nature of this corporation's activities and the purpose of the fundraising, it would be essential to include expert reports in the prospectus as to the viability of the mine and its potential gold yield. Investors will also need to be able to assess the reliability of the financial statements and projections for the project and it would be usual, therefore, to include a statement from the auditors. The requirements of s 710 are deliberately general to account for the varying nature of each corporate fundraising activity. Thus, the ultimate test of what is needed for an informed decision will depend largely on the amount, purpose and prospects of the company and its project. What reasonable investors and their advisers 'require' and 'expect to find' will vary in the same way.

Those who provide statements in the prospectus may also be liable for defects relating to their statements under ss 728 and 729: see *ASIC v Sino Australia Oil and Gas Ltd (in liq)* [2016] FCA 934. There are defences, however, where those persons did not give permission for their statements to be included in the prospectus: s 733(3).

Examiner's Comments

9-12 Students should expand on the potential liability for defective disclosure documents as set out in Pt 6D.3. Better answers will be more explicit concerning the practical reality of offering new securities including descriptions of the role of underwriters, merchant banks, institutional investors and retail investors. It is also desirable to set out a brief table or dot-point list outlining the main steps in the public fundraising process: see s 717.

Students could note potential liabilities for misleading conduct or statements outside of the prospectus document under s 1041H or s 12DA of the ASIC Act.

Where courses have gone through the detail of exceptions under s 708 (although this is more common for advanced courses on securities law) it would be advisable to discuss the growing body of case law in this area: see, for example, *Gore v ASIC* [2017] FCAFC 13; *ASIC v Astra Resources PLC* [2015] FCA 759; *ASIC v Axis International Management Pty Ltd (No 5)* [2011] FCA 60; *ASIC v Great Northern Developments Pty Ltd* [2010] NSWSC 1087; *ASIC v Cycclone Magnetic Engines Inc* (2009) 71 ACSR 1; *ASIC v Sydney Investment House Equities Pty Ltd* (2008) 69 ACSR 1; *ASIC v Maxwell* (2006) 59 ACSR 373.

Keep in Mind

- The most common error in this type of question is to assume that a public issue of shares also necessarily involves the corporation listing on a securities exchange. Public companies do not have to list in order to make a public offer of shares (listing can be expensive) but it will provide a ready and efficient market for the sale of shares in the company. Public offers, particularly from a listed company, will generally also be accompanied by an underwriting agreement to ensure a sale of the shares.

Question 39

Worldwide News Ltd issued a prospectus in which it offered ordinary shares to the public. The purpose of the issue was to finance the expansion of Worldwide into television broadcasting. The prospectus stated that Worldwide was an applicant for a new television broadcasting licence and, if granted, Worldwide claimed there would be substantial earnings arising from the venture. The prospectus included a report from an auditor which confirmed that the income and profit forecasts were fair and reasonable based on information provided by the directors. The prospectus also included an advice from the solicitors for Worldwide that there was no chance that Worldwide would be unsuccessful in its application for a broadcasting licence.

Worldwide's application for the licence was refused and it now appears that the solicitors' advice was negligent in that it failed to take account of the rules regarding foreign ownership of television broadcasting licences in Australia. Over two million shares were issued pursuant to the prospectus offer.

Who, if anyone, faces liability for the statements in the prospectus and what are the possible outcomes?

Time allowed: 40 minutes

Answer Plan

Liability for statements contained in a prospectus is a complex mix of common law and statutory liability. Liability can be both civil and criminal. It is essential, in order to answer this broad-based question, to break it up into two parts: who may sue and what is the cause of action.

Actions available to investors

- Outline potential common law remedies.
- Discuss potential causes of action under Ch 6D: ss 728 and 729.
- Explain who may be liable under these causes of action.

Actions available to ASIC

- Consider whether any statutory contraventions have occurred and what ASIC's role would be in pursuing actions based on these contraventions.
- What remedies/orders would ASIC be likely to pursue?

Answer

Investors

9-13 A subscriber for shares pursuant to the prospectus will undoubtedly be disappointed when the broadcasting licence is refused. It is likely that the projections for earnings will fall and probably the value of the shares will fall. The investor will clearly be facing some kind of loss. At common law, investors who relied on a prospectus which is subsequently found to contain a misstatement have remedies in both contract and tort against the company and possibly for a breach of fiduciary duty against the directors or promoters of a company. On the basis of the principles set out in *Esanda v Peat Marwick Hungerfords* (1997) 23 ACSR 71, those persons responsible for the preparation of statements on behalf of the company in a prospectus could also be liable in tort to investors.

When an investor subscribes for shares and the offer to subscribe is accepted, there is a contract for the allotment of shares. If the contract was entered into on the basis of a false statement, regardless of whether the false statement was made innocently or fraudulently, the party induced has a right to rescind the contract. The right to rescind can be lost if there is delay or restitution is not possible or if the company commences to wind up. Alternatively, investors may sue the company for fraudulent misrepresentation or deceit and be awarded damages. In this case, the representation may not have been false when it was made but if the company becomes aware that it was false before the contract for allotment was entered and does nothing about it then it would be liable for the false representation: *Jones v Dumbrell* [1981] VR 199.

In *Derry v Peek* (1889) 14 App Cas 337, the directors of the company that had issued the prospectus had honestly believed that the representation in the prospectus was true. The representation was, in many respects, similar to the representation in the question as it was based on the granting of permission or licence by an administrative body. The directors were not liable in deceit in that case because there was no fraudulent or reckless intent in making the statement — rather, it was carelessness. Thus, if the directors of Worldwide News Ltd have been merely careless then they won't be liable in deceit; however, if they become aware of the falsity of the statement and continue to accept subscriptions, their intent is then likely to be fraudulent or reckless.

Tortious liability for negligent misstatement would, however, still be a problem. Certainly, the directors and the company owe a duty to prospective investors regarding the reliability and truthfulness of the prospectus. If it can be shown that there was negligence in permitting the statement to be published in the prospectus, and the investors relied on the statement in making their decision to invest, then the directors and the company would be liable: *Hedley Byrne & Co Ltd v Heller & Partners Ltd* [1964] AC 465. The solicitors would also be liable on the basis that they would have known that their opinion or advice was in the prospectus and that it would be relied upon: *Esanda v Peat Marwick Hungerfords* (above).

In addition to the common law remedies, the Corporations Act makes provision for the civil liability of various persons involved in the preparation and publication of prospectuses. Common law remedies have long been considered inadequate or too difficult to obtain to properly protect investors from mistakes and omissions in prospectuses.

The key section is s 729 which provides that a person who suffers loss or damage by conduct of another person in contravention of s 728 (misleading or deceptive statements or material omissions) may recover the loss or damage from that person or any other person involved in the contravention. See, for example *ASIC v Sino Australia Oil and Gas Ltd (in liq)* [2016] FCA 934.

Section 729 imports a notion that the loss suffered must have a causative link to the contravention. Section 729(1) provides a right to compensation for a person who suffers loss *because* of a breach of s 728. The investors would therefore need to prove that they relied upon the misstatements in the prospectus in order to obtain compensation: see generally *Ingot Capital Investments Pty Ltd v Macquarie Equity Capital Market Ltd* (2008) 68 ACSR 595; *Wealthsure Pty Ltd v Selig* [2014] FCAFC 64. Under s 729, all persons involved in the contravention would be liable, although the scope of each individual's liability would be determined by which category they fall into under s 729(1). The company, its directors and the underwriter are liable for any contravention, while a person named in the prospectus is liable for the inclusion of the statement. All persons involved in the contravention are liable only for that specific contravention. Section 79 defines the categories of persons involved in a contravention as persons who aid, abet, counsel or procure, or persons who induce, or are knowingly concerned in or who conspire to contravene the section. Being involved in the contravention in the sense set out in ss 729 and 79 therefore requires some intent or knowledge of the contravention. An expert who merely consents to the inclusion of their opinion in a prospectus may well not have this measure of intent. Section 729 also lists as the persons liable not only the company and its directors and promoters, but also any person named in the prospectus with their consent. Whether the solicitors who provided the statement did so as professional advisers, as the solicitor in respect of the prospectus, or simply because of their expertise does not matter, as they would come within at least one if not all three of these categories. The solicitors could be liable under item 5 of the liability table in s 729(1) as it was their statement regarding the licence application that was potentially misleading.

Having established who can be liable, it is necessary to verify what the cause of action may be. Section 728 establishes various causes of action to sue under s 729. Liability is most likely to arise under s 728(1)(a). First, s 728(1)(a) covers misleading or deceptive statements. The High Court stated in *Parkdale Custom Built Furniture Pty Ltd v Puxu Pty Ltd* (1984) 149 CLR 191 at [8] per Gibbs CJ that this term means 'being led into error'. In this case, investors would be likely to believe that the licence application was certain to be granted, which is incorrect. Prima facie, it seems therefore that the company, directors and solicitors would be liable in a civil proceeding for a contravention of s 728 under s 729. The statement was clearly false and, given that the projected earnings were based upon the granting of the broadcast licence, it is certainly a material statement in the prospectus and it would be misleading or likely to mislead.

They would be liable, of course, unless they could make out one of the defences available to them. The range of defences include reasonable reliance on information (s 733(1)), withdrawal of consent to be named in the prospectus (s 733(3)), genuinely unaware of defect (s 733(4)) and due diligence failed to notify of the defect (s 731).

In summary, therefore, the company, its directors and the solicitors may be liable at common law and would face action for rescission of the contract, possible breach of fiduciary duty and negligent misstatement respectively. More certainly, however, the company, its directors and the solicitors would be liable for loss or damage to investors who bring action under s 729 of the Corporations Act. It is not possible to conclude whether any of these persons would be able to make out any defence to the action because of the lack of information; however, it is likely, given that the solicitors are said to have been negligent in the preparation of their advice, that they would not be able to make out a defence of due diligence. The directors may escape liability under s 733.

ASIC

9-14 As the key regulator in the securities market, ASIC has a range of powers both under the Corporations Act and the ASIC Act. ASIC has the power to issue a stop order in respect of an issue of securities in circumstances where it becomes aware that a prospectus would breach s 728: s 739. These powers are in addition to ASIC's power to bring proceedings for the contravention of any provisions of the Corporations Act, in particular the prospectus provisions.

Many of the provisions of the Corporations Act which prohibit certain activity or require corporations to perform certain duties are converted into offences by s 1311. Section 728(3) (misleading or deceptive statements or omissions that are materially adverse to investors) is governed by s 1311 and the maximum penalty for a contravention is provided in Sch 3 as 15 years' imprisonment.

The prospectus for Worldwide News contains a material statement that is false or misleading. The terms of s 729 are such that anyone involved in the contravention of s 728 may be civilly liable to compensate investors who have suffered losses because of the contravention.

The solicitors may be liable under s 729 as they were involved in the breach. Their liability is limited to losses flowing from their breach of s 728.

Persons sued under s 729 have a defence of due diligence and reasonable belief: s 731.

In summary, apart from the power to place stop orders on the issue of securities, the directors, the corporation and the solicitors could face civil or criminal penalties for breach: s 729. The criminal penalties for these offences are set out in Sch 3 of the Corporations Act.

Examiner's Comments

9-15 The range of duties and corresponding statutory regime for civil liability is similar to the regime under the Australian Consumer Law (ACL) (formerly the Trade Practices Act 1974 (Cth)). However, there is a basic philosophical difference between the regulation contained in the Corporations Act to protect investors and consumer protection legislation. Investor protection is achieved by disclosure of accurate information. If the information turns out to be false or misleading then the persons who provide the information will be liable unless they can show that they did everything reasonable to ensure the accuracy of the information. Consumer protection legislation, however, is concerned only with the effect that the information has upon the consumer and there is no defence of due diligence for breach of s 18 of the ACL. It could be possible to discuss potential statements or conduct by the company outside of the specific prospectus (such as statements on the company's website) which could give rise to liability under s 1041H of the Corporations Act.

Finally, it is worth noting that there is a duty upon those who issue or authorise a prospectus and those persons listed in s 730 (including experts) to inform the corporation that there are false or misleading statements or that there are changes which affect the truth of statements in the prospectus or that there is a significant new matter. This is clearly designed to then lead to the provision for supplementary or replacement prospectuses and the ability to correct false or misleading statements: s 719.

This answer could also discuss the possibility of the company's directors being found liable for breach of their directors' duties by causing the company to breach Ch 6D: see *ASIC v Sino Australia Oil and Gas Ltd (in liq)* [2016] FCA 934; civil penalty decision in [2016] FCA 1488; see the discussion in *ASIC v Sydney Investment House Equities Pty Ltd* (2008) 69 ACSR 1; *ASIC v Maxwell* (2006) 59 ACSR 373.

Keep in Mind

- The Corporations Act imposes civil and criminal liability for defective disclosure documents. Students should ensure that they adequately distinguish between conduct that attracts civil and criminal penalties and conduct that only attracts civil penalties.
- Care must be taken to precisely identify the defendants who may take advantage of each of the defences and the applicable standard of diligence in relation to each one.
- Disregard of disclosure law by directors through ignorance or lack of proper understanding is not an excuse and will not be tolerated: *ASIC v Sino Australia Oil and Gas Ltd (in liq)* [2016] FCA 1488 at [12].

Chapter 10

External
Administration

Key Issues

10-1 The majority of this book, and indeed the majority of corporate law subjects, are concerned with companies that are solvent and where the business is managed by, or under the supervision of, the board of directors. This chapter discusses how corporate law addresses the problems of companies that are insolvent. Insolvent companies enter what is called 'external administration' which is where an independent and external manager (an accountant who is registered by ASIC to work as an external administrator) takes over the running of the business and, except for 'debtor in possession' restructuring for small businesses under Pt 5.3B of the Corporations Act (in effect from January 2021), the directors lose their authority to manage the company but are not replaced.

There are five different types of external administration regimes:

1. *Receivership:* This is usually initiated by a major financier (such as a bank) enforcing its security rights over the debtor company's assets but may also be ordered by the court.
2. *Schemes of arrangement:* These allow the company and its creditors to enter into a compromise or arrangement to restructure the company's debt obligations. These are used for large and very complex corporate insolvencies (which are usually a small number each year). For most insolvency situations, a deed of company arrangement (which may follow a period of voluntary administration) can usually achieve a similar outcome and is generally easier and cheaper to undertake. As a result, schemes will not be discussed in detail in this chapter.
3. *Voluntary administration:* This provides a brief period of relief from debt repayment obligations (through a moratorium against claims) and attempts to allow the company's creditors to save some or all of the business or at least provide a better return than an immediate liquidation. A deed of company arrangement (DOCA) is one of the potential outcomes following from a period of voluntary administration.
4. *Small business restructuring:* On 1 January 2021, the federal government's post-Covid small business restructuring reform

— 217 —

package came into effect. The new Pt 5.3B of the Corporations Act provides for a restructuring process for eligible companies (small businesses with debts up to $1 million) that allows such companies to retain control of the business, property and affairs while developing a restructure plan with creditors with the assistance of a small business restructuring practitioner. It also provides for a simplified liquidation process, to allow for a faster and cheaper procedure, for eligible small businesses.

5. *Liquidation:* This terminates the company's business by the liquidator selling all of the assets to try to repay debt and then deregistering the company after all the assets have been realised.

It should be noted that, although this chapter is focused on insolvent companies, liquidation may also be used by solvent companies to distribute the assets of the business and wind up the company's affairs. This is called a 'members' voluntary liquidation' (see Corporations Act Pt 5.5 Div 2) and is only available if the company's directors make a declaration of the company's solvency. This chapter will concentrate on insolvent companies entering external administration. Creditors may also use voluntary liquidation under Pt 5.5 Div 3 (called a creditors' voluntary liquidation (CVL)).

In most cases other than a members' voluntary liquidation, court-ordered liquidation or receivership (which may be ordered because of fraud or other illegality), the external administration arises because the company is experiencing a liquidity problem and is unable to pay its debts on time. Section 95A of the Corporations Act defines 'solvency' and 'insolvency' with reference to the debtor company's ability to pay its debts as and when they become due and payable; that is (rephrasing s 95A), a company that is unable to pay its debts as and when they become due and payable is not solvent and is therefore insolvent for the purposes of the Corporations Act. In some situations, this may be difficult to prove in court (in order to obtain the appointment of a liquidator, for example), so the Corporations Act provides a range of 'presumptions of insolvency'. In liquidation proceedings, a company will be presumed to be insolvent if any of the events in s 459C occur (the most common being a failure to comply with a statutory demand within 21 days). In recovery proceedings (such as liquidators pursuing voidable transactions or insolvent trading), the company will be presumed to be insolvent if it fails to keep proper financial records: s 588E(4). See, for example, *Re Balmz Pty Ltd (in liq)* [2020] VSC 652; *Re Swan Services Pty Ltd (in liq)* [2016] NSWSC 1724. There are no presumptions of insolvency for voluntary administration. The purpose of the provisions for deemed insolvency upon the failure to maintain proper records was explained in *Trinick v Forgione* [2015] FCA 642 at [209] by Siopis J who said it was:

... to assist a liquidator in bringing recovery actions (including recovery actions against former directors for insolvent trading) when it is necessary to prove insolvency and the company's financial records are not available.

Aside from presumptions of insolvency, the debtor company must be shown to be unable to pay its debts. This is assessed according to the commercial realities of the situation which, as Palmer J said in the leading case of *Southern Cross Interiors Pty Ltd (in liq) v DCT* (2001) 53 NSWLR 213; [2001] NSWSC 621 at [54], 'will be relevant in considering what resources are available to the company to meet its liabilities as they fall due, whether resources other than cash are realisable by sale or borrowing upon security, and when such realisations are achievable'. It is clear that s 95A is focused on a 'cash flow test' rather than a 'balance sheet test' (that is, measuring available cash resources against debt levels rather than asset values against debt levels): *Southern Cross Interiors Pty Ltd (in liq) v DCT* (2001) 53 NSWLR 213; [2001] NSWSC 621. The applicable principles interpreting s 95A are well known, and were recently summarised by Black J in *Re Humur Pty Ltd* [2020] NSWSC 1759 at [17]–[18]; *Re Swan Services Pty Ltd (in liq)* [2016] NSWSC 1724 at [136]–[139]. See also the discussion in *Quin v Vlahos* [2021] VSCA 205 at [42]–[63]; *Treloar Constructions Pty Ltd v McMillan* [2017] NSWCA 72 at [76]–[83].

In *Bentley Smythe Pty Ltd v Anton Fabrications (NSW) Pty Ltd* (2011) 248 FLR 384; [2011] NSWSC 186, Ward J reviewed the authorities on s 95A and said (at [49]): 'The s 95A test requires ascertainment of the company's existing debts, its debts within the near future, the date each will be due for payment, the company's present and expected case resources and the date each item will be received'. For example, the debtor company may be unable to generate sufficient cash flow to pay its debts but may have sufficient assets to enable it to obtain medium-to-long-term loans to pay its ongoing debts. In such a situation, the company would not be insolvent. It is important to note that insolvency concerns being unable to pay debts rather than refusing to pay a particular debt because of a dispute with the creditors. However, a consistent failure to pay debts over a long period of time suggests that the company is insolvent. As Palmer J said in *Hall v Poolman* (2007) 65 ACSR 123; [2007] NSWSC 1330 at [266]:

> There is a difference between temporary illiquidity and 'an endemic shortage of working capital whereby liquidity can only restored by a successful outcome of business ventures in which the existing working capital has been deployed'. The first is an embarrassment, the second is a disaster.

This is an elaboration of what the High Court said in *Sandell v Porter* (1966) 115 CLR 666 (a case under the Bankruptcy Act 1966 (Cth)). Proving insolvency (or impending insolvency) is not necessary for receivership. Receivership arises when the debtor company defaults on its loan obligations (such as failing to make interest payments or allowing its assets to decline below a minimum required value) and the secured lender exercises their right under the debt contract to appoint a receiver to take control over the secured assets. In such a situation, the company's directors generally lose their management powers and the receivers take control of the business. Receivership can also arise under a court order (see s 1323) where the court believes that the assets of the company are in jeopardy (see *ASIC v Berndale Capital Securities Pty Ltd* [2019] FCA 595 for a collection of judicial authorities), although this is an extreme remedy and will only be awarded where there is a clear need for receivership.

The Corporations Act does not provide a complete code to regulate receivership as most appointments are done privately and the terms will be set by the secured loan documentation. Receivership, essentially, is only a temporary or partial external administration. The receiver only has authority to control those assets which are the subject of the security and for the purpose of satisfying the secured creditor's debt. However, it is common for security documents to grant a receiver the power to manage the business for the purpose of protecting the security. Once this role is performed, the receiver 'leaves' the company and the company has whatever is left after the security has been satisfied. Of course, if the security covers a large proportion of the company's assets, or if it is the whole of the company's business, then it is likely the receivership will result in a completely depleted company which will only have the option of then being wound up. It is also possible that a company will be placed in either liquidation or a voluntary administration during receivership.

Receivership also has a public quality about it, as the Corporations Act requires publication of the appointment by lodging a notice at ASIC and ensuring that the fact of the appointment appears on all company documentation. This in itself can cause further financial distress to a company. It should be noted that other types of external administration also have notice requirements but they also protect the company's assets from litigation by a moratorium against claims.

A receiver, once appointed, will have obligations under the Corporations Act to report contraventions and other misconduct to ASIC should such matters come to the knowledge of the receiver. Receivers may also seek guidance from the court as to the manner in which they may exercise their powers. Most importantly, receivers are classified as officers of the company under s 9 and as such they owe the same statutory duties to the company as are owed by directors: ss 180–184. In addition, receivers are required to exercise a duty to obtain the market price or best possible price on a disposal of company assets under s 420A. For summary of the legal principles underpinning s 420A, see *Re Australasian Barrister Chambers Pty Ltd (in liq)* [2017] NSWSC 597 (appeal dismissed in *Re Australasian Barrister Chambers Pty Ltd (in liq)* [2017] NSWCA 117).

Schemes of arrangement

10-2 A scheme of arrangement under s 411 allows a company to restructure its capital by entering into an arrangement with its members or to enter into a compromise with its creditors about the repayment of a debt owed by the company to a particular creditor or class of creditors. A scheme requires court approval on two occasions. The court's approval must be obtained to present a scheme proposal to the company's members or creditors. After the scheme proposal has been approved, the court must also approve of the actual scheme agreed to by the members or creditors. For the differences between schemes and voluntary administration, see the High Court judgments in *Mighty River International Ltd v Hughes* (2018) 265 CLR 480; *Lehman Brothers Holdings Inc v City of Swan* (2010) 240 CLR 509. In the *Lehman* case, the High Court observed (at [73]):

> The structure and detailed terms of Pt 5.1 [schemes] are quite different from those of Pt 5.3A [voluntary administration]. In particular, court approval in advance is always required under Pt 5.1; in Pt 5.3A the role of the court is only belated and occasional ... after the deed of company arrangement has been entered, and even then only if the creditor complains. The much more ample oversight of the court under Pt 5.1 contrasts with the significant things which can be done under Pt 5.3A [such as entering into a deed of company arrangement] without court sanction.

Voluntary administration

10-3 Voluntary administration (VA) is a procedure which was introduced to avoid the drastic nature of liquidation and provide a speedy and cost-efficient means of professional administration of a company which is in financial difficulty but may not be hopelessly insolvent. The object of VA is to either save some or all of the business or, if that is not possible, to obtain a better return for the creditors than they would receive from an immediate liquidation: s 435A. The typical period for a VA is under 25 business days from appointment. The administrator must call an initial creditors' meeting within eight business days of appointment (where he or she may be replaced by the creditors and a creditors' committee may be appointed), and then call a final creditors' meeting within five business days before or after the 20-business-day 'convening period' which typically begins on the next business day after the administrator is appointed: s 439A. It is at this meeting that the creditors decide the company's future.

The court may extend the convening period where the administrator demonstrates there is some need to do so; for example, in *Mighty River International Ltd v Hughes* (2018) 265 CLR 480, Nettle and Gordon JJ referred to a number of cases and concluded (at [73]):

> Generally speaking, courts have been disposed to grant substantial extensions in cases where the administration has been complicated by, for example, the size and scope of the business, substantial offshore activities, large numbers of employees with complex entitlements, complex corporate structures and intercompany loans, and complex recovery proceedings, and, more generally, where the additional time is likely to enhance the return to unsecured creditors. Provided the evidentiary case for extension has been properly prepared, there has been no evidence of material prejudice to those affected by the moratorium imposed by the administration, and the

administrator's estimate of time has had a reasonable basis, the courts have tended to grant extensions for the periods sought by administrators. ...

For a summary of the legal principles applicable to an application for an extension of the convening period for the second meeting of creditors under s 439A, see *Re Strawbridge (in their capacity as joint and several voluntary administrators of each of Virgin Australia Holdings Ltd (admins apptd) (ACN 100 686 226)) (No 2)* [2020] FCA 717 at [64]–[68].

The VA is usually initiated by the company's directors (s 436A) but may also be started by a liquidator or a substantial security holder: ss 436B and 436C. Importantly, the directors' opinion of insolvency under s 436A must be 'bona fide and genuinely formed': *Kazar v Duus* (1998) 88 FCR 218. Directors may breach their general law and statutory duties by appointing an administrator for collateral purposes: *Re Bean & Sprout Pty Ltd (admin apptd)* [2018] NSWSC 351. For a collection of judicial authorities and discussion of legal principles under s 436A, see *Re Windows on the World Steel Windows Pty Ltd (In Administration)* [2020] VSC 880.

One advantage for the board of directors in appointing an administrator is that they may be able to claim a defence to insolvent trading (under s 588H(5)) and will also receive protection from personal guarantees given over the company's debts under s 440J (at least for the period of the VA). The effect of a VA is that the power of the board of directors is suspended and all the affairs of the company are in the control of the administrator: s 437A. The administrator can also deal with property that is held by the company but is subject to a security interest held by someone else or is owned by someone other than the company: see Pt 5.3A Div 8. Importantly, the procedure is designed to cover all of the company's creditors, secured and unsecured. To enable this and to ensure minimal distraction to the administration process, there is a moratorium on all enforcement proceedings against the company (see s 440D), although major secured parties may still enforce their rights during the initial 13-business-day 'decision period': s 441A. A secured party who begins enforcement before the appointment of an administrator may continue with their enforcement: s 441B.

The administrator's duties are to examine the affairs of the company, to report to the members and creditors of the company and to advise on whether to wind up the company, hand it back to the control of the directors (which rarely occurs) or to come to an arrangement with creditors resulting in a formal deed of company arrangement. If creditors agree to a deed, they then agree to have their claims against the company limited by the conditions of the deed which will usually involve an extension of time to repay and/or a reduced return or a release of the debts subject to a payment being made to compromise the claim: see ss 444A, 444C and 444D. The administrator usually becomes the deed administrator and implements the terms of the deed which might be a sale of the business or continuing to trade for a period of time.

Small business restructuring

10-4   Due to the significant impact of Covid-19 on the economy, and the expiry of a host of temporary Covid-19 insolvency relief measures at the end of December 2020, the government introduced the Corporations Amendment (Corporate Insolvency Reforms) Act 2020 (Cth) on 1 January 2021 to help small businesses survive financial pressures. The new debt restructuring procedure in Pt 5.3B of the Corporations Act has potential to incentivise corporate rescue and to prevent unnecessary destruction of valuable and viable businesses in the SME sector.

Part 5.3B of the Corporations Act draws heavily on the established voluntary administration framework in Pt 5.3A and shares many of its features; however, these have been adapted to suit small businesses.

Section 452A sets out the object of the new Pt 5.3B which is to provide for a restructuring process for eligible companies (namely, with total debts that do not exceed $1 million and which have up-to-date tax lodgments). Section 452A allows such companies:

- to retain control of the business, property and affairs while developing a plan to restructure with the assistance of a small business restructuring practitioner; and
- to enter into a restructuring plan with creditors.

To enter into the restructuring process, the board of an eligible company must resolve (via a written resolution) that the company is, or is likely to become, insolvent and that a restructuring practitioner should be appointed: s 453B.

While a company is under the restructuring process, the company directors retain control of the company's business, property and affairs and are responsible for ensuring compliance with the new legal regime (new ss 453K and 453L). Significantly, for the first time, directors in eligible small companies will be able to trade their way out of financial difficulty without the need to appoint an external administrator to take temporary control of the business. The change in law reflects a 'debtor in possession' model of insolvency law — in this respect, akin to the Chapter 11 bankruptcy model used in the United States. Part 5.3B reflects a fundamental change from the 'creditor in possession' model reflected in Pt 5.3A.

An independent small business restructuring practitioner, representing a new class of registered liquidator, is given a key role under the new law. They are expected to help the directors to develop a rescue plan and are expected to assess the continued viability of the business: ss 453E–453J.

During the entire restructuring process, the law offers small businesses valuable breathing space: ss 453R–453X. Legal action against the company by suppliers, lenders and other creditors to enforce payment of debts owed to them is temporary suspended, akin to the equivalent provisions in Pt 5.3A. As with voluntary administrations, there is also a stay upon the enforcement of 'ipso facto' contractual clauses.

A majority of creditors by value, excluding related-party creditors, must accept the plan for it to be binding. The restructuring process ends if the plan is not approved. If the rescue plan is voted down by creditors, the company will be liquidated under the new streamlined process.

Liquidation

10-5 Finally, the fifth type of external administration to be dealt with in this chapter is the most invasive of all — liquidation. Liquidation occurs after a company has been wound up. Companies may be wound up voluntarily for a number of reasons, or compulsorily by the court. There are a number of grounds for winding up a company under s 461, some of which were dealt with in the chapter on members' remedies: see **Chapter 8**. By far the most common ground for winding up a company is insolvency: s 459A.

The procedure for winding up a company is provided for under the Corporations Act. As noted above, s 459C provides for a presumption of insolvency if certain events occur, usually the failure to comply with a statutory demand. A statutory demand is a formal notice by a creditor to the company to repay an outstanding debt (it must be due and payable) of at least $4000 (increased from $2000 from 1 July 2021) within 21 days. Failure to pay in accordance with the demand then gives rise to a presumption of insolvency which the creditor can then rely on to ground an application to wind up the company. There are a number of opportunities for companies to avert this process by applying to set aside the demand. This may be done under s 459G to have the demand set aside under the grounds in either s 459H (offsetting or disputed amounts that reduce the undisputed debt below $4000) or s 459J (setting aside the demand because of a defect or on other grounds). There is a voluminous body of case law on ss 459H and 459J; for a useful summary of the main legal principles derived from the leading cases, see the judgment of Black J in *Re Malosi Group Pty Ltd* [2021] NSWSC 633.

The debtor company may also defend the winding up application (for example, on the ground that the company is solvent: see, however, the limitation in s 459S).

If the court orders that the company be wound up, it appoints an official liquidator to call in the company's assets to create a fund out of which the liquidator is required to pay the company's creditors. A liquidator has more extensive powers than either administrators or receivers because the liquidator may sue the directors for breaching their duties to the company (such as ss 180–183), may take action against the directors for insolvent trading (s 588G) or may recover amounts paid, or property transferred, by the company prior to the liquidation commencing (known as 'voidable transactions': ss 588FA–588FJ). A liquidator may also take advantage of the vesting provisions relating to PPSA security interests that are not properly perfected within a particular time of the liquidation (ss 588FK–588FO) or where a security interest is granted in favour of an officer of the company and they seek to enforce it within six months of its creation (s 588FP).

Once all of the debts are paid, or as much as can be paid out of the company's realisable assets, the company is deregistered and ceases to exist. The Corporations Act provides a detailed ranking of priority payments (see, in particular, s 556) which runs in rough order as follows:

- liquidation costs;
- prior external administration costs;
- liquidator's remuneration;
- employee wages;
- personal injury claims; and
- employee leave and redundancy.

Only after all of these priority creditors have been paid in full do any unsecured creditors receive any distribution. Of course, secured creditors receive the first payment as they are able to seize the company's property to pay off their debts. (Note that there is an exception for circulating security interests which must satisfy employee entitlements prior to paying the secured amount: s 561.) For hopelessly insolvent companies without sufficient assets even to pay these priority creditors, the Commonwealth Government established the Fair Entitlements Guarantee Scheme (previously known as GEERS) to cover employee entitlements to a certain limit (with the Commonwealth then assuming the priority position of the employees): Fair Entitlements Guarantee Act 2012 (Cth).

The powers of the liquidator to call in and take control of the company's assets are set out in the Corporations Act, along with the power to commence or defend proceedings in the name of the company: s 477. The order of priority of payment is also prescribed by the Corporations Act and the liquidator is also able to seek guidance or direction from the court as to the exercise of any of his or her powers.

A liquidator must be independent of the company, its directors and shareholders and individual creditors and must act impartially in the discharge of his or her duties and responsibilities: *Re FW Projects Pty Ltd (in liq)* [2019] NSWSC 892 (see collection of authorities at [100]). For extensive discussion on the role of a liquidator, see *ASIC v McDermott; Re Conalpin Pty Ltd (in liq)* [2016] FCA 1186; *ASIC v Edge* (2007) 211 FLR 137. In *Edge*, Dodds-Streeton J said (at [44]):

> The extensive powers vested exclusively in the liquidator entail a corresponding vulnerability in the creditors, members and the public. The liquidator is a fiduciary on whom high standards of honesty, impartiality and probity are imposed both by the Act and the general law. As an officer of the company, the liquidator has a statutory duty of care, diligence and good faith.

Courts have long held a broad supervisory jurisdiction over the conduct of court-appointed liquidators: see *Hall v Poolman* [2009] NSWCA 64; *ASIC v Macks (No 2)* [2019] SASC 17 at [48]–[51]. This power was extended over all kinds of liquidators under the now repealed s 536 of the Corporations Act. Since the amendments made by the Insolvency Law Reform Act 2016 (Cth), the court's supervisory jurisdiction over 'external administrators' and 'external administration' is governed by the Insolvency Practice Schedule (IPS) to the Corporations Act (see s 5-15 and s 5-20 of the IPS).

The content of ss 90-5, 90-10, 90-15 and 90-20 of the IPS in the Corporations Act serve the public interest by promoting the regulation, supervision, discipline and correction of liquidators in the interests of honest and efficient administration of companies in liquidation. See, for example, *Djordjevich v Rohrt* [2021] VSC 178 for discussion of the legal principles applicable to these statutory clauses. It is important to remember that corporate insolvency is a very complex area of corporate law. In most corporate law courses, there is only time to cover the basics, including:

- types of appointment (who may be appointed and how they are appointed);
- impact of appointment on key stakeholders such as directors, the company, creditors and employees;
- powers of external administrators; and
- duration and termination of procedure.

When attempting questions on corporate insolvency, be careful to focus on what the question is asking, particularly whether the question is concerned with only one type of appointment (such as VA or liquidation) or whether the question asks for a comparison between different appointments.

Before attempting the questions below, check that you are familiar with the following issues or terms:

✓	The advantages and disadvantages of liquidation, receivership, voluntary administration and schemes of arrangement.
✓	Who can appoint a liquidator (both court and voluntary appointments), a receiver (both court and private appointments), a voluntary administrator and a scheme administrator.
✓	The powers of secured creditors in liquidation, receivership and voluntary administration.
✓	The rights of unsecured creditors in liquidation, receivership and voluntary administration.
✓	How appointing a voluntary liquidator or voluntary administrator may assist directors avoid insolvent trading liability.
✓	What the system of payment priorities in liquidation is, and where employees, unsecured creditors and members fit on that priority list.

Question 40

ABC Pty Ltd is a manufacturer of smallgoods (that is, salami and processed meats). It owns a large factory and storage facility in Sydney and it has all the machinery and plant for the processing of smallgoods as well as trading stock.

In 2021, ABC Pty Ltd borrowed money from Basic Bank to upgrade manufacturing processes. As security for the loan, a security interest was granted over all of the company's current and future property including two expensive pieces of machinery (two sausage-making machines) that were acquired as part of the upgrade and stock-in-trade and book debts (receivables). It was a term of the security instrument that the loan would default if the value of stock-in-trade fell below $100,000.

ABC normally had around $200,000 worth of stock at any given time. The stock of ABC consists mostly of cured sausages and hams which have lengthy use-by dates but are perishables susceptible to spoilage if not stored properly.

ABC's largest customer was Safewise which ran a chain of supermarkets throughout New South Wales. As a result of a legal action launched against Safewise for alleged food poisoning arising from the consumption of an ABC salami, Safewise withdrew all ABC products from its shelves and returned them to ABC.

ABC now has a liquidity problem because of the loss of its major customer. Further, the smallgoods that were returned are of dubious quality because of possible poor storage and the implication from the legal action that the products are affected by bacteria. Accordingly, the value of the stock-in-trade plummets below $100,000. ABC defaults on its loan from Basic Bank which gives the bank the right to appoint a receiver. The directors of ABC are concerned about the company's viability. The company has outstanding tax liabilities.

Advise the ABC board as to their, and the company's, legal position.

Time allowed: 40 minutes

Answer Plan

This is a problem that is asking for a comparison between different types of external administration. The wording of the question simply states 'advise as to their legal position', so the board will want to know:

- what they can do as a board of directors;
- what the company's creditors can do; and
- how these possible outcomes will impact on them, the company and its stakeholders.

The company's current problems

- Is the company insolvent?
- What are the consequences of being insolvent?
- If insolvent, it is important to do something about it.

Options for the board

- The board cannot appoint a receiver as the board are not secured creditors; court appointment unlikely.
- The board cannot appoint a restructuring practitioner, under Pt 5.3B of the Corporations Act, as the company is not eligible. Although ABC Pty Ltd may have total debts of less than $1 million, a small business with outstanding tax liabilities is not an eligible company for the purposes of Pt 5.3B.
- The board can appoint a voluntary administrator under VA (advantages and disadvantages).
- The appointment of a liquidator is not the best option if the company can be saved.

Potential action by stakeholders

- Basic Bank appoints a receiver (how and why).
- Other unsecured creditors seek the court appointment of a liquidator (how and why).

Advice to the board

- Need to avoid insolvent trading; renegotiate with the bank, draw up a rescue plan that would satisfy the safe harbour provisions or put the company into VA.

 Answer

10-6 The board of ABC has requested advice regarding their legal position and the company's legal position based on the facts as disclosed in the question. I will advise first on the company's position, then on the board's position, and finally on potential action that may be taken by key stakeholders.

The company's current problems

10-7 The facts state that ABC is having a liquidity problem due to the withdrawal of a major customer. This raises the question as to *whether the company is insolvent*. If the company is insolvent then a number of consequences may arise, including potential liability for the board for insolvent trading, the appointment of an external administrator and potential closure of the business. These will be discussed further in **10.8** and **10.10** below.

Solvency is defined in s 95A of the Corporations Act as the ability of the company to pay all of its debts as and when they become due and payable. In determining whether the company is able to pay its debts, the courts apply a test of commercial reality: *Southern Cross Interiors Pty Ltd (in liq) v DCT* (2001) 53 NSWLR 213; [2001] NSWSC 621. This concerns the practical ability to use assets to generate funds to pay off debt which may involve asset sales or obtaining loan finance. Unfortunately, ABC has already granted a security interest over all of its current and future assets which means that their disposal will be subject to the terms of the loan with Basic Bank. Given the facts state that the stock-in-trade can fluctuate, it is clear that the loan security agreement with Basic Bank allows for circulating assets to be bought and sold without the bank's permission. It is unlikely that the loan allows for the sale of the sausage machines as these are non-circulating assets but this should be of little concern as the company would most likely not want to sell these as they form the core of the business — although a sale and leaseback may free up some cash resources to help the business through a difficult time.

ABC is unlikely to be able to obtain further finance from Basic Bank because it is in default. The company's liquidity problems suggest that ABC has been unable to find another major customer. The company's ability to sell its trading stock to repay debts quickly might be doubtful given the quality issues set out in the facts of the question. Selling stock in a hurry is also likely to generate lower returns due to the forced nature of the sale. It may also be possible for the directors or shareholders to provide additional funding to support the business, although nothing in the facts suggests that this is likely.

Therefore, we assume that ABC is insolvent because it seems unable to pay its current debts and is unlikely to be able to do so in the future so it is insolvent as defined in s 95A. It is important for the directors of ABC to be aware that they face potential civil and criminal liability if they allow the company to trade while it is insolvent: s 588G. In this case, we are not told about whether they have sought any expert advice to determine whether the company can remain solvent, which may give them an opportunity to argue one of the defences under s 588H. Contravention of s 588G may give rise to ASIC bringing an action against the board for a declaration of contravention of a civil penalty provision (s 1317E) which may lead to a pecuniary penalty order (s 1317G) and/or a disqualification order (s 206C). If found to have contravened s 588G, the directors may be liable to pay compensation in respect of debts that were incurred during the period of insolvent trading: Pt 5.7B Divs 3 and 4.

Options for the board

10-8 Given the potential for insolvent trading liability and the company's deteriorating financial position, clearly the board of ABC cannot simply allow the company to continue trading. The directors do not appear to have security over the company's assets, or at least any security that would give them priority over Basic Bank's debt. Thus, they don't appear to have any power to appoint a receiver. If they were to seek a court-ordered winding up of the company (which directors may do as they have standing under s 459P), it would certainly mean the demise of ABC and ultimately their loss of employment. Liquidation would also likely trigger any personal guarantees that they may have given to secure the company's loans, although this is not mentioned in the facts of the question.

It may be that if ABC is given sufficient time to find a replacement for its major customer then it may be able to be saved, in which case liquidation would be a bad outcome for the company's stakeholders. The best option may be for the board to appoint a voluntary administrator. The board can appoint an administrator under s 436A by passing a resolution at a board meeting that:

(a) the company is insolvent or likely to become insolvent; and
(b) a voluntary administrator should be appointed.

The board must have reasonable grounds to believe that the company is insolvent or likely to become insolvent: *Kazar v Duus* (1998) 88 FCR 218; *Re Windows on the World Steel Windows Pty Ltd (In Administration)* [2020] VSC 880.

Appointing an administrator cannot be used merely as a delaying tactic to frustrate any action that Safewise might take against the company: *Blacktown City Council v Macarthur Telecommunications Pty Ltd* (2003) 47 ACSR 391. The creditors will have the opportunity to replace the administrator at the first creditors' meeting which is held within eight business days of the administrator's appointment: s 436E.

Once appointed, the administrator takes control of the company's property and a general moratorium is imposed on action against the company's assets that may be taken by creditors: s 440D. Such action may only be undertaken with the permission of the administrator or with the leave of the court, which is rarely granted as enforcement action is likely to distract the administrator from his or her job of investigating the company's affairs and advising the creditors as to their options for the company's future: *Foxcraft v The Ink Group Pty Ltd* (1994) 15 ACSR 203; see *Buurabalayji Thalanyji Aboriginal Corporation v Onslow Salt Pty Ltd (No 7)* [2020] FCA 572 for discussion of authorities on s 440D.

One exception to the moratorium that may be applicable here relates to rights of secured parties: see Pt 5.3A Divs 6 and 7. We are told that Basic Bank has a security interest in all present and future property which obviously covers 'substantially the whole of the company's property': s 441A. The bank could appoint a receiver during the 13-business-day 'decision period' that commences on the date of appointment: s 441A. This assumes that the security interest is enforceable under the PPSA (known as being 'perfected'), because if it is not then it may vest in ABC under s 267 of the PPSA.

If the bank appointed a receiver, the administrator's powers would be limited (s 442D) and the payment of creditors would need to await the completion of the receivership, unless the administrator could persuade the receiver and the secured creditor to support some form of debt restructuring or sale which may provide a better outcome for all creditors.

After investigating the company's affairs, the administrator must convene a final creditors' meeting within five business days before or after the 'convening period', which is generally 20 business days starting on the next business day after the appointment of the administrator, but may be longer due to public holidays or by court extension: ss 439A and 447A. The administrator provides a report to the creditors advising them on a preferable course of action which can only be (s 439C):

- terminating the administration and returning the control of the company to the directors;
- undertaking a DOCA; or
- placing the company into an immediate creditors' voluntary liquidation.

The board should be advised that putting the company into voluntary administration will not trigger any personal guarantees that they may have given to secure the company's debts: s 440J.

Potential action by stakeholders

Basic Bank

10-9 The bank's secured loan is stated to be in default, which gives the bank the right to appoint a receiver or other agent to take control of the secured assets. It is important that any procedures in the loan documentation that must be undertaken before the bank can exercise its right to appoint a receiver (such as giving prior notice to ABC) are completed. It is also important that the perfection requirements of the PPSA are complied with. This would include registration of the bank's interest on the PPSR. It is unlikely that the bank will have a PMSI over the machines as it has taken an all present and after acquired property security interest over the assets: PPSA s 14. If the bank fails to perfect its security interest the interest may vest in the company if it enters formal insolvency: PPSA s 266.

The receiver once appointed does not have title to the subject assets; the assets still remain the property of the company: *Re Scottish Properties Pty Ltd* (1977) 2 ACLR 264. Once the receiver has repaid or recovered the amount owed to the bank, he or she must return possession and control of the balance of the assets (if any) to the company. If the proceeds recovered from any sale of secured assets exceed the value of the debt, then the surplus must be returned to ABC: *Expo International Pty Ltd v Chant (No 2)* [1979] 2 NSWLR 820. Receivers are bound by the duty to serve the interests of the appointing creditor and by general law and statutory duties to exercise the power of sale with reasonable care: s 420A. It should be noted that a receiver is also an 'officer' of the company under s 9 of the Corporations Act and therefore owes duties to the company under ss 180–184.

In this situation it seems that the receiver would take possession of the whole business and manage it with a view to recovering the debt. Such an event would effectively overtake all of the powers of management of the board of directors. Receivers under these types of security arrangements usually have explicit powers to manage the company's undertaking and they are described as managing controllers under s 9. Despite the extent of the managerial power of these receivers, the company still legally exists and the board of directors remains an organ of the company, albeit with probably no real task to perform while the receiver is in control except that of assisting the receiver: *Hawkesbury Development Co Ltd v Landmark Finance Pty Ltd* [1969] 2 NSWR 782. Therefore, it is important that the board of ABC examine the loan documents for its loans with Basic Bank to determine when a receiver may be appointed, how that appointment must take place and what role and powers the receiver may have once appointed.

Apart from the loss of control over the assets of the company under a receivership, there is a requirement under s 428 that all of a corporation's public documents, such as letterheads and negotiable instruments, must indicate after the corporation's name that a receiver has been appointed. This immediately signals to outsiders that the company is in some financial difficulty and this requirement, apart from the loss of control of some or all of the assets, can have a detrimental effect upon a company's business. Indeed, if the company has granted other securities over other assets, then the appointment of a receiver under one security agreement will often constitute a default event in those other security agreements. The appointment of a receiver therefore may lead to the need for either the directors or the bank to appoint a voluntary administrator which will protect the company during the receivership and may assist the receiver to recover a better price when selling the assets.

Assuming the loan documents will give the receiver (if and when appointed) the power to manage the business, the board of ABC will still retain the ability to challenge the appointment of the receiver on behalf of ABC: *Ernst & Young (Reg) v Tynski Pty Ltd* (2003) 47 ACSR 433. This may occur when the secured creditor seeks to appoint a receiver when ABC is not in default of its loan obligations. However, here the question makes it clear that ABC is in default and it is assumed the bank could appoint a receiver at any time.

The bank may, however, not wish to appoint a receiver as this is likely to damage the business further and reduce the chance of obtaining full repayment. Given the deterioration of the trading stock it is unlikely that its sale will reach full retail price. Furthermore, the market for industrial sausage machines is likely to be highly specialised and a forced sale by a receiver may generate fire-sale prices.

Thus, it may be in the bank's best interests to support the appointment of a voluntary administrator who may be able to save the business and maximise the return to the bank. If the bank is unhappy with the result of the VA (such as a DOCA) then as a secured party it will not be bound by the DOCA unless it votes for the proposal: s 444D.

Other unsecured creditors

10-10 It is possible that ABC's other creditors, such as the ATO, are owed unpaid debts which they may be able to use to seek a court-ordered winding up: s 459A. As they are unsecured (and cannot appoint receivers) it may be possible to obtain a return from a liquidation, but such an option would take considerable time and money. Voluntary administration would seek to provide a better outcome for all creditors and may be the preferable option although unsecured creditors cannot commence this form of insolvency.

Advice to the board

10-11 My advice to the board is to seek urgent professional financial advice to determine the financial position of the business. If this advice does not allow the board to be confident that ABC is, and will continue to be, solvent, the board should appoint a voluntary administrator. If the administrator is able to develop a workable plan to save the business, it may be possible that the bank will not appoint a receiver and some of the business at least may be saved. The safe harbour provision in s 588GA provides incentive for the board to develop a course of action (such as a restructure or rescue plan) that is reasonably likely to result in a better outcome for the company. In this way, the board can seek to avoid personal liability for insolvent trading. It is assumed that the factors that prevent reliance on the safe harbour (the statutory exclusions in s 588G(4)) are not present.

Examiner's Comments

10-12 This question is very broad in scope and it is important to tailor your answer to the issues discussed in your course. It is important not to get too bogged down in detailing appointment processes and timelines if your course has, rather, stressed the impact of external administration on different stakeholders, for example. It is also important that you are able to summarise the key sections without quoting extensively or repeating them.

The use of cases for corporate insolvency questions will also vary with the emphasis given to the topic in each course. Given the limited time allotted to insolvency in most compulsory corporate law subjects, it is common for few cases to be considered in detail. Whilst it is always useful to be aware of cases for key principles, don't feel obligated to cite cases for every proposition if the class and reading materials are mainly focused on the legislation (which is quite detailed and complex).

Keep in Mind

- Do not overlook the different sources for the appointment of receivers and administrators.
- Remember to explain the different roles and powers of administrators and receivers and how they might overlap. Receivers have limited powers under a security agreement for the benefit of the secured creditor. Administrators have full power over the company's affairs for the benefit of the company and all its creditors.
- Remember to explain why directors and creditors might prefer one type of appointment over another.
- Remember the eligibility requirements for small businesses to rely upon the restructuring provisions in the new Pt 5.3B of the Corporations Act.
- The essential difference between voluntary administration and liquidation was explained by Young J in *Foxcroft v The Ink Group Pty Ltd* (1994) 15 ACSR 203 at 204–5:

  > There is, however, quite a big difference between a company in administration and a company in liquidation. A company in administration is seeking to continue to trade and is, in accordance with s 435A, seeking to maximise the chance of it remaining in business. A company in liquidation is one where the liquidator is seeking not to trade but to realise the company's assets as soon as possible for the best price, in order to be able to distribute the net available funds to the creditors and in some circumstances, the members.

Question 41

Ajax Ltd is a large mining company listed on the ASX. During the first quarter of 2021 it became apparent that Ajax was in financial difficulties. In July 2021, Peter (the managing director of Ajax) made several public comments about the level of Ajax's gold reserves which were incorrect. Peter made these comments in an attempt to lift the company's share price so that he could exercise a large number of options included as part of his remuneration package.

Richard is a professional investor who read Peter's statements in the *Business Review* newspaper in July 2021 and shortly thereafter purchased 5000 shares in Ajax through the stock market at the current trading price of $5 per share.

During August 2021 the financial position of Ajax deteriorates significantly. At the end of August, the company is forced to announce a profit warning to the market which sends its share price falling. The fall in public confidence also affects the company's ability to sell gold futures (a major source of income) because market sentiment is not confident of the company's ability to fulfil future orders. This results in the company being unable to pay its wages bill, resulting in an outstanding amount of $1 million in wages and $100,000 in unpaid holiday pay.

The workers go on strike at the end of the week and refuse to return to work until they are paid in full. The strike cripples the company and it defaults on its repayments to creditors at the end of August 2021. A major supplier applies for a winding up order from the court in early November 2021, with a liquidator taking over the company.

This effectively wipes out Richard's investment because the company's shares are removed from the ASX official list and have a nominal value of $0. Richard contacts Gorgon & Spacer (a leading plaintiff law firm specialising in class actions) to sue the company for failing to comply with its market disclosure obligations. Gorgon & Spacer believe that there may be 1000 other shareholders in the same position as Richard, with potential claims of around $50 million. Richard and the other shareholders who bought shares in Ajax during July and early August want to lodge proofs of debt in the administration and vote at the final creditors' meeting.

Advise the following parties as to their rights in this situation:

- Richard and other shareholders in his position; and
- the employees.

Time allowed: 40 minutes

Answer Plan

This question is concerned with the ability of key stakeholders (employees and shareholders) to claim creditor status in a liquidation. It requires a discussion of the impact of liquidation on the rights of these stakeholders (including bringing litigation, attending and voting at creditors' meetings and receiving dividends) and an explanation of the process for proving a debt in liquidation.

General impact of liquidation

- When does the appointment take effect?
- General consequences of liquidation for stakeholders (moratorium and liquidator's powers and creditors' role).
- Process of liquidation (brief overview).

Richard and the other shareholders

- Debts to shareholders are subordinated.
- Shareholders (as creditors) may submit a proof of debt, although they have no right to vote at a creditors' meeting.
- Requirements for proofs of debt.
- Subordinated position of shareholder claims as unsecured creditors.

The employees

- Impact of liquidation on contract of employment.
- Priority position for unpaid entitlements.
- Possibility of FEG payment.

Answer

10-13 I have been asked to advise Richard and the other Ajax Ltd shareholders, as well as the company's employees, now that Ajax is in liquidation.

General impact of liquidation

10-14 Before considering the specific impact of the company's liquidation on the employees and shareholders we should note the general impact of liquidation on the company and its stakeholders, as these issues will be shared by both the shareholders and the employees.

Once Ajax enters liquidation its assets will come under the control of the liquidator, who has various powers to pursue the beneficial liquidation of the company under s 477. This may include taking legal action on behalf of the company, including to sue the directors for breach of their duties (such as insolvent trading under s 588G) or to recover voidable transactions. It may be possible that Peter's actions to obtain options could be voidable as an unreasonable director-related transaction, as it occurred within a short time before the company's collapse: s 588FDA.

During the liquidation any dispositions of the company's property without the liquidator's or the court's consent will be void (s 468) and there is a general moratorium prohibiting claims against the company being pursued without the court's permission (s 471B). The liquidator acts as agent of the company and as such does not take ownership of the company's property: *Commissioner of Taxation v Linter Textiles Australia Ltd (in liq)* (2005) 220 CLR 592.

The appointment of a compulsory liquidator will not automatically terminate contracts with Ajax (*Smith v FCT* (1996) 71 FCR 150), although the liquidator does have power to disclaim onerous contracts: s 568.

The liquidator's role involves selling the company's assets to repay as much of its debts as possible and then seeking release from the court and an order deregistering the company: s 481.

Having considered the general impact of liquidation on Ajax it is now appropriate to discuss the impact on the shareholders and employees specifically.

Richard and the other shareholders

10-15 If the information released by Ajax to the market through its officers (such as Peter) has been misleading or deceptive, or may otherwise constitute a breach of the company's continuous disclosure obligations under s 674 (Ajax is a disclosing entity because it is listed on a licensed financial market: see ss 111AC–111AE), then Richard (and other shareholders in a similar situation) may have a statutory right to damages (see, for example, ss 1041I and 1325). Unfortunately for Richard, members cannot transfer their shares during liquidation without the permission of the liquidator or the court: s 468A. Richard is also prevented from easily selling his shares because the shares have been removed from the list of the securities exchange due to the company's insolvency.

While Richard and the other shareholders may technically have creditor status, s 563A classifies their claims as 'subordinate claims' (defined in s 563A(2)). This means that the claims cannot be paid in the liquidation until all other debts are paid in full: s 563A(1). Furthermore, Richard and the other shareholders may only receive information about the liquidation if they make a request in writing to the liquidator (s 600H(1)(a)) and may only vote at a creditors' meeting if the court gives them approval (s 600H(1)(b)). These provisions were brought in during 2010 to overturn the effect of the High Court's decision in *Sons of Gwalia Ltd v Margaretic* (2007) 231 CLR 160.

It would seem that Richard and the other shareholders will only receive any distributions from the liquidation if all other creditors are paid in full, which is unlikely. It may be possible for them to pursue the directors as being involved in the company's disclosure contraventions as such actions would not come within the company's liquidation and hence would not be subordinated. Of course, the directors might not have sufficient funds to justify taking such action.

The employees

10-16 Unfortunately for the employees, the appointment of a compulsory liquidator will serve as an automatic notice of termination of their employment: *Re General Rolling Stock Co* (1866) LR 1 Eq 346; see generally *McEvoy v Incat Tasmania Pty Ltd* (2003) 130 FCR 503. However, the employees are priority creditors in the liquidation and are entitled to priority payment for their wages, leave pay and redundancy pay: see s 556(1). Employees' priority entitlements also take precedence over the priority of a creditor with a circulating security interest: s 561. If any of the employees have worked as a director of Ajax or are related to directors of Ajax then their entitlements may be capped as they would fit within the definition of excluded employees: ss 9 and 556.

The employees will need to submit a proof of debt for their outstanding wages and leave pay and will be able to attend and participate in the creditors' meetings. If there are insufficient funds in the company to cover the employees' entitlements, it may be possible for them to receive a payment under the Fair Entitlements Guarantee Act 2012 (Cth).

○ Examiner's Comments

10-17 This question is a relatively straightforward application of the rules for proving debts, including what debts are provable as well as some discussion of the priority rules for paying debts in company liquidations. It is essential that you manage your time well on questions that involve many statutory provisions as it is easy to get bogged down in the detail of certain procedures and run out of time. Do not forget to tailor your answer to the parties who are seeking your advice.

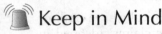 Keep in Mind

- Remember to recognise whether there is a provable debt.
- Note that provable debts and claims must exist before the liquidation commences.
- Do not get tied up in timelines, notices and procedural detail (unless such content was emphasised in your course).
- Employees of companies that become insolvent have always enjoyed special priority for their unpaid entitlements, primarily in recognition that their contribution to a company may enhance the value of assets the subject of a creditor's security: *Kirman v RWE Robinson & Sons Pty Ltd (in liq); Re RWE Robinson and Sons Pty Ltd (in liq)* [2019] FCA 372.

 Question 42

Lloyd and Bridget were directors of Deep Sea Fishing Excursions Pty Ltd (DSFE). The company owned two fishing vessels and other associated equipment. The fishing boats were acquired as a result of a loan made to the company by Bridget's father. Bridget's father had intended to give the money to Bridget as a wedding gift once it was clear that Bridget would marry Lloyd. However, Bridget and Lloyd disagreed over the management of the business and, as a result, the business did not prosper.

Bridget was worried about her father's money and so she arranged for the company seal to be affixed to a secured loan document in favour of her father over one of the fishing boats. This secured loan was then perfected by her father under the requirements of the PPSA. About two weeks after the secured loan document was executed and registered, the company was ordered to be wound up by the court on grounds of insolvency arising from a statutory demand that was not paid on time.

The liquidator held discussions with both Lloyd and Bridget to determine the quickest way to realise the company's assets and pay creditors. Bridget offered to buy the boat, which was not covered by the security, to her father. Her offer was below market price, but it would have given a reasonable (and quick) return to the creditors.

Lloyd complains to the liquidator and argues that he cannot sell the boat to a director and that Bridget's father's security is void.

Bridget retaliates by saying that the company would never have been wound up if Lloyd had not continued to purchase fishing equipment when they could not afford it.

Advise the liquidator.

Time allowed: 45 minutes

Answer Plan

This question is concerned with the powers of company liquidators, particularly their ability to sell assets and to commence litigation on behalf of the company. In the aftermath of a winding up order, the former directors of a company will frequently make claims upon the liquidator regarding what they are permitted to do and what should be done about other directors. A liquidator needs to be clear about his or her duties and responsibilities under the Corporations Act. The liquidator of DSFE has a number of issues to deal with in this situation.

Overview of liquidation

- Impact and role of compulsory liquidators.

Powers of liquidator

- General and specific powers of liquidators.

Voidable transactions

- Is the security interest in favour of Bridget's father void or voidable?

Insolvent trading liability

- Are Bridget and/or Lloyd liable for insolvent trading?

Conclusion

- Recap the main points.

Answer

Overview of liquidation

10-18 Although the role of the liquidator is to wind up the affairs of the company by selling assets to pay off debt, the liquidator is appointed in a number of different capacities. It has been said that the liquidator is an agent of the company (*Re Timberland Ltd* (1979) 4 ACLR 259); an officer of the corporation (s 9); and an officer of the court (*Sydlow Pty Ltd v TG Kotselas Pty Ltd* (1996) 14 ACLC 846). The liquidator has also been characterised as being in a fiduciary position owing duties to the company, its creditors and its members. Due to this the liquidator may find it difficult to know whose interests are to receive precedence when there is a conflict; however, at the very least the liquidator must be independent and show impartiality: *Re National Safety Council of Australia (Victoria Division)* (1989) 15 ACLR 355; *ASIC v Franklin (liquidator); Re Walton Constructions Pty Ltd* [2014] FCAFC 85.

The power and responsibility imposed on the liquidator comes with concomitant obligations under both general law and statutory obligations to act with due care and diligence (see *Asden Developments Pty Ltd (in liq) v Dinoris (No 3)* [2016] FCA 788) and to act for the benefit of the company's creditors: see generally *ASIC v Edge* (2007) 211 FLR 137.

Powers of liquidator

10-19 In determining whether the proposed activity of a liquidator is permissible, it is necessary to determine the powers and the specific duties relating to the exercise of that power. Generally, the liquidator of an insolvent company has three functions:

1. to call in all the assets of the company and finalise its affairs;
2. to distribute the company's assets equally amongst creditors; and
3. to investigate what precipitated the company's misfortune to determine whether any company property was disposed of improperly or whether any person ought to be prosecuted for their conduct.

In order to carry out the second of these functions, the liquidator is empowered to deal with the company's assets in a wide variety of ways. When a liquidator is appointed, the company's assets do not become the property of the liquidator — rather, the liquidator is an agent in respect of these assets and may deal with them just as the directors may. The company in liquidation retains beneficial ownership of its property: *FCT v Linter Textiles Australia Ltd (in liq)* (2005) 220 CLR 592. Importantly, the liquidator has a power of sale over the assets: s 477(2)(c). Because the liquidator is an agent and in a fiduciary position, he or she will owe certain duties in the exercise of the power of sale.

Apart from being categorised as an officer under the Corporations Act and subject to the statutory duties under it, the liquidator owes duties to act honestly (*Re Ah Toy* (1986) 2 ACLC 483); to avoid a conflict of interest (*Re Timberland Ltd* (1979) 4 ACLR 259); and he or she must not act to favour any particular person or group, but must act impartially (*Re Intercontinental Properties Pty Ltd* (1977) 2 ACLR 488). In carrying out the power of sale, therefore, the liquidator must have regard to these duties or risk a complaint to the court and potential removal under s 90-15 of the Insolvency Practice Schedule (Corporations) of the Corporations Act.

The question is whether the liquidator can sell the company assets to any person at any price. While there is nothing specific in the Corporations Act which restricts the class of persons to whom a liquidator may sell company assets, there is a problem in maintaining the appearance of impartiality if the asset is sold to a director of the company. The problem becomes more acute when the offered price is below market value. Courts are reluctant to interfere in decisions made by liquidators as a result of business or commercial judgment: *Northbourne Developments Pty Ltd v Reiby Chambers Pty Ltd* (1989) 19 NSWLR 434.

Thus, considerations of whether the offer made by Bridget would produce a reasonable return to creditors will carry some weight in support of the liquidator selling to her; however, liquidators appointed by the court are expected to carry out their duties in a manner and appearance of absolute impartiality, and any challenge to that impartiality will be viewed seriously and may warrant an order removing the liquidator: *Re Timberland Ltd* (1979) 4 ACLR 259. The court has the power to investigate the conduct of a liquidator under s 45-1 of IPS of the Corporations Act: see *Hall v Poolman* (2009) 75 NSWLR 99.

On balance, it would be unwise for the liquidator to sell the boat to Bridget at this price. The liquidator would be well advised to advertise the boat for public sale and accept the best offer or tender for it. If he receives no acceptable offers then he may proceed with the sale to Bridget.

Voidable transactions

10-20 The second problem for the liquidator is the claim by Lloyd that the security interest granted to Bridget's father may be set aside. Part 5.7B Div 2 deals with voidable transactions (s 588FE) and also transactions that are void (s 588FJ).

Despite the fact that Bridget's father may have lent the money to the company at an earlier time, the security for the loan was not perfected until one month prior to the winding up order. The existence of a security over an asset of the company means that the secured creditor can realise the security first, and only the balance, if any, after the sale of that asset is then available to the liquidator for distribution to unsecured creditors. Secured creditors are not bound by the stay that operates during liquidation: s 471C. In an insolvent company, the liquidator is anxious to call in, and has a duty to call in, all available assets in order to pay the creditors. In the course of calling in assets, the liquidator has power to commence court action to recover company property which is held by or controlled by others: s 477.

One particularly important set of powers for a liquidator is to recover voidable transactions. Liquidators may recover unfair preferences, uncommercial transactions, unfair loans and unreasonable director-related transactions: see s 588FE. Liquidators may apply to the court for orders under s 588FF which means that these transactions are voidable at the option of the liquidator upon the court making orders. Liquidators may also seek to set aside a security interest in certain circumstances. A circulating security interest may be set aside under s 588FJ; however, that does not apply to this question as Bridget's father's security interest is not in circulating assets: s 51C.

The liquidator may also recover the secured asset free of the security interest if it is unperfected within the timeframe set out in s 588FL. The question states that the security interest was perfected only two weeks before the company's liquidation. This means that the security interest will vest in the company because it was perfected too close to the liquidation. It may also be possible to invalidate the security interest by vesting it in the company if it can be established that Bridget is an associate of her father as a director of the company (see ss 15 and 588FP for a definition of associate).

It is also possible that the security given by the company to Bridget's father would amount to an unfair preference in accordance with the definition in s 588FA if the security would deliver to him a greater proportion of his debt than he would have received if he was an unsecured creditor: *Airservices Australia v Ferrier* (1996) 185 CLR 483. The liquidator may also argue that the transaction was uncommercial having regard to the benefit obtained by Bridget's father compared to the detriment suffered by the company (that is, granting a security interest in the boat as opposed to simply retaining the contractual debt obligation): s 588FB; see *Crowe-Maxwell v Frost* [2016] NSWCA 46.

Both unfair preferences and uncommercial transactions are classified under s 588FC as insolvent transactions if they also, relevantly, were a transaction entered into when the company was insolvent (s 588FC(a)(i)) or the transaction itself caused or was one of the matters causing the insolvency (s 588FC(b)(i)). It is important to establish whether or not this creation of the security interest is an insolvent transaction, for it is insolvent transactions which may be set aside by the court under s 588FE.

The granting of the security would not have caused or contributed to the insolvency, and so it would be necessary to show that the granting of the security was done when the company was in fact insolvent. Given that the court ordered the winding up approximately one month after the security interest was granted, and taking into account the time between an application and an order, it is likely that the security interest was granted when the company was unable to pay the statutory demand and it may well have been insolvent. If this is the case, then this unfair preference or uncommercial transaction would also be an insolvent transaction and it will be voidable (s 588FE) and liable to be set aside or discharged under s 588FF. It is also possible to argue that the transaction is an unreasonable director-related transaction under s 588FDA (see *Crowe-Maxwell v Frost* [2016] NSWCA 46; *Vasudevan v Becon Construction (Australia) Pty Ltd* [2014 VSCA 14) which may be set aside under s 588FE(6A) within four years prior to the relation back date (that is, the date of the application to wind up the company: see s 9 definition of 'relation back day'). Importantly, s 588FDA has the same criterion as s 588FB but does not require proof of insolvency (*Re IW4U Pty Ltd (in liq)* [2021] NSWSC 40), and there is no defence available.

It would seem in this case that the company has received little benefit for granting a security interest to Bridget's father and he has received a significant benefit (that is, the security interest) for providing no extra value to the company. It is likely that this transaction could be set aside by the liquidator.

Insolvent trading liability

10-21 The third issue for the liquidator is the claim by Bridget that Lloyd continued to purchase equipment when the company could not afford it. Potentially, this would amount to a breach of Lloyd's duty to prevent insolvent trading under s 588G. However, as Bridget was a director at the same time, it would seem that she too would be liable in respect of the insolvent trading transactions. This section is quite clear in its expression and it places a duty upon directors to be aware of the company's financial position at all times. The test of whether a director was aware that the debt would lead to insolvency or that the company was insolvent is an objective test in that it imposes the 'reasonable person in a like position' standard upon directors in relation to the incursion of the debt: s 588G(2); see *Re McLellan; Stake Man Pty Ltd v Carroll* [2009] FCA 1415. Section 588G is a civil penalty provision and it also carries criminal consequences for dishonest or reckless conduct. Proceedings under this section are generally prosecuted by ASIC, although a creditor who suffers loss as a result of insolvent trading transactions by the company may recover from the director, with the written consent of the liquidator, an amount equal to the debt incurred by the company: s 588R. The liquidator may also recover from the director the amount of the debt owed to the creditor as a debt owed to the company: s 588M(2); see *Treloar Constructions Pty Ltd v McMillan* [2017] NSWCA 72.

The liquidator would need to examine which debts were incurred during the company's demise to determine which ones either led to insolvency or occurred when the company was insolvent. However, proceedings to recover these amounts from either director need to be commenced within six years of the beginning of the winding up: s 588M(4).

The defences available to Bridget and Lloyd are set out in s 588H and they relate to the directors' knowledge of the company's affairs. The question does not contain information to indicate whether either Bridget or Lloyd could make out any of the defences; however, it seems reasonable to assume that as the only two directors who clearly had control and participation in the company's affairs, they are unlikely to make good any of the defences. Nor is there any evidence of the directors coming up with a corporate rescue plan that would reasonably likely lead to a better outcome for the company. For this reason, the safe harbour provision in s 588GA will be unavailable to them.

Conclusion

10-22 In summary, it would be unwise for the liquidator to sell the boat to Bridget as this may be a breach of his or her fiduciary duty as a liquidator, and it may compromise the liquidator's impartiality.

The security in favour of Bridget's father is liable to be set aside by the liquidator because it has vested in the company due to the timing of the perfection or the relationship between Bridget and her father. The liquidator may also apply to have the transaction set aside on the basis that it is an unfair preference, uncommercial transaction or unreasonable director-related transaction.

Finally, if there are debts incurred which have contributed to the company's insolvency or which were incurred when the company was insolvent, then both Bridget and Lloyd are personally liable in respect of these debts. The liquidator or the relevant creditor may recover these amounts equal to the debts incurred so long as they commence proceedings within six years of the winding up.

 ## Examiner's Comments

10-23 In relation to avenues of complaint about the liquidator's exercise of powers, see ss 90-10, 90-15 and 90-20 of the Insolvency Practice Schedule to the Corporations Act. The court may inquire into the external administration of a company either on its own initiative or on the application of the company, the external administrator, ASIC or a creditor. The court has wide powers to make orders, including orders replacing the external administrator or dealing with losses resulting from a breach of duty by the external administrator. As part of the court's supervisory power, the liquidator's actions may be the subject of an inquiry on the basis that the liquidator is not acting faithfully or not adhering to his or her duties under the Corporations Act or at common law. The court's powers are unlimited in this inquiry (s 90-15) and will be directed to matters of a disciplinary nature.

A complex area for further discussion is raised by the difficulty for a liquidator to prove that a transaction occurred at a time when the company was insolvent: s 588FE. The presumption of insolvency which arises from a statutory demand only exists in relation to the question of insolvency for the purpose of a winding up application. The presumptions under s 588E do not aid the liquidator in cases other than those where the directors have failed to keep proper books of account. In this question there is nothing to suggest that this has occurred.

 ## Keep in Mind

- Do not confuse the terms 'void' and 'voidable' in relation to the security in favour of Bridget's father.
- 'Voidable' means that it is valid until set aside by the court. For this to happen, the liquidator must take action to achieve an order in this regard from the court.
- Do not forget that unfair preferences and uncommercial transactions alone are not voidable transactions. They are only voidable if they are also insolvent transactions.
- The test of unreasonableness, under s 588FDA, is an objective test (what a reasonable person in the company's circumstances may be expected not to do): *Crowe-Maxwell v Frost* [2016] NSWCA 46.

- Liquidators are officers of the court and are, accordingly, expected to conduct themselves with independence, impartiality and integrity: *ASIC v Franklin (liquidator); Re Walton Constructions Pty Ltd* [2014] FCAFC 85 at [61]; *Ziziphus Pty Ltd v Pluton Resources Ltd (Recs and Mgrs Apptd) (in liq)* [2017] WASCA 193.

Question 43

Hunter Valley Coal Ltd (HVC) has been experiencing severe financial difficulties over the last two years with the result that it has incurred substantial losses and is unlikely to recover profitability. Mindful of their duty to avoid insolvent trading, the directors of HVC decide to appoint a voluntary administrator, Max Rayne (MR), on 1 July 2021.

HVC has three classes of creditors:

1. LeftBank Ltd, with secured debts of $50 million;

2. unsecured creditors, including employees owed $50 million; and

3. secured debts owed to the directors of HVC in respect of a loan made by the directors to the company on 29 June 2012 worth $50 million.

All secured debts have been properly perfected under the PPSA.

The first creditors' meeting approves the appointment of MR as administrator despite the protests from unsecured creditors that MR has a long business association with the company's bank and is a business partner with the wife of one of the directors of HVC.

After an uneventful investigation period, MR convenes the final creditors' meeting for 18 July 2021. At the final creditors' meeting MR proposes that the creditors enter into a DOCA with HVC which will sell all of the company's assets to the secured creditors for $100 million which will be used to repay in full the debts of the secured creditors, with nothing left for unsecured creditors. The secured creditors agree unanimously to approve the execution of the deed and the unsecured creditors all disapprove of the deed with the result that the resolution approving of the deed is passed after MR uses his casting vote as chairman of the creditors' meeting.

The employees are particularly unhappy about the DOCA because they have learnt that the directors of HVC have established a new mining company that plans to use the assets sold under the deed to keep mining in the Hunter Valley, but with different employees who will be paid less than the HVC employees. The new mining company proposal was put forward by the investment banking arm of LeftBank Ltd and will be established using a stock market listing that will generate substantial fees for LeftBank. MR's insolvency firm has been appointed as a highly paid consultant of the new company.

Advise the employees as to their rights under the DOCA.

Time allowed: 1 hour

Answer Plan

This question requires students to discuss the rights of unsecured creditors (particularly employees) during a voluntary administration and a DOCA. There are also issues of administrator independence, timing of creditor meetings and seeking to set aside a DOCA.

Overview of voluntary administration (VA)

- Purpose of VA.
- Impact of VA on stakeholders.
- Duration and outcomes of VA.

Implementing a DOCA

- Requirements for holding a valid final creditors' meeting and executing a DOCA.

Setting aside a DOCA

- Discussion of s 445D grounds and role of court.

Administrator independence

- Independence requirements and removal of the administrator.

Conclusion

- Recap main points.

Answer

Overview of voluntary administration

10-24 Voluntary administration has the primary purpose of saving some or all of a business that is insolvent or likely to become insolvent: s 435A(a). If the business cannot be saved, then the object of voluntary administration is to provide a better return than would result from an immediate winding up: s 435A(b). The administrator may be appointed by a range of parties (ss 436A–436C); in this case, by the company through its board of directors. The facts do not state whether the directors followed the required procedure of passing a resolution that the company was insolvent or likely to become insolvent: s 436A. If this was not done, it may be argued that the appointment of MR was invalid. In such a case the court could remove him or may grant an order validating the appointment under s 447A.

The appointment of an administrator will transfer control over the business from the directors to the administrator: ss 437A–437D. The administrator is responsible for investigating the company's affairs to enable a recommendation to be provided to the creditors at the final creditors' meeting as to the future of the company: ss 438A and 439A.

The effect of voluntary administration is to impose a moratorium (or stay) on claims against the company, unless the administrator or the court grants consent: s 440D; see also *Foxcraft v The Ink Group Pty Ltd* (1994) 15 ACSR 203. The moratorium also applies to the rights of secured creditors (s 440B), although there are various exceptions for particular securities: Pt 5.3A Div 7. This is designed to give the company breathing space and time to enable the administrator to investigate the company and provide a recommendation to creditors without being caught up in litigation that would delay the process and deplete company resources. This moratorium would thus prevent the unsecured creditors (including the employees) from suing the company during the period of the VA.

Implementing a DOCA

10-25 At the final creditors' meeting, which must be held within five business days before or after the end of the convening period (ordinarily 20 business days from the appointment of the administrator: s 439A), the creditors must choose whether to:

- end the administration and return the control of the company to its management;
- put the company into a creditors' voluntary winding up; or
- recommend that the company enter into a DOCA.

In this case, the final creditors' meeting was held on 18 July 2021. This was only 13 business days after MR was appointed as voluntary administrator. As noted above, the meeting must be held no earlier than five business days before the end of the 20-business-day convening period. The meeting was thus held two business days earlier than is permitted under law. However, this could be remedied by an order under either s 447A or s 1322 (see *Australasian Memory Pty Ltd v Brien* (2000) 200 CLR 270 where s 447A orders were made validating a final meeting held several days too early).

It is unusual for a secured creditor to vote for a DOCA at a final creditors' meeting — if they do not vote they are not bound by the DOCA: s 444D(2). However, unlike in liquidation where a secured creditor is not permitted to vote in respect of a secured amount, in voluntary administration secured creditors may vote if they wish: see Corporations Regulations 2001 (Cth) reg 5.6.24(4). In order to approve a DOCA the creditors must vote by a majority in number and in value of outstanding debts. This may be calculated by the chairman of the meeting on the voices: reg 5.6.19. Alternatively, a poll may be held to calculate the precise number of votes and the value of those votes: reg 5.6.21. However, in this case all of the unsecured creditors voted against the DOCA, so the majority in number requirement could not have been satisfied. MR, as the chairman of the meeting, may exercise a casting vote where there is a discrepancy between the majority in number and value (with one for and one against): reg 5.6.21(4). It should be noted that the administrator is an officer of the corporation (s 9) and therefore owes fiduciary duties to the company's creditors as a whole to act fairly between them and to avoid conflicts of interest: ss 181–183. It could be argued in this case that MR has exercised his casting vote for the improper purpose of pushing through the DOCA to secure a position on the board of the new company. We are not told if MR knew about this at the time of the final creditors' meeting, but the non-disclosure of the identities behind the DOCA would suggest that he was aware. It is possible to apply to the court for an order to challenge the result of the exercise of the casting vote.

Setting aside a DOCA

10-26 The mere fact that the unsecured creditors were out-voted by the secured creditors at the final meeting is not a ground for setting aside the DOCA. The Corporations Act provides a range of factors in s 445D that may allow a court to terminate the DOCA. In this case, it would seem that insufficient information was provided to the creditors (that is, the identity of those putting forward the DOCA) or that the information provided was misleading or deceptive: see s 445D(a)–(c). It could also be argued that the DOCA is unfairly prejudicial to the interests of the unsecured creditors (s 445D(f)) on the basis that they are receiving nothing from the DOCA.

Unfair discrimination may be established where the creditors receive a lower return than they would receive from an immediate liquidation of the company: *Lam Soon Australia Pty Ltd v Molit (No 55) Pty Ltd* (1996) 70 FCR 34. This is because the object of voluntary administration is to provide a better return than liquidation (s 435A(b)), although if the discrimination is necessary to save the business, then this may be permitted: see *Lam Soon* (above); *Commonwealth v Rocklea Spinning Mills Pty Ltd* (2005) 145 FCR 220. However, both of these authorities were decided under laws operating prior to the 2007 insolvency amendments which introduced s 444DA into the Corporations Act. This provision provides that eligible employee entitlements must be given the same statutory priority that they would receive under liquidation. In this case, it seems that all employee creditors have received nothing and the court may set aside the DOCA for infringing this principle on the basis that they would have received something under liquidation and were therefore discriminated against: s 445D(1)(f) or (g). It may also be argued that the employees may have received no return in liquidation as the assets of the company would only satisfy secured claims. In such a case the employees could receive payment under the Fair Entitlements Guarantee Act 2012 (Cth) and hence s 444DA(5) could be satisfied: see *Re Fitzgerald; Advance Healthcare Group Ltd (admin apptd)* (2008) 68 ACSR 349. This claim is doubtful, though, as the directors' security could be challenged as a voidable transaction (such as an uncommercial transaction under s 588FB or as an unreasonable director-related transaction under s 588FDA). Furthermore, if either of the security interests are circulating security interests (see s 51C) then the employee entitlements (but not other unsecured claims) that have priority under s 556 would need to be satisfied before payment could be made in liquidation to the secured creditors: s 561. A failure to do this in VA could establish unfair discrimination to support setting aside the DOCA under s 445D.

Administrator independence

10-27 It is a fundamental principle that external administrators (including voluntary administrators) must be independent and be seen by the community as acting independently: *Re Biposo Pty Ltd* (1995) 17 ACSR 730; *ASIC v Franklin (liquidator); Re Walton Constructions Pty Ltd* [2014] FCAFC 85. Certain persons are prohibited from acting as voluntary administrators of particular companies under s 448C; however, the facts do not disclose any relationships that would support the view that MR could be disqualified on this basis. Voluntary administrators are also required to give to the company's creditors a 'declaration of relevant relationships'. This is defined in s 60 to include prior relationships between the administrator or their firm and the company or its associates. Associates are defined in ss 11 and 15 but do not include the wife of a director. It would appear that MR did not need to disclose his prior relationship but it does add to the perception that he may not be independent or act in the best interests of the creditors as a whole. We are not told that MR did in fact issue this declaration, which may give rise to an offence under s 1311. Clearly, the court could make an order under s 447B on application by ASIC to protect creditors during administration — for example, by removing MR as deed administrator on the basis of improper conduct in failing to comply with his obligations under Pt 5.3A (for example, holding the final meeting on time, inadequate reporting and favouring particular creditors): see further *ASIC v Edge* (2007) 211 FLR 137. As noted above, if MR has been acting improperly under a conflict of interest, he may be liable for breach of fiduciary duties.

Conclusion

10-28 It seems that the employees have a solid case against MR to have the DOCA set aside and MR removed as deed administrator.

Examiner's Comments

10-29 This question covers a broad range of issues including meetings, the role of external administrators and the rights and powers of stakeholders (particularly secured and unsecured creditors). Any one of these topics could be the primary focus of the question and students should seek to prioritise their consideration according to how much time is given to each of the topics in their course.

Keep in Mind

- Remember to mention whether meetings are properly held.
- Remember to consider the court's extensive powers — particularly under s 447A which confers plenary powers on the court to do whatever it thinks is just in all the circumstances: *Australian Memory Pty Ltd v O'Brien* (2000) 200 CLR 270; *Correa v Whittingham* [2013] NSWCA 263.
- Remember to consider that the employees may receive a nil distribution in liquidation due to the lack of unsecured assets.

Question 44

Short Essay Question:

'Property owners are unfairly discriminated against in a voluntary administration.'

Discuss.

Time allowed: 30 minutes

Answer Plan

This essay question requires students to critically evaluate the impact of VA on property owners. This will require a brief overview of VA, defining the scope of the term 'property owner' and an analysis of the legal position of property owners during VA.

Introduction

- What is VA (initiation, duration and outcomes)?
- Comparative benefits of VA (compared with liquidation and receivership).

Impact of VA on property owners

- Define property owners.
- Effect of moratorium during VA.
- Protection from the court.
- Rights during transition to DOCA or liquidation.

Are property owners unfairly treated during VA?

- Consider both for and against arguments.

Conclusion

- Recap main points.

Answer

Introduction

10-30   VA was introduced in order to provide a mechanism for facilitating corporate rescue rather than immediate liquidation. The previous use of both receivership and official management had failed to save companies in financial distress from collapsing. The introduction of VA in 1993 represents parliamentary recognition of the value of attempts to save struggling companies. These benefits include saving jobs, preserving going-concern values (such as work in progress and goodwill) as well as the broader benefits to the customers and suppliers of businesses connected to the struggling enterprise. However, the legislative goal of trying to save businesses does not come without compromises, particularly in regard to the company's creditors for whom the administration may be seen as an unjustified limit on their contractual rights of enforcing repayment. Furthermore, many businesses will remain unviable even after a VA, thereby merely wasting scarce company funds. In the writer's view, these compromises do not represent 'unjust discrimination' because they provide a net benefit to the Australian economy.

What is VA?

10-31   VA is a type of corporate external administration which involves the appointment of an independent expert administrator who is registered with ASIC as having sufficient knowledge and experience in corporate insolvency practice to work as a registered external administrator. The Corporations Act imposes a range of independence requirements on administrators to ensure that the insolvency process is managed for the benefit of creditors as a whole: see, for example, ss 436DA and 448C. Furthermore, administrators are officers of the corporation under s 9 and are therefore bound by fiduciary obligations: see, for example, ss 181–182.

VA is designed to be a quick and efficient process so as to minimise the impact on stakeholders (particularly creditors). The ordinary timeframe for VA is within 25 business days of the date of appointment: s 439A. During this time the administrator takes over the running of the company (s 437A) and carries out an investigation of the company's financial position and makes a recommendation to the company's creditors at the final meeting: s 439A. The creditors then decide on the company's future: s 439C.

How does it affect property owners?

10-32   The appointment of an administrator imposes an automatic moratorium on claims against the company for the duration of the administration: s 440D. This extends to third parties with rights over the property used by the company (including secured creditors, lessors and suppliers with retention of title claims — provided these are properly perfected under the PPSA: s 440B) and applications to wind up the company: s 440A. During the period of the VA, property owners may not take back their property without the permission of the administrator or the court. The property owners (particularly lessors) may, however, serve notices of termination on the administrator so that as soon as the administration ends, they can proceed to recover their property: s 441J. Ordinarily, the owners' rights will resume once the company exits administration; for example, through a DOCA: s 444D. However, the court has the power to limit the powers of such owners in order to facilitate the successful operation of the deed under s 444F.

These provisions have been considered on a number of occasions. In *Re Java 452 Pty Ltd* (1999) 32 ACSR 507, the court noted that the parliament had specified a clear preference to suspend the rights of owners of property used by the company for the duration of the administration so as to not limit the chances that the company may be saved through a DOCA. This was reinforced by the possibility that an order may be made under ss 440H (during administration) and 444F (during a DOCA). The court stressed the importance of seeking to balance the goals of VA with the prejudice that may be caused to property owners, although if they conflicted, 'the will of the parliament must prevail'. Similar comments were made in *Canberra International Airport Pty Ltd v Ansett Australia Ltd* (2002) 41 ACSR 309. See also *Strazdins Re DNPW Pty Ltd v Birch Carroll & Coyle Ltd* (2009) 178 FCR 300 for a discussion of these matters under a DOCA. Moreover, courts have repeatedly emphasised that s 444F should be construed with the object of Pt 5.3A in mind — this means, in effect, preserving the company and its business to the extent possible: *Cook, in the matter of The Natural Grocery Company Pty Ltd (administrator appointed)* [2020] FCA 433; *Re Hi-Fi Sydney Pty Ltd (Admin Apptd)* [2015] NSWSC 1312.

It is also important to note that the rights of property owners whilst suspended are not extinguished or reduced by VA. For instance, an order under s 444F may only be made where the court is of the view that the interests of the owner will be protected. Furthermore, the power of the administrator to deal with the property is limited to the ordinary course of business (which arguably the owner has already consented to in entering the initial contract) or otherwise with the approval of the court or the owner of the property. In the writer's view, property owners are not unfairly discriminated against during a VA. The protection given to dealing with their assets outside of the ordinary course of business removes any unfairness to the limitations imposed on their exercise of property rights.

Are property owners unfairly treated during VA?

10-33 When compared to their rights in a liquidation or receivership, where they may take action over unsecured assets, it would seem that property owners are treated comparatively harshly in a VA.

However, there is little discrimination as all creditors are bound by the moratorium. The only exception to this is major secured creditors, who could appoint a receiver during the 13-business-day decision period: s 441A. These creditors are normally large banks or finance companies who have supplied essential funds to the business over a period of time. It could be argued that the business could not exist without its major source of funding. Furthermore, the major secured creditor will usually be monitoring the progress of the borrower and may well have had an opportunity to appoint a receiver much earlier than the commencement of the administration but chose not to enforce their rights to give the company a chance to reorganise its finances. It is clear that the support of the major secured creditors is needed if any rescue plan is to succeed. Therefore, it is argued that property owners are not unfairly discriminated against simply because major secured lenders can enforce their charge during the initial stages of VA.

More importantly, the property used by the company that is owned by someone else (such as supplies under a retention of title clause or premises leased by the company) is typically an essential component of the business. Without this property, the goal of trying to save the business would be unachievable. This is especially because there is usually more value in selling a business as a going concern than there is in selling some or all of a terminated business. The attempt to preserve enterprise value (particularly goodwill and work in progress) is a key feature of voluntary administration and justifies limiting the rights of property owners.

Conclusion

10-34 This essay has discussed the nature and purpose of voluntary administration, with a particular emphasis on trying to save the business. It has been argued that a limitation on the rights of property owners whose property is needed for the successful implementation of a rescue package is essential and promotes a valuable policy goal that benefits the broader community. The limitations imposed on property owners have been outlined and it has been argued that there are also a range of protections built into the system which are sufficient to disprove the view that property owners are *unfairly* discriminated against during a VA.

Examiner's Comments

10-35 This essay requires a critical assessment of the treatment of property owners during a VA. This involves not merely a description of how a VA operates and what rights property owners have during this procedure but rather a personal view on whether the limits imposed on property rights are justified.

Keep in Mind

- Do not simply describe how the law operates without directly answering the question.
- Be sure to provide critical analysis.
- Remember to support arguments by citing statutory and case references — do not rely on general statements without supporting your arguments.

Index

Index

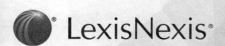

Related LexisNexis Titles

Anderson, Dickfos, Nehme, Hyland & Dahdal, *Corporations Law*, 5th ed, 2016, ISBN 9780409343298

Austin & Ramsay, *Ford, Austin & Ramsay's Principles of Corporations Law*, 17th ed, 2018, ISBN 9780409345537

Baxt, Black & Hanrahan, *Securities and Financial Services Law*, 10th ed, 2021, ISBN 9780409352795

Farrar & Hanrahan, *Corporate Governance*, 2016, ISBN 9780409344028

Fitzpatrick, Symes, Veljanovski & Parker, *Business and Corporations Law*, 4th ed, 2019, ISBN 9780409351101

Gooley, Dicker, Russell & Zammit, *Corporations and Associations Law*, 7th ed, 2020, ISBN 9780409351705

Grantham, *The Law and Practice of Corporate Governance*, 2020, ISBN 9780409348927

Hargovan, Adams & Brown, *Australian Corporate Law*, 7th ed, 2021, ISBN 9780409350739

Hargovan, *LexisNexis Case Summaries: Corporations Law*, 2nd ed, 2021, ISBN 9780409352283

Hargovan, *LexisNexis Study Guide: Corporations Law*, 4th ed, 2020, ISBN 9780409349498

Harris, *Company Law: Theories, Principles and Applications*, 2nd ed, 2015, ISBN 9780409338782